ROMANO-BRITISH CEMETERIES AT CIRENCESTER

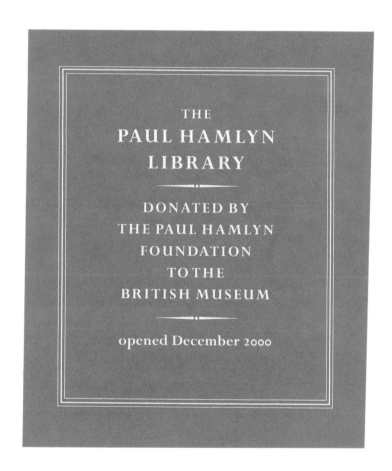

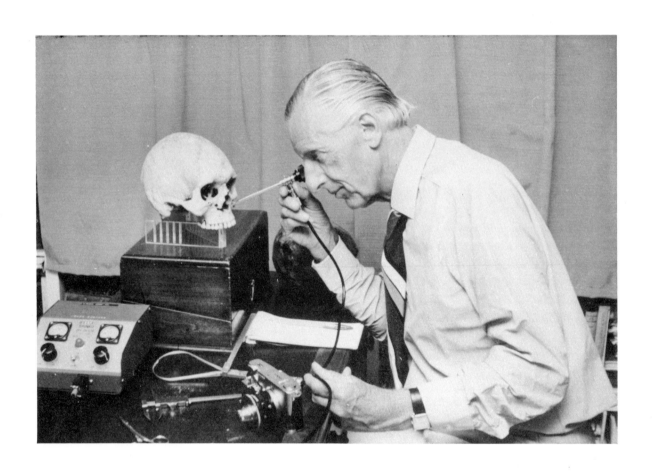

This volume is dedicated to the memory of

Calvin Wells
(1908–1978)

CIRENCESTER EXCAVATIONS II

ROMANO-BRITISH CEMETERIES AT CIRENCESTER

by Alan McWhirr, Linda Viner and Calvin Wells

WITH CONTRIBUTIONS FROM

Dorothy Charlesworth, T.C. Darvill, Brenda Dickinson, Margaret Guido, B.R. Hartley, M. Hassall, M. Henig, R.H. Leech, D. Mackreth, R. Reece, Valery Rigby, T. Slater, Clare Thawley, T. Waldron, D.J. Wilkinson

AND ILLUSTRATIONS BY

Nick Griffiths

Published by
Cirencester Excavation Committee
Corinium Museum, Cirencester, England
1982

The publication of this volume has been financed
by the Department of the Environment.

Produced by
Alan Sutton Publishing Limited,
17a Brunswick Road, Gloucester.
Printed in Great Britain by
Page Bros (Norwich) Ltd.

CONTENTS

THE HUMAN BURIALS by Calvin Wells

LIST OF PLATES

(★ denotes that a metric scale was used in the photograph)
Frontispiece: Calvin Wells at work with arthroscope looking at sinuses

LIST OF FIGURES

LIST OF TABLES

ACKNOWLEDGEMENTS

Prior notification of the construction of the western relief road around Cirencester allowed a series of excavations to be planned over a number of years and as a result many people became involved in the work of the Committee both during and after the excavation programme. The work of five seasons, between 1969 and 1974 is reported in this volume, plus an excavation in 1976 directed by Dr. R.H. Leech on behalf of the Committee for Archaeology in Avon, Gloucestershire and Somerset. In addition, T.C. Darvill carried out excavations on the site of Querns House kitchen garden in 1978 prior to the construction of the new ambulance station, and we have taken the opportunity of including his report in this volume. D.J. Wilkinson observed a number of areas during construction work to the west of the town, most recently in 1981, and his reports are also included, as are the observations of T.J. O'Leary, R. Downey, D.J. Viner and R.J. Zeepvat to whom the Committee is indebted.

The difficult excavation of the Bath Gate Cemetery was in the hands of a number of skilled supervisors, and but for their devotion, the work of interpretation would have been impossible. They were David Viner (1969–70), Mark Webber (1971) and Linda Viner (1972–4). Work on the cemetery to the north of the Fosse Way, the road itself and the adjacent building was supervised by J.A. Derry (1971–2), David Wilkinson (1973–4) and Roger Leech (1976). Photography was the responsibility of R. Peers (1971), C.J. Shuttleworth (1972–4), Roger Leech (1976) and Tim Darvill (1978), with some additional aerial views taken by J. Hancock and R. Brown. The pottery shed was ably administered by the late Annie Anderson, Ian Lea and Helen McWhirr.

The bulk of post-excavation analysis was carried out by Valery Rigby and Linda Viner; with John Thawley and Ann Woods responsible for conservation. The illustrations for this volume are the work of Nick Griffiths. Without their support and continuing loyalty the production of this report would not have been possible; moreover it certainly would not have been completed without the editorial skills of Linda Viner who, in addition, has written much of the first section.

The crucial element of any cemetery excavation is the detailed study of the skeletal remains, and we could have wished for no greater authority than the late Calvin Wells who first became involved with Cirencester 'people' when Richard Reece asked him to examine the burials from the Oakley Cottage rescue excavations in 1960. We have respectfully dedicated this volume to the memory of Calvin Wells who despite his illness continued to work on the Cirencester material until shortly before his death in 1978. We are also greatly indebted to his widow, Freddie Wells, and wish to thank her for continued support throughout.

During the course of the excavations and post-excavation analysis many local people have helped in a variety of ways. The late John Whyte, tenant of the land on which we dug, and his son Alan were both stalwart supporters of our work; so too were the landowners, the then Cirencester Urban District Council and later Cotswold District Council, and Gloucestershire County Council. Equipment was generously loaned by all these authorities and by the late Harry Pitts of Cirencester, and Peter Berry of South Cerney.

The Committee was allowed facilities for observation when new offices for Christian Brann

Ltd. were under construction alongside the relief road and Gloucestershire County Council allowed similar access during the actual road construction. Thanks are also due to the Gloucestershire Area Health Authority for permission to excavate the site of the ambulance station and to observe the construction works. A traditional feature of excavations in the town has been the way in which the Cirencester Archaeological and Historical Society has regularly provided guides to show the many visitors around our sites and throughout Miss D.M. Radway organised this task with great skill.

Finance for the excavations was provided by a number of bodies, but primarily from the Department of the Environment. Generous grants were also received from Gloucestershire County Council, Cirencester Urban District Council, Cotswold District Council, Cirencester Archaeological and Historical Society, the Bristol and Gloucestershire Archaeological Society, and individuals visiting our excavations. The Department of the Environment again provided nearly all the resources for post-excavation work, and without this continued support the production of this series of *Cirencester Excavations* would not have been possible. Our particular thanks must go to Miss S.A. Butcher and Dr. C.J. Young who have been involved with the Committee's work for many years. Both have appreciated the problems in processing the material from such large urban excavations. More recently the Committee has worked closely with P. Gosling, the Department's inspector now responsible for our area, who, like his predecessors, continues to keep a close and interested eye on the archaeology of Cirencester.

In the course of compiling specialist reports, the help of the following is gratefully acknowledged: for pottery Valery Rigby, Brian Hartley, Brenda Dickinson, Katharine Hartley, Scott Anderson, David Peacock, Janet Richardson, Alan Vince, Mike Fulford, and Chris Young; for all other materials Linda Viner, Margaret Guido, Don Mackreth, Richard Reece, Mark Hassall, Martin Henig, Clare Thawley, Glenys Lloyd-Morgan, Leo Biek, Don Bailey, Mark Maltby, Guy Grainger, Jane Timby, and Justine Bayley. The glass report was completed by Dorothy Charlesworth in 1978, and the Committee would wish to record the great debt it owes her for the detailed catalogue of glass from all sites excavated by the Committee since 1960 which she completed shortly before her death. Lead analysis of the human bones was conducted by Tony Waldron; with C14 analysis of samples carried out by the Harwell Laboratory, Abingdon. Hallam Ashley, of Norwich, was responsible for photography of the human remains under Calvin Wells direction. An historical analysis of the post-Roman development of The Querns has been provided by Dr. Terry Slater.

The Committee continues to benefit in having Professor S.S. Frere as its chairman and a group of dedicated members some of whom have attended meetings for well over a decade. In particular Miss Joyce Barker has been a member since the formation of the Committee and is always willing to give advice and to help whenever asked.

Finally a word of thanks must go to all Cirencester people who helped the work of the Excavation Committee no matter how small the contribution may have seemed.

Alan McWhirr
March 1982

INTRODUCTION

Large-scale development of the area to the south-west of Cirencester in the period 1969–1981, provided an opportunity for Cirencester Excavation Committee to investigate an extensive tract of ground lying between the walls of *Corinium Dobunnorum,* and the amphitheatre. (Fig 1).

Excavation prior to the construction of the western relief road, completed in 1974, resulted in the recovery of over 450 Romano-British burials from the extensive Bath Gate cemetery lying either side of the Fosse Way as it leaves the Roman town heading towards Bath. Evidence of stone quarrying in the area before the third century was obtained in excavations both to the north-west and south-east of the amphitheatre, with subsidiary roads branching from the Fosse being constructed to serve the industry. An extra-mural building north of the Fosse sealed by the later cemetery may have had a craft or industrial function. (Fig 2).

Construction of the eastern by-pass produced evidence for at least thirteen burials outside the Verulamium Gate, and the opportunity therefore has been taken in this report to collect together all the evidence of the known pattern of Roman cemeteries around *Corinium.*

Intensive and detailed anatomical analysis of all available skeletal material by Calvin Wells has contributed a great deal to the study of palaeopathology of the Roman community of *Corinium Dobunnorum,* once the second largest town in walled area in Roman Britain.

It was felt that numerous excavations and observations over such a large area in the period 1969–1981, and under differing conditions, did not lend itself readily to individual site reports, given also the current physical and financial restrictions of publication. Therefore, a thematic approach has been adopted, whereby a study of observable chronological development in the area of the Querns has been assessed, using a variety of sources. For example, evidence of stone extraction in the Roman period was recovered from a number of locations, and has been grouped together in the text to provide an overall view of the industry in the area. More detailed discussion of individual excavations can be found in the site records, microfiche copies of which are stored at the National Monuments Record, London. The all-encompassing descriptive term "the Querns" has been used throughout the text to denote that area of land, west of the Roman town, south of the Tetbury Road, north of Cotswold Avenue, Chesterton, and with the Roman amphitheatre at its centre (see p. 27 for derivation of name). The Bath Gate Cemetery is defined as the area of Roman burial lying immediately outside and to the west of the Roman town gate of that name, the site of which was confirmed in 1974.

EXCAVATION CODES

Excavations in the area of the Querns and Bath Gate Cemetery in the period 1969–1976 and 1978 were assigned site codes CS, CT, EA and DW. An abbreviated year code (for example 69 for 1969, 70 for 1970) follows the site code abbreviation when it has been necessary to refer to the work of a specific season. In addition, for site CS, the year code is followed by a trench number (arabic). Layer numbers form the last element in the code.

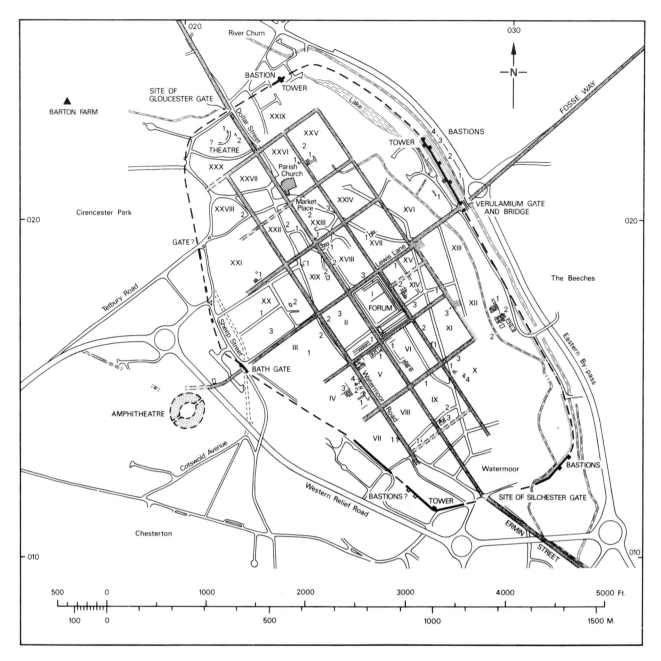

Fig.   1.   Cirencester: Roman Town Plan

For example: CS 72–3 8 7 refers to site CS, excavated 1972–3, trench 8, layer 7.
CS 71 2 refers to site CS excavated in 1971 layer 2 (only one trench was opened in 1971, and therefore no trench number was allocated).
In discussion of site CT, year and trench codes have been deleted in some instances, and the reference CT 116 for example refers directly to layer 116 on site CT. (If the year of excavation is important this has been inserted and the code given would be CT 73 116).
Fig. 3 shows the positions of the trenches referred to in the text.
Imperial measurements used during the excavation of CT 69 and CS 70–74 have been converted to metric to be consistent with modern practice.
All site books, finds, pottery, analyses, detailed archive and photographic records are stored at the Corinium Museum, Cirencester, and are available for study on prior application to the staff of the museum. The National Monuments Record, London, hold a microfiche facsimile of the site records, available for study on prior application.

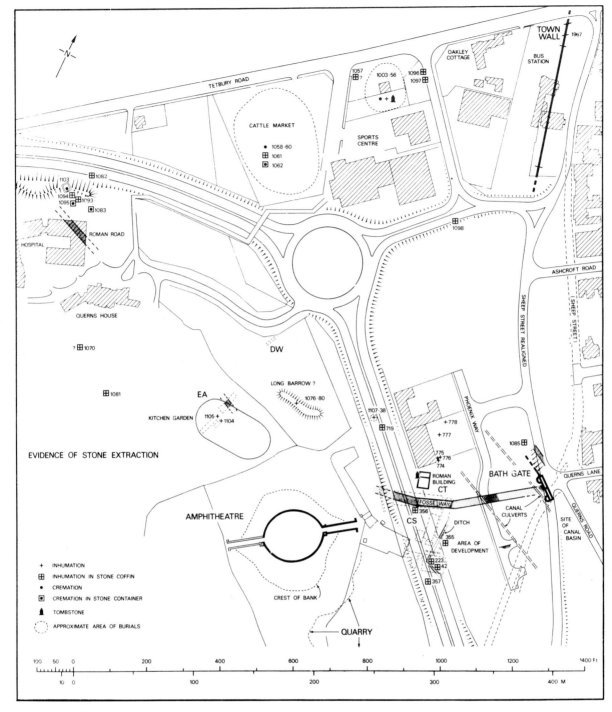

Fig.   2.   Roman and modern features to the west of the Bath Gate

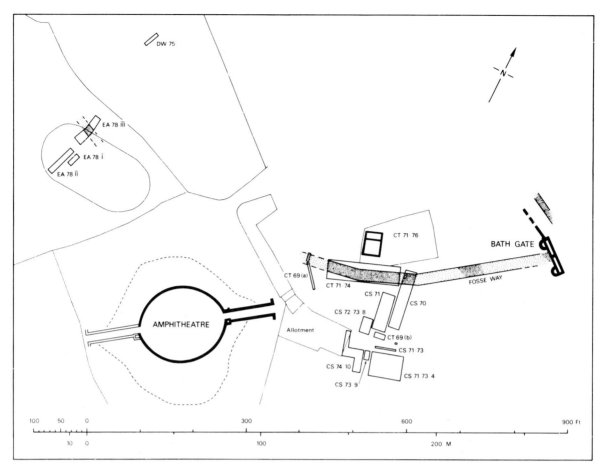

Fig.   3.   Trenches excavated 1969–1980

MICROFICHE

Following advice from the Department of the Environment, and in particular Advisory Note 25 dated 28 July 1980, this report initially written for text publication has been extensively revised for a text/fiche publication. Plans and sections appear in the printed part of the report so that they can be used in conjunction with the fiche. Specialist reports are split between text and fiche with the bulk of these reports appearing on fiche. The printed part of this report contains details of the excavation and the overall conclusions. There is also a discussion of the skeletal material by Calvin Wells based on his examination of over 400 skeletons, the detailed results of which are contained on fiche.

The production of a text/fiche format is an experiment tackled by few excavators and consequently the Committee is anxious to hear how it is received by the archaeological world.

Fiche are referred to by number, for example, in this volume where there are 5 fiche, fiche one is 1/5, fiche three is 3/5. The individual frames contained on each fiche are referred to by a letter followed by a number. The first row is lettered A, the second B, the seventh being G. The frames in each row are numbered 1 to 14 from left to right. Thus 2/5 C04 refers to row C fourth frame along in the second fiche of five fiches.

GEOLOGY AND TOPOGRAPHY

Cirencester lies at the south-eastern end of the long dip slope of the Cotswold Hills, geologically composed of richly fossiliferous rocks of the Middle Jurassic Age. The geology of the immediate Cirencester area has been little studied in detail by geologists because of the rarity of natural exposures. A history of geological study in the area has been discussed by Hugh Torrens in *Cirencester Excavations I* (Torrens, 1982, 72–78). Within the area investigated archaeologically and the subject of this volume, the underlying natural rock is oolitic limestone.

The landscape to the west of the town is dominated by the banks of the Roman amphitheatre, rising above and incorporating the upcast of Roman quarrying activities in the area, figs. 4 and 5. In 1969 the principal area investigated by the Committee was bounded on the east by the trackbed of the former Kemble-Cirencester branch railway, and Sheep Street;

1. Aerial view of The Querns, August 1973

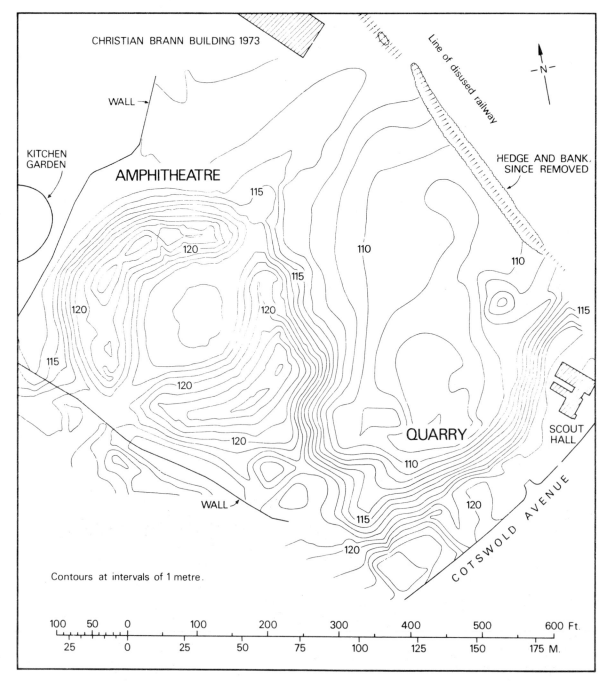

Fig.   4.   Contour survey of amphitheatre, quarry and Bath Gate cemetery (based on a survey commissioned by
the Department of the Environment)

Querns Hill and Cotswold Avenue to the south; the Amphitheatre to the west; and Tetbury
Road, the Cattle Market and Sports Centre to the north. Construction of the western relief
road necessitated the realignment of Sheep St, Querns Hill and Tetbury Road, with attendant
building development in the area served by the new Phoenix Way, and realigned Sheep Street,
of light industrial, office and residential grades.

Lying outside the Roman town walls in the vicinity of the amphitheatre, the area was one of
potential archaeological importance particularly with regard to a study of the cemetery pattern
and Roman road alignments. As shown by the contour survey of the area east and north-east of
the amphitheatre, fig. 4, a natural ridge ran from the north-eastern entrance of the amphitheatre
towards the then supposed site of the Bath Gate of the town (subsequently confirmed in
excavations in 1974, see McWhirr, 1978, 71–2, fig. 4). South of this line a large semi-circular

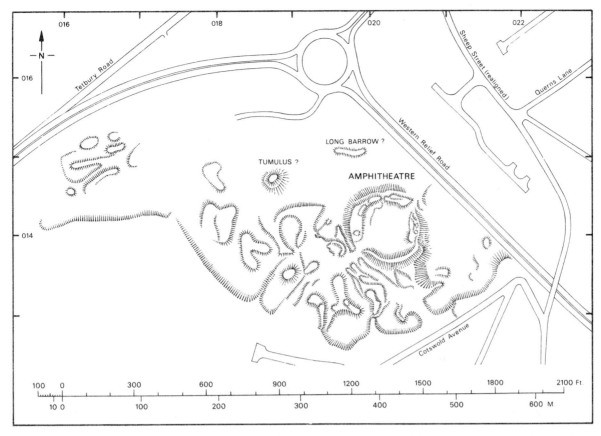

Fig.   5.   Earthwork survey of the Querns (based on O.S. 1921 1:2500, with modern roads superimposed)

hollow existed, flanked on the west by the banks of the amphitheatre and to the south by a steeply sloping face *c.* 10 m. high. The topography of the land further to the east had been obliterated by an embankment and cutting to take the bed of the railway constructed in 1841.

Evidence for the quarrying of stone in Roman times is discussed p. 31. The delays experienced in publishing *Cirencester Excavations I* (see Wacher and McWhirr, 1982, 17) are equally applicable comments for this volume. Plans to construct an ambulance station in the former Kitchen Garden of Querns House provided the Committee with an opportunity in 1978 to investigate the area to the north-west of the amphitheatre. Actual construction was not started until 1981 when the Committee continued its observations in the area. But for the delays in publication, the results of this work could not have been included in this present volume, where they form an important contribution to our understanding of the geological and topographical history of the area.

HISTORICAL SUMMARY OF THE QUERNS

The area to the west of the town is commonly referred to as the Querns, and this account of the history of that area is included in an attempt to show that the landscape visible before the construction of the ring road was an ancient one possibly little altered, except for some property boundaries, since the Roman period.

PRE-ROMAN PERIOD

Finds of an obviously pre-Roman origin have not been recorded from the area, although five burials recovered by Buckman and Newmarch (1850, 12; Gazetteer burial nos. 1076–1080 mf. 5/5) were, they believed, from a long barrow, marked as such on the O.S. maps of the area, figs. 2 and 5. The site in question is a long oval mound to the north of the amphitheatre. Witts (1883, 76 no. 8) records that this partial opening consisted of two transverse cuts through the mound. The burials, arranged east-west, were in a fragmentary state, although Beecham (1886, 257) was able to add that they were male, and that they were flexible and bent so that 'they were probably killed in an encounter, and would appear to have been buried immediately after death'.

The basis for identifying burials 1076–1080 as pre-Roman appears simply to be their presence below a long oval mound reminiscent of long barrows of the Severn-Cotswold type. Leslie Grinsell (O'Neil and Grinsell, 1960, 75, Cirencester i) regarded it as a very doubtful long barrow considering its low-lying position and the presence of extensive quarrying activity (both Roman and post-Roman) in the vicinity. The Committee's work would appear to further substantiate Grinsell's view and in the light of evidence to be presented in greater detail p. 31 and microfiche 5/5, these five individuals should probably be considered as Roman in date.

Similarly, O'Neil and Grinsell (1960, 108, Cirencester [4]) considered the "tumulus" as marked on fig. 5 at SP 01870147 to be highly questionable as a round barrow. The conical mound, 4.6–6.1 m. high, has a modern octagonal tiled platform on top, and is probably to be connected with quarrying, the tile platform perhaps representing the remains of a summer house constructed as part of the garden landscaping of the area for Charles Lawrence. A second postulated round barrow (O'Neil and Grinsell, 1960, 108, Cirencester [5]) at SP 01800136 is very large and shapeless, and would again be best interpreted as the result of quarrying.

ROMAN PERIOD

The earliest dated finds recovered from the excavations are of an early military character, (see mf. 2/5). Unstratified and unassociated with any burials, these objects were probably casually lost either in the cemetery area or elsewhere in the town, subsequently arriving in rubbish

26

deposits cleared from the town centre — a practice which is very evident from a study of the pottery recovered during the excavations.

Quarrying in the Roman period is discussed later, p. 31, but on present evidence this would appear to be one of the first extractive industries in the area, creating a landscape of irregular humps and hollows. The earliest firmly dated structure is the amphitheatre, situated 800 m. south-west of the town, and now a grass-covered mound in the care of the Department of the Environment (Wacher, 1981). The banks survive to a height of 7.62 m. surrounding an elliptical arena approximately 47 m. by 41 m. with entrances at each end of the long axis. Excavations were first carried out by Mr. T.C. Brown in 1868 when a section was cut through the banks (Brown T.C., 1869, 106); while the north-east entrance and arena were investigated by Wacher in 1962–3, (Wacher, 1963, 23; 1964, 17); with further sectioning of the banks in 1966 (Brown and McWhirr, 1967, 185).

In 1868 Mr. T.C. Brown reported that to his 'knowledge the arena had never been opened, whilst cuttings in other mounds by Mr. Lawrence (of Querns House, see p. 29) had discovered several coins, lachrymatories, pottery, and some stone coffins' (Brown T.C., 1869, 107). The amphitheatre as suggested by Brown (p. 102) probably resulted from the upcast of rubbish from quarrying activity. The presence of such a large public monument would imply the existence of a road giving access from the town. Elucidation of the road systems serving the cultural, industrial/agricultural and burial functions of the area was obtained in excavations to be described in greater detail in this volume.

The cemetery appears to have continued in use into the fifth century although evidence from excavations in 1961 would appear to suggest that the municipal care of the town was in decline by that time. Two burials, recovered from the ditches of Ermin Street (Gazetteer burials nos. 5001, 5006, mf. 5/5) in the centre of the Roman town, and discarded without proper burial point to both a breakdown of civil administration and to a decline in the town population. The presence of later timber buildings, with fifth or sixth century pottery and the blocking of the entrance has led Wacher to suggest a shift of population to the amphitheatre for defensive purposes during the troublesome years of the fifth century (Wacher, 1974, 312–315). The place-name evidence of Chesterton is of relevance here, see below. (Wacher, 1974, 314; Rivet and Smith, 1979, 321–2).

POST-ROMAN PERIOD by Terry Slater

Historical evidence for the use of the Querns in the post-Roman period is not available before 1086, whilst the fields are not referred to specifically until 1288, therefore information must be sought from less direct sources for the early history of the area. Place-name scholars demonstrate that 'Querns' derives from an Old English word *crundel,* which means quarry. It was not until the sixteenth century that the medieval name of 'Crundles' began to change to the modern Querns (Smith, A.H., 1964, 65). The evidence of quarrying is clear in the area even today, but the main period in which these quarries were exploited was the early Roman. They were the sources of the stone used for many of the buildings in the town and since both amphitheatre and cemetery occupy the floor of the quarry it seems likely that it was already going out of use as an active excavation in the Roman period.

The other place-name of significance is Chesterton, the name of the manor and tything in which the Querns is situated. Wacher's excavations in the amphitheatre seem to suggest that it was converted in the fifth century A.D. into a fortified enclosure (Wacher, 1963, 15–26; 1964, 9–19; 1976, 15–17). Its embankments would have made a much more readily defended area than the two miles of wall once the town population had begun to shrink. This suggests that the *ceaster* of the first element of Chesterton makes reference to the amphitheatre rather than the adjacent Roman town and that Smith's interpretation of 'farm near, or belonging to, the Roman town' might be modified (Smith, A.H., 1964, 64).

It is probable that Chesterton was part of the large royal manor of Cirencester until the late-Saxon period, but before Domesday it had been granted to a subject and its manorial descent thenceforth remained separate. In 1086, the two-hide manor was held by William de Baderon (Taylor, 1889, 280–4). In the early thirteenth century, Chesterton was purchased by the Langley family whose principal Gloucestershire manor was the adjacent Siddington St. Peter, and it remained in their hands until 1459 (Coss, 1971, charter 45; 1974). Though its manorial and judicial administration remained separate from Cirencester through the medieval period, and though the tithes were granted to St. Peter's Abbey, Gloucester, in the late eleventh century (Hart, 1863–67, 70), Chesterton remained part of the ecclesiastical parish of Cirencester and did not acquire a church or chapel of its own. The boundary of the manor and tything of Chesterton followed the pre-1975 line of Tetbury Road, Sheep Street and Querns Lane, so that the Querns occupied its extreme northern corner (Fig. 6).

The Querns is exceptionally well-documented through the medieval period because of the survival of charters belonging to both Cirencester Abbey and the Langley family. It also gains mention in the national archives in the prolonged disputes between abbot and townspeople in the fourteenth century. Before about 1200 A.D., the Querns was divided into two parts: a rough and thorn-grown pasture of some sixty acres (24 ha.), which included the Roman amphitheatre and cemetery area and extensive remains of the quarries, and a ten-acre (4 ha.) meadow called Athelmead. There is no mention in the documents of active quarrying in the Querns, so it seems likely that stone was by then obtained from elsewhere, including, not least, from upstanding Roman walls (Brown and McWhirr, 1966, 240–53).

The meadow of Athelmead occupied the elongated level strip of land between Sheep Street and a watercourse which, in the late eighteenth century, supplied the Thames and Severn Canal basin. The watercourse originates as a part of the water defences of the Roman city and was diverted in the early Norman period to fill the moat of the medieval castle. Though the castle was destroyed by Stephen in 1142 (Potter, 1955, 141; Fuller, 1890–1, 103–119), the moat, known as Law Gutter, survived until the late-eighteenth century as a street name and ditch. Athelmead, too, survived as a valued meadow, and subsequently as a market garden, until the coming of the railway in 1841.

These two enclosures, the overgrown quarry and the meadow, were used as common pasture by the townspeople of Cirencester and the tenants of Chesterton. The other town common, Watermoor, occupied an equivalent position outside the south gate of the Roman defences, where a second Roman cemetery is known. Common grazing of this kind would seem a logical use for these rough, hillocky areas with, in the early years of Saxon settlement, large stone tombstones still protruding through the scrub and long grass. As well as pasture, the Athelmead part of the Querns common was used as the site of the town archery butts since the name of Sheep Street derives from an Old English word, *scytta,* meaning archer (Smith, A.H., 1964, 63). Common rights, once established, were difficult to extinguish. At Watermoor they survived until 1825, but in the thirteenth century successive abbots of Cirencester were engaged in a systematic consolidation and development of their town properties through judicious agreements and exchanges with lesser land-holders. As part of this process, Abbot Henry of Munden concluded agreements in 1286 with Bartholomew Archibald, Lord of the small manor of Archibalds in the town, and with Sir Geoffrey Langley, Lord of Chesterton, whereby they gave up their rights, and the rights of their tenants, in the common grazing of the Querns and Athelmead in exchange for Abbey meadowland elsewhere (Devine, 1977, charters 188, 357). Abbot Henry was thus able to properly enclose the Querns with a stone wall in 1292 and began to utilise it as a rabbit warren (Ross, 1964, 99–119; Fuller, 1884–5, 298–344).

In order to safeguard the abbey from subsequent legal action by the tenants of Cirencester, who had lost their accustomed grazing, a pardon was purchased from Edward II in 1315 (Calendar of Patent Rolls, 9 Ed. II). For this reason, the townspeople were unable to press their legitimate complaint presented in the great petition to the Crown made in 1342 (Ross, 1964, 99–119), the legal ramifications of which continued for more than half a century, as they sought to extract themselves from the yoke of the abbot's Lordship.

The Querns continued in use as a rabbit warren until the Dissolution of the Abbey, since in 1538, one Clement Rede, yeoman of Cirencester, was appointed 'keeper of the game of conyes

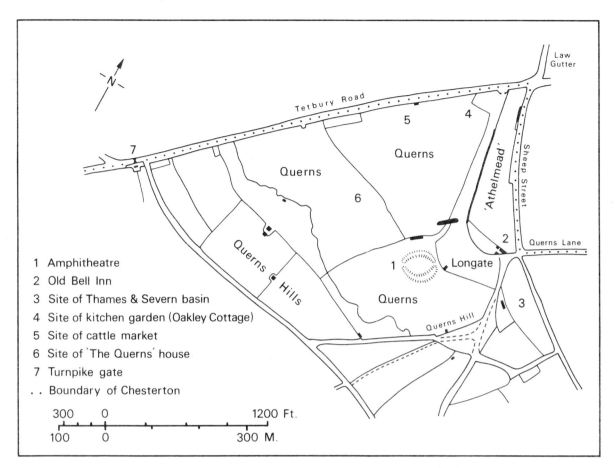

Fig.   6.   The Querns, 1777 (based on G.C.R.O. Bathurst MSS D2525, Plan of Chesterton 1777)

being within the lese or pasture called corners' (Fuller, 1890–1, 103–119). The Langley charters show the principal gate to the warren to have been opposite the west gate of the Roman town, whilst a reference to 'Ravensgate' in a charter of 1392 possibly refers to the medieval or Saxon name for that west gate. It would be an appropriate association for a gate leading to a large cemetery since the raven is linked with a number of pagan religious cults, including the Roman Mithraic, and is often particularly associated with death (Gelling, 1978, 130–161).

At the Dissolution, the Querns was included in the western of the two great estates into which the abbey lands were divided and in the late seventeenth century it thus passed into the ownership of the Bathurst family. An estate plan of 1777 provides the earliest cartographic evidence of the area (G.C.R.O., Bathurst MSS D2525, Plan of Chesterton 1777 — part reproduced here, fig. 6). It shows that the Querns was used as pasture land and had been sub-divided into three large and one smaller enclosures. Athelmead was a market garden, except for its southern end beside Crundlesgate, which was occupied by the premises of the Old Bell Inn. The plan shows the area just before it was to be radically altered by the nineteenth-century expansion of the town.

In 1789, a branch of the Thames and Severn Canal was opened to Cirencester. It terminated in a basin at the foot of Querns Hill and the watercourse which had irrigated Athelmead for a millenium and more, was culverted to provide water for the canal (Household, 1969, 63–8; G.C.R.O. Thames & Severn MSS, 175/16 no. 45, plan of canal feeder). By 1807, Earl Bathurst's kitchen garden had been laid out beside the Tetbury Road on part of the Querns (G.C.R.O. Bathurst MSS D2525, Plan of Chesterton 1807), and in 1826 much of the northern portion of the Querns was leased to a Cirencester solicitor, Charles Lawrence. Within this area he built himself a large ornamental villa, designed by P.F. Robinson (now the Querns Hospital), and laid out park-like gardens with lodges, stables, avenue and walled kitchen garden

(Slater, 1978, 129–144). In 1841, Earl Bathurst sold Athelmead to the Great Western Railway Company for the terminus station and coal yards of their branch line from Kemble. The remaining street frontage on Tetbury road was used for a new cattle market in 1867, the site being donated by Earl Bathurst (Beecham, 1887, 205–6; 229–20). The southern portion of the Querns, including the amphitheatre, continued to be leased as pasture into the present century. The twentieth century has seen the fields to the west of the Querns developed for housing, the closure and redevelopment of the railway area, the conversion of the Querns house to a hospital, and finally the division of the site by the western relief road which was the stimulus for the excavations forming the subject of this volume.

THE EXCAVATIONS

EXTRACTION OF STONE

INTRODUCTION

Mr T.C. Brown reported as early as 11th August 1868 the following thoughts to the British Archaeological Association during its visit to Cirencester (Brown, T.C., 1869, 102) . . . "the Querns (probably Coerns), which is particularly deserving your attention. It was the place of quarries. There the Romans dug stone, and of the rubbish formed the amphitheatre; and among the hills and valleys, extending over many acres, there have been found stone coffins, cinerary urns, skeletons (some with fetters on), and rude sarcophagi made of two sections of the shaft of a column hollowed out to receive an urn. The Romans, a people delighting in games out of doors, in the Querns not only amused themselves, but there also buried their dead; and no doubt it was the common place to which all the people resorted".

Stone for buildings, walls and streets was required early in the Roman period, and the town shows a great flourish of construction in stone in the late first century. Oolitic limestone was used for the two military tombstones found in 1935–6 outside the South Gate (Gazetteer nos. 2003–2004, mf. 5/5), and it must therefore have been quarried locally within twenty years of the Conquest. The wealth of columns, capitals and bases, sculptures and inscriptions in the Bath and Cirencester regions in oolitic limestone points to working of the stone on a large scale. Dunning believed that Cotswold quarries had been opened up by the sixties of the first century (Dunning, 1936, 4) to supply the monolithic blocks five feet long which formed part of the monument of Classicianus, Procurator of Britain. The Roman sculptor Sulinus attested by *RIB* 105 at Cirencester and *RIB* 151 at Bath, would have known the local quarries of the region well. Exploitation of the stone, from either quarry source, or disused buildings within the town continued throughout the Roman period, stone representing the principal building material in Cirencester where little evidence of tile as a structural component other than in hypocausts or roofs has been found (see McWhirr, 1978, 77, pl. XXXVIIa, however, for its use in a half-timbered wall). It has been estimated that some 2,414 cubic metres of stone would have been required to build the defensive town wall, and re-furbishing of the town defences in the third century may have resulted in the re-exploitation of former quarries, despite secondary uses as burial grounds having been found for them. Thus in EA 78 disturbed human skeletal fragments were recovered from quarry backfill, the implication being that the winning of stone took precedence over the preservaton of burial grounds.

EA 78 (QUERNS HOUSE, KITCHEN GARDEN) by Tim Darvill

In 1978, in advance of development of the site for a new ambulance station, limited excavations were undertaken in the former kitchen garden of the Querns House, about 100 m. north–west

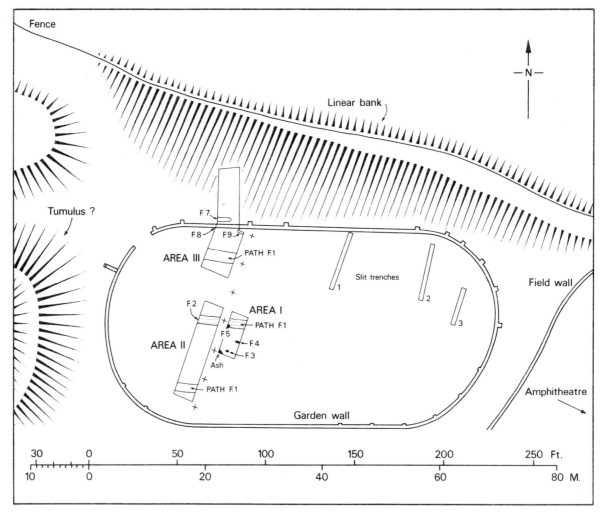

Fig. 7. Trenches excavated EA 78, Querns House Kitchen Garden

of the amphitheatre, fig. 3. Built about 1830 the oval kitchen garden with its high surrounding wall continued under cultivaton until the mid 1960's when the Gloucestershire Area Health Authority acquired the Querns House for use as a hospital.

Within the limits of a 'rescue' excavation it was hoped that a number of research topics might be studied — the development of extra-mural activity, specifically the possibility of Roman quarrying; and elaboration of the road systems within the area. A number of trenches were opened-up across the site, fig. 7, using mechanical excavators, with subsequent manual excavation being concentrated in specific areas.

Evidence of the post-Roman soil horizon suggested that prior to 1825 the topography of the site consisted of a large hollow in amongst a series of mounds. In laying out the kitchen garden the area was flattened by cutting into the mounds and introducing a certain amount of new soil to level the site.

The top of the quarry fill in Area I revealed three shallow features filled with dark brown stoney loam, containing finds giving an aproximate *terminus ante quem* of A.D. 350–360 for the completed filling of the quarry. The quarry itself, F6, was found in both areas I and II as an apparently continuous face, fig. 8. In both cuttings the quarried area had been backfilled with a homogeneous layer of yellow/brown clay matrix, introduced into the quarry pit from above, working back from the quarry face, as evidenced by the tip lines. The homogeneity of the layer suggested that it was deposited in a fairly continuous operation, and may well have derived from the clearance of further areas for quarrying.

In Area I excavation by hand produced a corroded coin of third-fourth century date, pottery

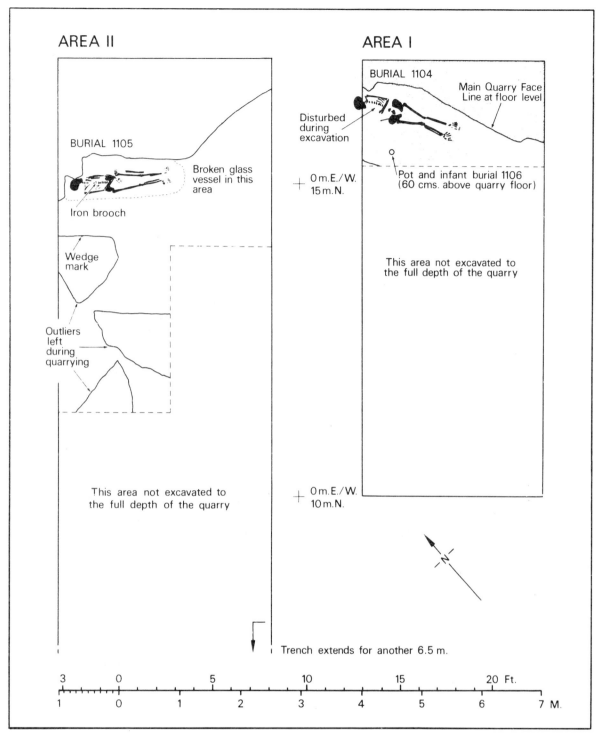

Fig.   8.   Plan of EA 78 areas I and II

of third century date and burials with associated finds. Burial 1104 had been placed supine on
the floor of the lowest bed of stone before quarry backfilling was begun as no intrusive slot
could be detected. The burial was that of an adult male on a north-south orientation dictated by
the line of the quarry face against which he was lying, wearing a pair of hobnailed shoes or
boots, and clutching a small unidentifiable iron object in his right hand. Burial 1105, in Area II,
was deposited in very similar circumstances lying supine on the lowest bed of rock and parallel
to the rock face. In this case, however, a slot had been roughly cut from the lowest tip line, the
burial inserted, and the grave backfilled with the material which had been dug out. The adult

2.   EA 78 I quarry face

3.   EA 78 I quarry face

could not be accurately sexed. Over the central chest region was an iron brooch. The third burial, 1106, was recovered at a higher level, just below the lower tip line about 60 cm. above the quarry floor. No cut through the tip line could be detected suggesting that it was inserted during the infilling process. The body was that of a birth-sized infant, accompanied by a complete narrow-necked Black Burnished cooking jar, of middle–late third century date. Within the general matrix of the backfilling were many fragments of human bone, and the shattered sherds of a late first–early second century glass bottle.

The quarry face itself was of a varying height, rising in the east of Area I to about 1.5 m. above the quarry floor, but only 0.5 m. high in the west of Area II. The Great Oolite, because of its bedding and jointing is very suited to extraction in blocks for working up into squared building stones. The face of the quarry in Area I, pls. 2 and 3, was cleaned with particular attention when cylindrical pick or wedge marks were noticed where the stone had been cut off the face. The working surface of the quarry face was stepped, typical of removing Cotswold stone in usable blocks, and of course dictated by the bedding and cleavage planes in the rock. In all about 20 examples of these wedge slots were noted, all semi-circular in shape about 1 cm. in diameter. Where several occurred as a group they were spaced at 30–35 cm. intervals and all were on the edges of the face step.

The practice of working to a face is usual in stone extraction, but in this case the height of the face was limited by the depth of the band of stone, which changed immediately below the lowest exposed bed at this point to a much softer rock, which when wet became slightly plastic, and which would have been useless for building. In Area II much of the rock had been removed down to the top of this softer band, which formed the floor of the quarry, with only occasional outliers of the harder limestone remaining. Wedge marks were also recorded round these outliers of stone.

Area III, fig. 9, was located to test the hypothesis that the Fosse Way skirted the amphitheatre on the north side, to join up with a section of road found in the grounds of the Querns Hospital in 1973 (McWhirr, 1978, 64). A road was discovered but its scale was inappropriate to it being the Fosse Way, and its construction was not the same as the sections in the Querns 1973 excavations, and CT 71–2, (p. 46). It would appear that quarry waste of limestone brash was levelled out and rammed hard to form the surface of the road, F10, layer 26, about 6.3 m. wide, figs. 9 and 11. Water washing down over the exposed surrounding stone deposited a fine light grey silt over the southern side of the road. Subsequently a layer of limestone brash was laid over the southern part of the road restricting its width to c. 3.4 m., and resulting in the concentration of rutting close to the bank. Repairs to the road were carried out, and a gully leading from the road was presumably scraped out to try and prevent water staying on the surface. After the abandonment of the road, further silting and rain wash from surrounding slopes and exposed stone left a thick wedge over the road, containing much residual Roman pottery and human bone. It is probable therefore to conjecture the line of the Fosse running to the north of Area III and between the ?long barrow. The relative chronological positions of the quarry and the roadway were difficult to assess because they could not be stratigraphically linked, due to the logistical necessity of maintaining access to the site.

To summarize the stages of development of the area it would appear that initial activity on the site was the opening up of the area for stone extraction, working to a quarry face and thus producing the mounds of debris which characterize the area to the present day. Within area III the mounds were levelled to produce the wide road to give continuing access to quarry areas located within Areas I and II. As sources of usable stone were exhausted backfilling in redundant areas continued with burials being placed on convenient ledges. Quarry rubble and slope-wash reduced the width of the road in Area III, which probably continued to give access to other parts of the working area.

To append actual dates to this suggested chronology is very difficult. The majority of the pottery is obviously redeposited as is the whole of the quarry fill, except for the pot associated with burial 1106 dated to the middle–late third century. No dating evidence was obtained from the road, as the re-deposited material in the silting is valueless for dating. None of the pottery from the quarry fill need be later than the late third century, thus providing the only clue to the

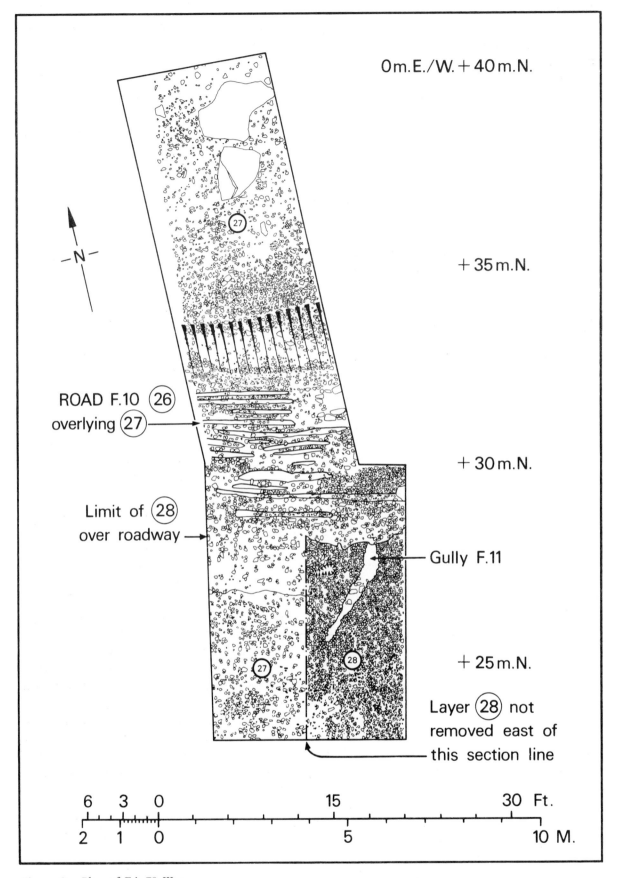

0m. E./W. + 40 m.N.

+ 35 m.N.

ROAD F.10 ㉖
overlying ㉗

+ 30 m.N.

Limit of ㉘
over roadway

Gully F.11

+ 25 m.N.

Layer ㉘ not
removed east of
this section line

-N-

Fig.   9.   Plan of EA 78 III

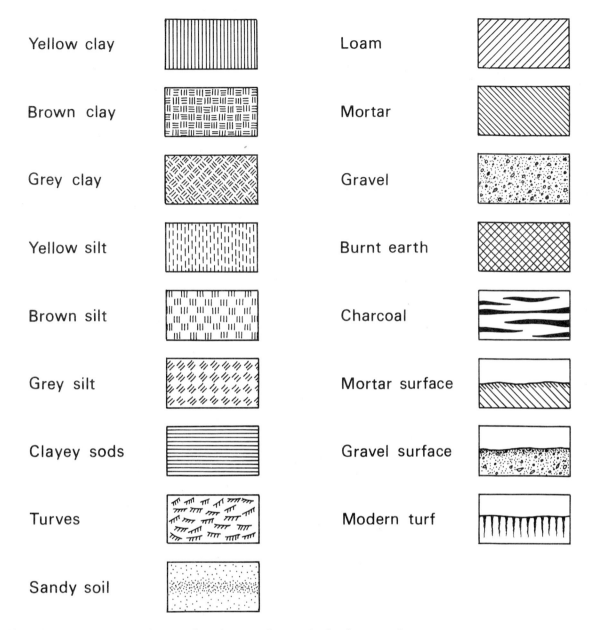

Yellow clay

Brown clay

Grey clay

Yellow silt

Brown silt

Grey silt

Clayey sods

Turves

Sandy soil

Loam

Mortar

Gravel

Burnt earth

Charcoal

Mortar surface

Gravel surface

Modern turf

Fig. 10. Key to conventions used to denote soil types in the drawn sections

date of the working. Little time elapsed between the termination of the stone extraction and back-filling as the quarry face was 'fresh' with no evidence of frost shattering which would be expected if the face had been left exposed over a winter. Demand for stone in the third and fourth centuries might have been high if the chronology proposed by Wacher is accepted for the re-furbishing of the town defences with the wide stone wall (Wacher, 1974, 302). The final clue as to the date of the quarries comes from the small but useful group of coins, derived from post-quarry filling features. The three coins range in date from A.D. 330–360, suggesting that by the mid-fourth century the quarry was backfilled — a pattern well in accord with the evidence from within the quarry.

1981 OBSERVATIONS by David Wilkinson

Construction work for the Ambulance Station with preliminary site clearance and installation of services began in May 1981, and permission to carry out archaeological observation was

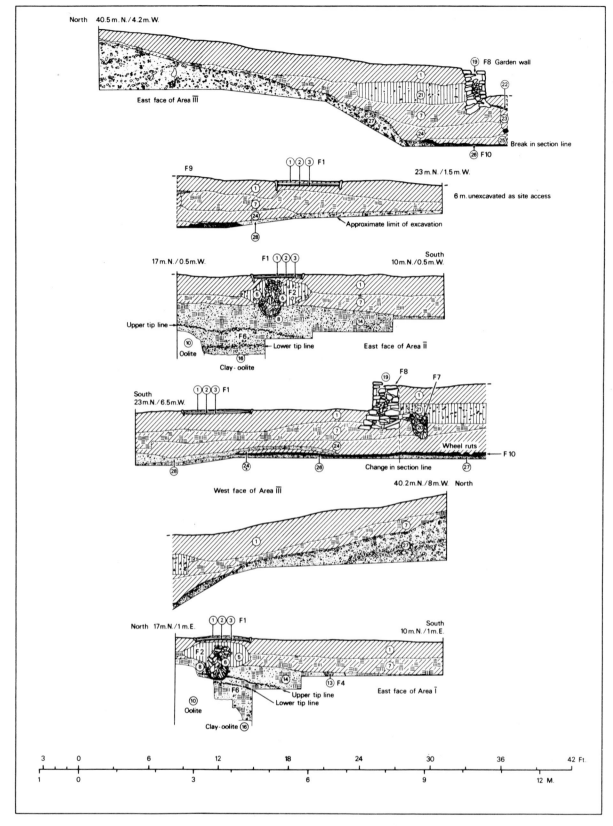

Fig. 11   Section EA 78 III

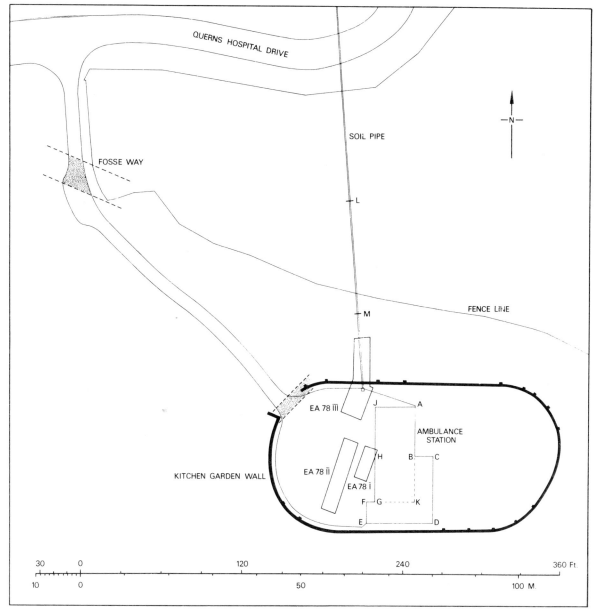

Fig. 12. Plan of 1981 observations

granted by the Gloucestershire Area Health Authority and the contractors Newcombe Beard Ltd.. The information retrieved by site visits, and recording of mechanically cut sections has augmented details recovered during excavations in 1978, p. 38.

SITE PREPARATION

The construction of a new site access from the north (fig. 12) involved the removal of *c*. 60 cm. of topsoil along the proposed route. About 25 m. from its junction with the main access road to Querns House, brash was exposed below a brown clay subsoil. Although no good worn metalled surfaces could be recognised, this may represent the top layers of a road or track, aligned north-west to south-east.

Similar layers of brash, composed of stones in a sandy clay, were exposed at the entrance to the walled garden. The top surface of this material was up to 25 cm. higher than the reduced level of 113.30 m. and may yet again represent a track or road. Fig 12.

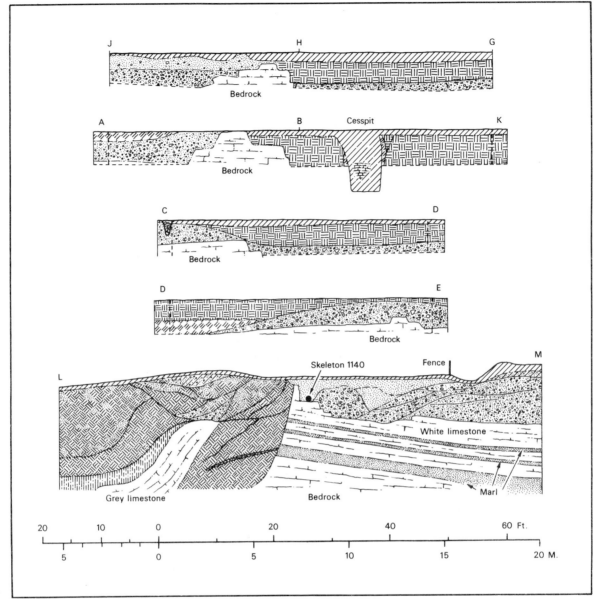

Fig. 13. Sections, 1981 observations

FOUNDATIONS

The excavation of trenches for the building foundations involved the removal of up to 2 m. of material following a general reduction in ground level of between 40 cm. and 1 m. to 113.30 m. O.D.. Diagrammatic section drawings were made of some of the trench sides and these are illustrated in fig. 13. The letter codes refer to those in fig. 12. In the course of its operations the JCB removed material down to the level of the bedrock which survived to a much higher level at points just north of 'H' and 'B', an indication that to the south much had been removed in quarrying. It is also to be noted that the fill on the north side of this surviving limestone ridge was composed in the main of brash, whereas that to the south was composed predominantly of silts and clay. It can be postulated that quarrying took place in the northern area first, working southwards to a face, to be followed by quarrying in the southern area working northwards. The waste from this second working was dumped into the disused quarry to the north. In contrast, the southern quarry when abandoned filled naturally with material washed from the surrounding higher ground.

The limestone ridge to the west of 'J-G' corresponds to F6 discovered in EA 78 I and II.

Excavations in 1978 in Area III showed that the brash had been deposited during the Roman period, probably during the late 3rd century. It is possible to suggest that at least 1.3 m. and probably more than 3 m. of stone has been quarried from the bedrock in the area of A-B.

SERVICE TRENCH

Excavation of a north-south trench for a soil drain to connect the ambulance station with the soil drain north of the roundabout provided much valuable information, particularly of the underlying geology. The fill of the trench to the north of the drawn section, fig. 13, was in the main of brown clay. In places the clay was silty, grey or with a fine gravel admixture. At the northern end, traces of grey limestone were observed in the bottom of the trench, at 110.0 m. O.D..

Fig.13 L-M represents a 25 m. length of the east side of the trench. There is little doubt that the trench crossed the line of a geological fault with a dip of 11° south and a strike of 283°. (Information provided by Dr. J. Harpen of St. Paul's College, Cheltenham). The white limestone bedrock, with intervening beds of marl, had been uplifted in relation to the clays and the grey limestone. At the time of writing it has not been possible to define the grey limestone as being from the Forest Marble or Kemble beds. It would appear that the Romans were conscious of the presence of the fault line and had begun their quarrying adjacent to it. It is not clear, however, if layers of white limestone were removed from the section illustrated, although failure to observe an old ground surface suggests they had.

The oxidised appearance of the upper clay deposits at the north end would suggest waste material deposited as a result of soil clearance prior to quarrying. Unfortunately the trench at this point was excavated in two stages. A trench about 3 m. wide was cut down to a level of 114.5 m. O.D. prior to a narrow trench 80 cm. wide being excavated for the drain itself. It can be seen that this split level occurs at a crucial point and since the stratification could not be clearly seen, allows for alternative interpretations.

It is clear that quarry waste was being dumped onto the surviving surface of the white limestone and that the large agger so created along the south side of the boundary fence clearly contained surfaces and was used as a road. The top surfaces of the road had however been disturbed by the root action of trees. Some of the layers of brash on the north side of the road were little more than tips of waste and the road had no definite edges. Some washed material from the road was deposited on the north side although the deposits were very mixed.

The JCB removed a skeleton from the upper spit of the soil drain trench leaving only the lower legs and feet in the baulk. The bones which survived in situ together with some loose bones from the spoil heap were allocated burial number 1140. Associated with the burial were a few sherds of Roman pottery and the position of the lower legs would suggest orientation east-west.

In section the southern end of the soil drain pipe trench crossing EA 78 III, revealed definite metalled surfaces, with perhaps more within the layer described as 'gravel and stones'. These appear to have been laid on top of the brash derived from quarry working.

In conclusion, it can be seen that the line of the Roman road observed during the construction of the access road and in the soil pipe trench can be linked with the previously recorded segments to the east and north-west. It continues about 14 m. to the north of the walled garden as observed in the soil drain trench and thus well to the north of the 1978 excavations in EA III. This road can now be regarded as being the Fosse Way.

The road surfaces recorded at the south-east end of the new access road, and at the southern end of the soil drain trench (and EA 78 III) represent spur roads and tracks leading off the main road into the quarries. These ephemeral tracks would presumably have only short useful lives as quarried areas were abandoned, backfilled and new ones opened. All the mounds in the area can be regarded as quarry waste heaps until proved otherwise. This suggests that the area of Roman quarrying may have been in the region of ten acres (4ha.). The level of the stone above sea level prior to quarrying is likely to have been 116 m. at the north side of the quarry and could have been as high as 125 m. at the southern edge in the region of Cotswold Close. The level of the quarry base as revealed in the foundation trenches of the ambulance station was 111.3 m. O.D.

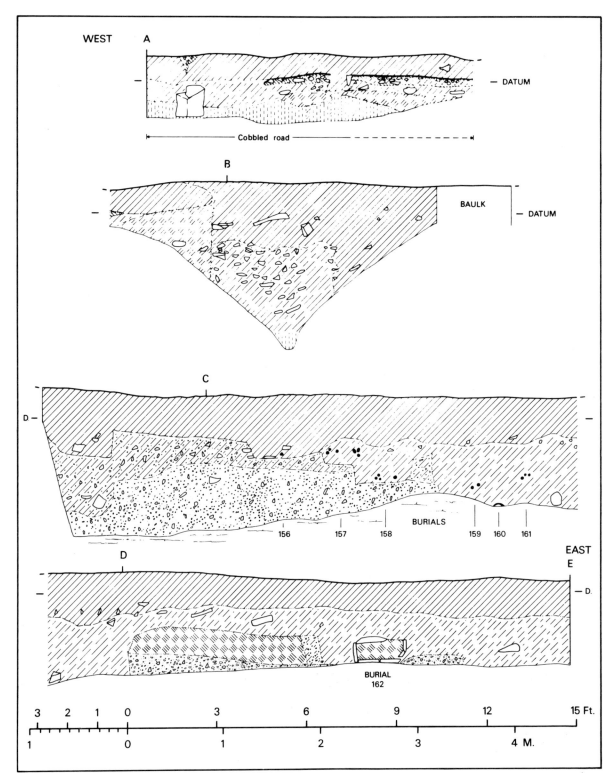

Fig. 14. CS 71–3 4, west-east section

AREA SOUTH OF FOSSE WAY by Linda Viner

The area to the south-east of the amphitheatre, fig. 4, is dominated by the steep sides of a semi-circular hollow, 10 m. high. Archaeological investigation of the face was not feasible, but there is the strongest supposition that the whole area forms the remains of a worked quarry, first exploited by the Romans.

In excavations south of the Fosse Way, 1969–74, positive evidence for quarrying activity as found in EA 78 was not observed, although in a west-east section cut mechanically along the north face of CS 71–3 4, a bench of oolitic limestone was uncovered at a depth of 1.37 m., fig. 14, extending southwards for 0.92 m.. No evidence of tooling on the exposed surfaces was detectable. The limestone rubble overburden covered the step to a depth of 0.61 m. and was of a similar nature to that recorded in EA 78, layer 14. Small fragments of animal bone, and abraided sherds of Roman pottery recovered from the bucket of the JCB indicated the redeposited nature of the rubble waste. In contrast to the area north-west of the amphitheatre there was no evidence to suggest that the quarry was being exploited whilst burial was taking place in the area. The accumulation of deposits of brown-black earth over the area — both naturally and augmented by positive dumping from elsewhere — appears to have levelled-out the quarry area before burial took place. Roman burials were located c. 50 m. from the sides of the hollow, in CS 70 exploratory trenches A–D, cut into black earth, with the deepest actually cut into the underlying quarry rubble. The documentary evidence, p. 28, does not suggest active medieval quarrying in the area, and the absence of quarry rubble sealing these burials so close to the face would tend to support this.

Evidence for a service road into the quarry area was recorded in CS 71–3 4. A compacted layer of stone with tile and iron fragments embedded in its surface was observed, with rutting on a north-south alignment. Grey-green silt had been washed into a dip in the road (as seen in section fig. 15, layer 3) presumably carried by rainwater washing down the slope to the north. An attempt to level out the site was made, layer 2, with a few large stones tossed into the silt to give a foundation for patches of smaller stones. Subsequent burials in the vicinty cut through this secondary road surface, and were found lying on top of the earliest road, for example burials 273 and 263, fig. 15. The track itself seems to have been a branch from the Fosse Way, and was used to take stone out of the quarry.

A V-sectioned ditch was traced in three trenches, CS 70 fig. 16 section H-G, CS 71 3, and CS 71–3 4 fig. 14, running in a north-south direction before turning south-east in CS 71–3 4. Its date and precise function remains uncertain. The road surface described above extended to the lip of the ditch in CS 71–3 4 with no clear-cut division between the road surface and the rubble sides of the ditch. In section, the earliest phase of the ditch appears to be contemporary with the road and therefore presumably with the quarrying activity.

Pottery from the ditch would indicate that it had been allowed to silt up with black earth from the mid-third century, and burials, such as 134, discovered lying along its length must post-date that date. However, it may have remained open in the earliest stages of the areas' use as a cemetery as north-south burials were recorded lying parallel to it; and two stone coffins 223 and 42 were similarly parallel to it on a NW/SE alignment as it turned south-east, fig. 2.

Evidence for extraction of limestone by tunnelling in the Roman period could not be proved, and the abundance of outcrops probably allowed for extensive surface workings, without the need to go underground. In 1975 construction of the relief road, and in particular the realignment of Querns Hill over a new road bridge led to the discovery of tunnels and shafts in former arable land known locally as 'The Bumpy Fields'. Local stories of tunnels have been current for many years, linking the Bull Ring (amphitheatre) in turn with the town, parish church or Lord Bathurst's mansion. The 1975 discovery has confirmed at least the presence of quarrying tunnels, but of uncertain date. A date of 1836 painted/scratched on the roof of one of the tunnels would imply that they were at least accessible, if not actually being worked, at that time.

The great variation in the depth at which limestone rubble was encountered in the areas

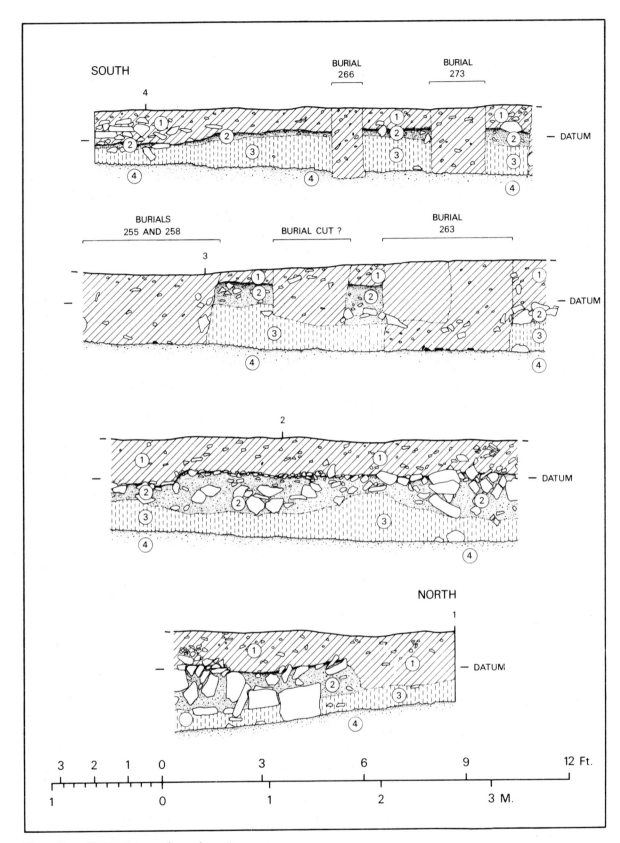

Fig.   15.   CS 71–3 4, south–north section

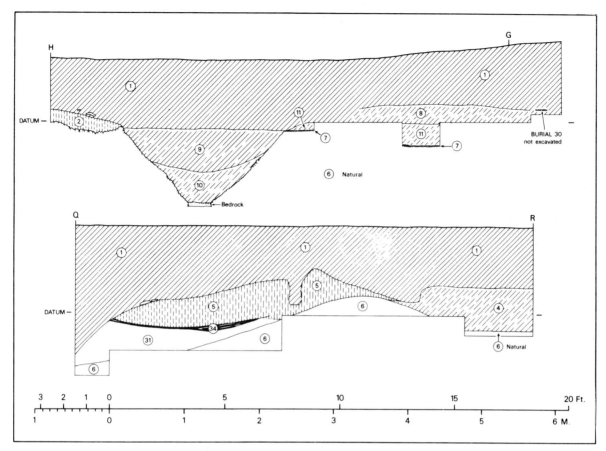

Fig. 16. CS 70, west-east sections

sampled provided further evidence to substantiate extensive quarrying. In parts of CS 71–3 4 black earth overburden was 0.76 m. thick, and in places as little as 0.23 m.. Similar depths were encountered in CS 73 9 and CS 74 10 to the west, but only 10 m. north in CS 73 8 a total depth of 1.84 m. of black soil had to be removed before limestone rubble was uncovered. Density of burial was also greatest in this trench — the Roman grave diggers on the site evidently knew either from previous knowledge, or practical experience the areas with the greatest depth of black earth. CS 74 10 was extended northwards in an attempt to correlate the natural rock profile with that of CS 72–3 8. Certainly in the north of the trench a depth of *c*. 1.60 m. of black earth sealed limestone rubble with burials 328 and 322 at depths of 1.52 m. and 1.42 m. respectively. In the small area uncovered there was certainly not the density of burial as found in CS 72–3 8. Sections suggested that this may have been the outer lip of a large hollow infilled with black earth, and because of the relatively greater depth of easily dug soil was the most heavily used area. It has often been noted in medieval graveyards that continued use over long periods has raised the height of the ground surface to completely encircle the church and create an island plateau in relation to the level of the surrounding ground. This phenomenon must have also occurred in heavily used Roman cemeteries, and could further account for the greater depth of black earth.

ROMAN ROADS WEST OF THE TOWN
by
Alan McWhirr

Prior to this series of excavations the Roman road pattern west of the town was considered fairly easy to understand. It had always been assumed that a road linked the town with the amphitheatre and that the Fosse Way was on the same line as the former Tetbury Road; other than that no other roads were suspected. When, therefore, it was planned to construct the relief road around Cirencester it was decided to test these assumptions where this road cut across the assumed Roman roads. The field between the amphitheatre and the disused railway line was trial trenched in 1969 (CT 69 (a), fig. 3) and one such trench was dug close to the amphitheatre across a pronounced ridge, which was thought at the time to conceal the road from the town.

The trench was placed to cut the southern side of the ridge and later extended when it was found necessary to explore surfaces beyond its northern end. A slight change in direction was made in the final extension in order to section at right angles features already found. A metalled surface, probably of first or early second-century date, was found on the southern side of the ridge and although is was not continuous over the whole of the excavated area it was shown to have been at least 4.5 m. wide and appeared to be aligned on the amphitheatre entrance. On a different alignment and at a higher level were at least two metalled surfaces, the latest of which was marked by a series of wheel ruts which clearly indicated that the traffic was passing to the north of the amphitheatre.

A more complicated system of roads was revealed than had been expected and so when plans were made to excavate large areas of the Roman cemetery in the same field the opportunity was taken in 1971–2 to section the ridge in the east of the field adjacent to the former railway line and this work was carried out under the supervision of Dr. J.A. Derry.

The first section of road uncovered was similar in character to that found in the northern part of the 1969 trial trench. It was well-worn and in places there were wheel ruts which had been repaired (pl. 4). Beneath was another road surface showing evidence of heavy use and again rutted, but with a very different make-up from the one above it (pl. 5); much larger stone being used as a base. Both of these roads were of similar width and made from the local limestone. During their life the soft limestone surfaces had weathered and been worn away by wheeled vehicles causing a considerable build-up of road silt on either side, but more noticeable to the north of the road where it was over a metre thick in places.

The earliest road surface to be encountered in 1970 appeared much wider than the others and was again resting upon a base of large stone, probably waste from the nearby quarries. As there were no ruts it was not clear in which direction the traffic was moving, although there were slight indications that it was on a different alignment from the later roads. No dating evidence came from this section.

The 1970 excavations indicated the need to examine even greater areas if constructional details and alignments were to be fully understood and so in 1971 an area of about 40 by 12 m. was opened up, the overburden being removed by machine. The road surface then exposed was thoroughly examined during the subsequent two seasons and various sections were dug across the road to investigate its make-up. The latest surface uncovered was found to consist of a much-worn small-stoned metalled layer, heavily rutted, with some of the deepest ruts being patched to prolong the life of the road, thus avoiding the need to lay a completely new surface.

The sections dug across the road showed features which were quite different from those of the 1970 section, in that the number of surfaces were fewer and the general make-up more conventional. The western section was very poor; the stone used in its make-up was crudely packed and not compacted, with evidence of some slippage on the north side. The central section was of better construction although the base layers were not graded in the same way as they were in the 1970 section. In this section there appeared a small ditch sealed by the upper levels but above another metalled layer, associated with which was a thin metalling (10 cm.), on

4.   Fosse Way 1972, ruts

5.   Fosse Way 1971, section

6. Kerb of Fosse Way

7. Road section observed at the Querns, 1973

an alignment different from the main road surfaces but possibly similar to the earliest one found in the 1970 section. This appeared to be unconnected with the main structure and coincided with the Lewis Lane/amphitheatre line, probably representing an early road from the town to the quarries and amphitheatre. The later road was at an angle of about 15° to the early one and the direction of its ruts indicated that it was by-passing the amphitheatre.

The final stage in examining the road was to remove the accumulation of road silt on the north side. A metre of silt had built up during the road's existence and under it a kerb consisting of two courses of limestone was revealed (pl. 6). This clearly defined edge of the road enabled its exact line to be plotted and changes of direction to be seen. One such change occurred in the 40 m. stretch of road metalling exposed, which took the road to the north of the ampitheatre. This supported an earlier feeling that the road was too well made to be just a service road for the amphitheatre.

When the topsoil was being removed in March 1973 prior to the construction of the Querns Maternity Hospital (fig. 2), a 22 m. stretch of a well-built Roman road was noted and with the co-operation of the contractors, Espley-Tyas, records were made during the course of their work. Finally the whole area designated for the new hospital was removed and two oblique sections left at the edge of the excavated hole (pl. 7). The road was about 6 m. wide and along the exposed length varied in its make-up, being some 93 cm. thick at the town end and reducing to 54 cm. at the west of the contractor's machine-dug hole. Within this accumulation of road material at least three different road surfaces were recorded.

The character and direction of the excavated road which emanated from the Bath Gate along with the stretch of road on the site of the Querns Maternity Hospital in 1973, which almost certainly links with the excavated section, gives the general direction of the road and some indication of its importance. The road aims for the modern Tetbury Road, which is the traditional course for the Roman Fosse Way, suggesting that, at some date, the Fosse Way was diverted just to the west of the town to enter it via the Bath Gate. The presence of first and second century burials alongside the Tetbury Road close to the town indicates that a way out of the town existed there at that time. Perhaps the diversion occurred when the Bath Gate and town defences were erected towards the end of the second century, although there is no reason why the original course could not have been maintained to lead to a small gate. Whatever the case, it seems clear that in the third and fourth centuries the main road from Bath branched off across the Querns to the Bath Gate. There is no direct dating evidence from the excavations for the road itself, but the presence of road silt in levels pre-dating the construction of the building shows that the road was there before *c*. A.D. 280.

Other metalled tracks of a less substantial nature have been found pre-dating the Roman cemetery (p. 43), during the excavation of the Querns Kitchen Garden (p. 35) and beneath the roadside building (p. 55). All these appear to be associated with the exploitation of the Querns for building stone.

ROADSIDE BUILDING
by
Roger Leech and Alan McWhirr

INTRODUCTION

1972–1974 Excavations, CT 72–74. (ADM)

The building was discovered in 1972 during excavation of a large area of the Fosse Way south-west of the Bath Gate (fig. 3). To the north of the Fosse three cobbled surfaces were found, the uppermost of which on investigation proved to be sealing an earlier building.

In April 1973 construction work for Christian Brann's new premises in Phoenix Way took place, just to the north of the building discovered in 1972, unbeknown to the Excavation Committee, in which the site was cleared to a depth of about two metres. As no advance warning had been given no archaeological observation took place but fortunately Mr. D.J. Wilkinson, who at the time was carrying out rescue work at the Querns Hospital in Tetbury Road, noticed the contractors at work and was able to arrange for some recording to take place. The levelling of the site had left standing a two-metre vertical face at the southern end of Christian Brann's site, just to the north of where excavations were carried out in 1972. This vertical face was cleaned and carefully examined by Messrs. R.R. Downey and T.J. O'Leary who also collected together oral information regarding other discoveries made during the levelling. They recorded walls belonging to the structure found in 1972 and from the wall foundations recovered part of an inscription of a tombstone which may indicate the settlement of veterans at Cirencester (mf. 2/5). Skeletons were visible in the upstanding section and comments from those working on the site suggested that others were found further to the north, but not in great numbers.

During the summer of 1973, an eight-week season was devoted to the excavation of the masonry structure to establish its plan and chronological sequence. It was shown that the walls formed part of a building which was probably used for craft or light-industrial purposes (fig. 17). As future excavations did not seem likely at the time, the opportunity was taken in 1973 to excavate a limited number of areas in depth to date the building and to see if earlier structures existed beneath. In the event however, it was possible for the Committee to carry out further excavations in 1974 with the knowledge that the site was due to be developed that year and so for this reason certain objectives were set and excavation was carried out with these in mind. It was decided to uncover as much as possible of the latest phase of the building and to take other selected areas down to natural to establish the chronology of the site. Approximately 75% of the inside of the building was excavated to the latest floor level and three areas dug to natural. Despite the urgency created in 1973 and again in 1974 the major part of the site remained undeveloped for well over two years although some disturbance took place at the western end during the construction of the western relief road between 1974 and 1975.

The 1971–4 excavations of the building and road were given the site-code letter CT with features/layers numbered 1–99 being reserved for the road and 100 to 278 for the building.

After the construction of the relief road Christian Brann proposed extending their premises further south on to the site of the Roman building which necessitated levelling the whole plot by one to three metres, involving the complete removal of the Roman building. The news of this development broke at a time when the Excavation Committee was not in a position to mount its own excavation and so arrangements were made with the Committee for Rescue Archaeology in Avon, Gloucestershire and Somerset (CRAAGS) to undertake the levelling operations on behalf of Christian Brann under archaeological supervision. This work was directed by Dr. R.H. Leech.

1976 Excavations, CT 76. (RHL)

In the limited time available it was impossible to excavate carefully by hand the entire part of

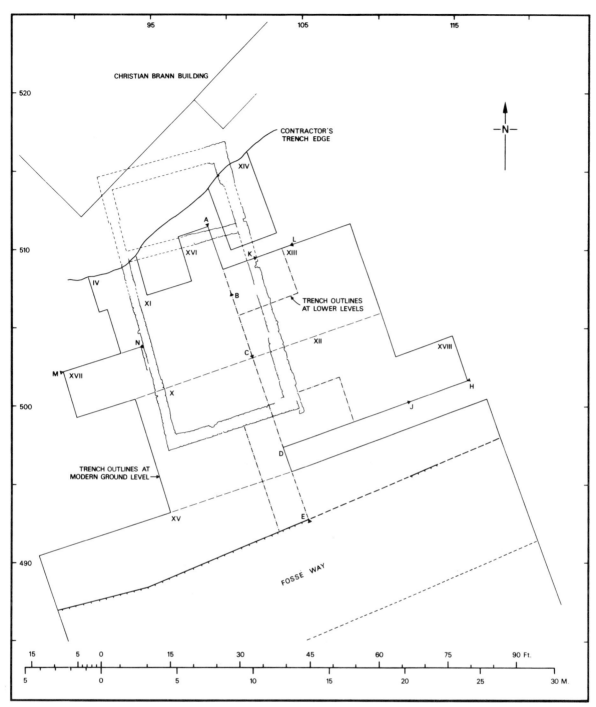

Fig. 17. CT 72–4 trench outlines

the site not previously examined, so arrangements were made with the contractors in order that the excavation could commence with some of the mechanical earthmoving operations that would subsequently have been necessary. This earthmoving, which was therefore carried out under archaeological supervision, comprised (a) the removal of recent spoil heaps and tipped material, (b) the cutting back to a vertical face of the trench (trench 1, fig. 18) left alongside the Christian Brann Building in 1973, (c) the removal of all layers above the silts traced in 1971–4, except in the two baulks left running at right angles to one another across the width and length of the site. The surfaces of the silt layers were trowelled over before (d) the cutting of four trenches (trenches 2–4, and 6) parallel with the axis of Phoenix Way and approximately at right angles to the Roman Fosse Way (fig. 18). The two on the south-west of the plot (trenches 2 and

3) were cut to the surface of the natural subsoil; the two on the north-east side (trenches 4 and 6) were cut to the depth that it was intended to excavate for the new building on this plot. All the exposed sections were cut back by trowelling prior to recording, the bottoms of several of the trenches, particularly the one alongside the Christian Brann Building, were taken down further by hand. In addition a large part of the central two baulks was excavated very carefully by hand from the existing ground surface downwards.

All features (including layers, pits, walls) were given a unique number, commencing at 300 so as to avoid confusion with the numbers given to the layers in the 1972–4 excavations. In accordance with the recording system of the Excavation Committee finds were given a separate number unique to CT 76, while burials were separately numbered from 720. The positions of plans, sections, features and recorded finds arc indicated by the excavation grid which was based on the Ordnance Survey co-ordinates. Thus the full map reference for 100/500 on fig. 18 is SP 402100 201500.

Section A-B (fig. 19) was cut from the existing ground level to the surface of the natural subsoil and provides a link between the 1976 excavation and the earlier examination of the Fosse Way and cemetery to the south. Section C-D (fig. 20) was partly cut to the surface of the subsoil and, but for a two-metre gap, would link sections A-B, E-F and F-G (figs. 19 and 21–22) to the remaining areas examined in 1976.

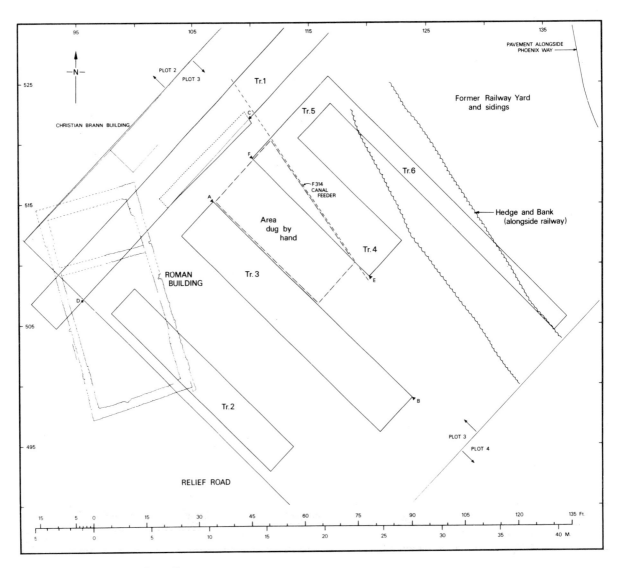

Fig. 18. CT 76 trench outlines

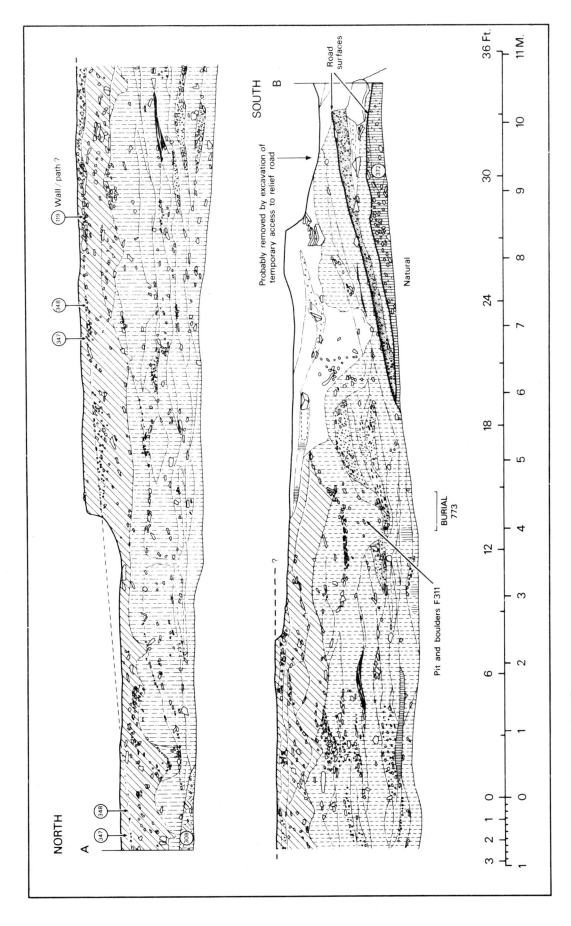

Fig. 19. CT 76 section A–B (see fig. 18)

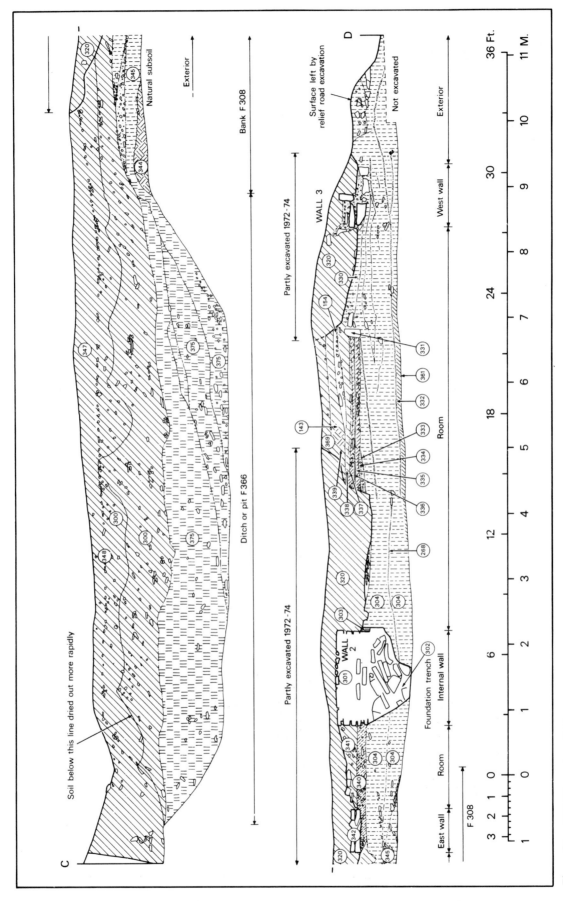

Fig. 20. CT 76 section C-D

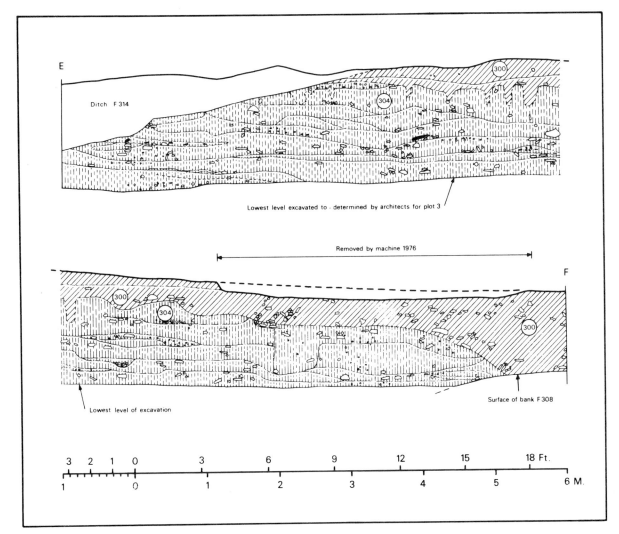

Fig. 21. CT 76 section E-F

SUMMARY OF CHRONOLOGY

Period   I Features and layers pre-dating the construction of the building, A.D. 145/161–280
Period   II Construction of the building around A.D. 280
Period III Use of building c. A.D. 280+
Period IV Layers post-dating the use of the building
Period   V Cobbled layer covering most of the building and surrounding area; after c. A.D. 330
Period VI Use of site as a cemetery

1972–1976 EXCAVATIONS (RHL and ADM)

PERIOD I

The earliest features noted comprised a series of surfaces with ruts just above natural, a quarry pit or ditch cut into natural and an early road surface (fig. 23).

The ruts were first found in 1974 in trench XVII/XI, and in the subsequent 1976 excavation in trench 1, just to the north of XVII/XI, and again in trench 3. In XVII/XI these ruts cut into a

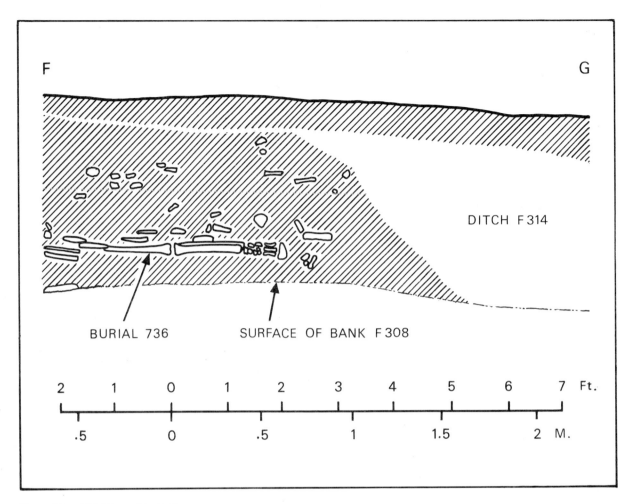

F   G

DITCH F 314

BURIAL 736   SURFACE OF BANK F 308

2   1   0   1   2   3   4   5   6   7 Ft.

.5   0   .5   1   1.5   2 M.

Fig.   22.   CT 76 section F-G

surface of small stones, not considered to be natural, ranging in size from 5 × 5 cm. to 1 × 1 cm., the majority being of the smaller size. Nearly all the stones showed signs of wear, and running west-south-west to east-north-east across the trench was a series of ruts some as much as 5 cms. deep. Others were very shallow and hardly noticeable except under certain conditions. There were two main ruts which could be traced for the entire length of the trench and were approximately 0.88 m. apart. In trenches 1 and 3 it was thought that the ruts marked the line of an early road using the surface of the subsoil as metalling (for a discussion of the roads see page 46).

There seems little doubt that the ruts just described were made by wheeled vehicles and that a prepared surface was used to provide a firm base for vehicles. The general direction of the ruts leads to where the main north-east/south-west street of the town meets the town defences, i.e. at the site of the Bath Gate.

A more substantial road, probably belonging to this period, was found in the 1976 excavations at the south-east end of trenches 2 and 3. It consisted of a low embankment 0.20 m. high of crushed oolitic limestone and clay (fig. 23 layer 327) lying on the natural subsoil. It was recorded in four separate sections in trenches 2 and 3, (e.g. fig. 19), which provided evidence for its northern edge; the other side of the road was beyond the limits of the 1976 excavations.

On the north side of the site was a possible quarry pit or ditch (F 366) cut 1.20 m. below the surface of the natural subsoil and with a low bank (F 308) 0.50 m. high, consisting of layers of clay, silt and small stones, mixed with brown clay, on its east and south sides. In the area examined, it was impossible to be certain whether the feature was a pit or the corner of two

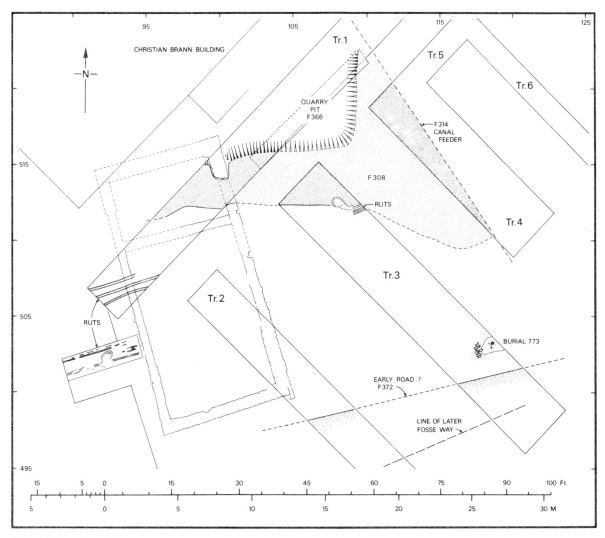

Fig. 23. Plan of road surfaces

ditches. It may have been dug as a pit for obtaining clay for use in the amphitheatre, or as a base for roads, or in building. The low bank (308) could be the remnants of the upcast quarried material.

There is no direct dating evidence to show when the above features were in use. As the majority of subsequent later layers seem to comprise rubbish from within the town, the datable material which they contain may have been lying around for many years before eventually being dumped. The coins and pottery from levels sealing the period I features and pre-dating the construction of the later stone building range in date from c. A.D. 145–280 and the problems of using this material for dating are fully discussed by Valery Rigby and Richard Reece elsewhere in this report. Despite these problems the features pre-dating the stone building must be earlier than A.D. 145–280.

As well as rubbish-like material which had accumulated over the site there was also a considerable amount of silt within which many tip lines were visible and are clearly seen on the sections (e.g. figs. 19, 24, and 25). These silt layers are the result of wear and weathering of the limestone surface of the Fosse Way to the south of the site. Thick deposits of silt extended as far as 12 to 15 m. to the north of the road. This is a clear indication of the way in which these relatively soft limestone road surfaces were eroded by traffic and weather. In the town, streets were constantly being repaired and when necessary completely new surfaces were laid directly

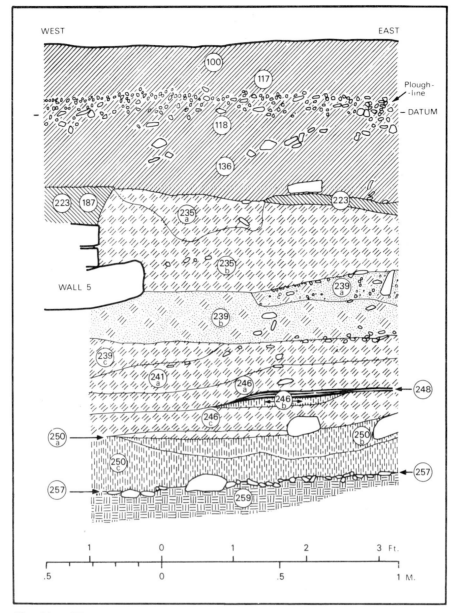

Fig. 24.   CT 72–4 section K-L (see fig. 17)

on the earlier worn-out one. The build-up of street surfaces is clearly illustrated in Dr. G.A. Webster's section across Ermin Street dug in 1958 (Webster, 1959) and more recently it has been possible to show that similar deposits of road silt accumulated in the town and could be used to bring the level of buildings up to that of the streets alongside (McWhirr, 1978).

Burial 773 (fig. 23) was in a grave cut from an undetermined level in the silt layers 0.20 m. into the natural subsoil below. The fill of the grave was entirely of silt, unlike the black soil which filled the later graves. Owing to lack of time during the 1976 excavations the burial was not removed. Above it at a higher level in the silt were a large erratic boulder and a number of smaller similar stones (F 311), which may have sealed burial 773, but cannot be proved to have done so since the stratigraphical relationship was removed by the machine-cut trench.

PERIODS II & III

Around A.D. 280 a stone building was erected and a detailed examination of the surviving walls during both series of excavations seems to indicate that the building was of at least two phases.

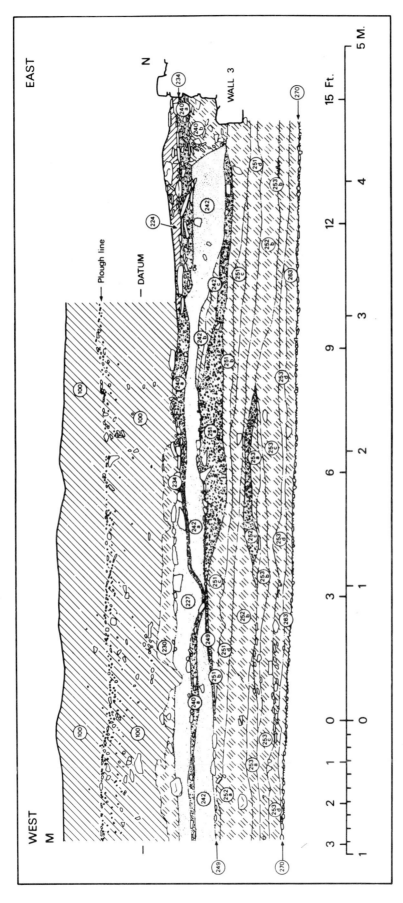

Fig. 25. CT 72–4 section M-N

8. Post-socket for timber upright in wall 5

The first phase probably consisted of the north wall (no. 1 on plan, fig. 26), parts of the east
(5) and west (3) walls and the internal wall (2). The southern limit of the building seems to have
been marked by two stone plinths which were placed in line with distinct structural changes in
the side walls (3 & 5). There was a re-alignment of wall 3 and on either side of this point the
construction of the wall is different. The coursing is not the same and to the north of this point
wall 5 was built to take timber uprights along the outside face whereas no such features were
noted to the south of the re-alignment, suggesting a later extension. These post-sockets were
taken down through the wall to offset level beneath which an extra stone had been provided to
support the timber upright, thus showing it to be an original feature (plate 8). The presence of
timber posts embedded in the wall implies a half-timbered structure with the stone walls
perhaps not being taken up to roof level. How the space between those timber uprights was
filled could not be determined; masonry panels not unlike a normal stone wall could have been
used as found in 1975 in Admiral's Walk, Cirencester, *insula VI* (McWhirr, 1978, 77). Alternatively the more traditional wattle and daub could have been used, although no indication of
such an infilling was found.

A re-examination of wall 5 during the 1976 excavations suggests that it consisted of three
separate sections. The southern and northern thirds (F 310, 353) were laid in deep foundation
trenches cut from the surface of the silt layers F 304 to the surface of the natural subsoil. The
greater depth of the northern section is explained by its being cut through the soft fill (F 375) of
ditch or pit F 366. The centre section of wall (F 342) was laid in a very shallow foundation
trench cut only 0.10 m. into the silt layers F 304. Assuming the existence of two phases, the
first phase seems to have been an open-fronted building facing onto the Fosse Way with presumably some form of timber shuttering at the front. The stone plinths could have supported a
timber upright to provide the necessary support along this side of the building for the roof.

The evidence as it stands implies at least two phases of building although a certain amount of
caution must be expressed about this interpretation, and the observations made during the 1976

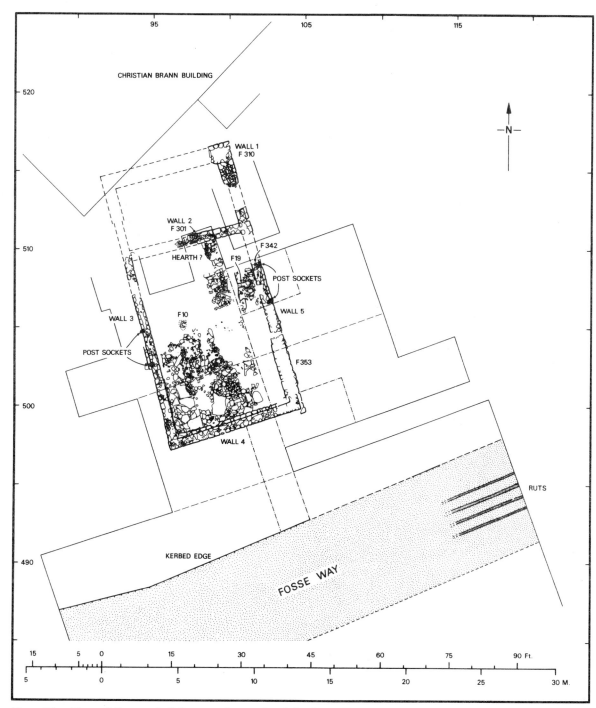

Fig.   26.   Plan of Roman building, to the north of the Fosse Way

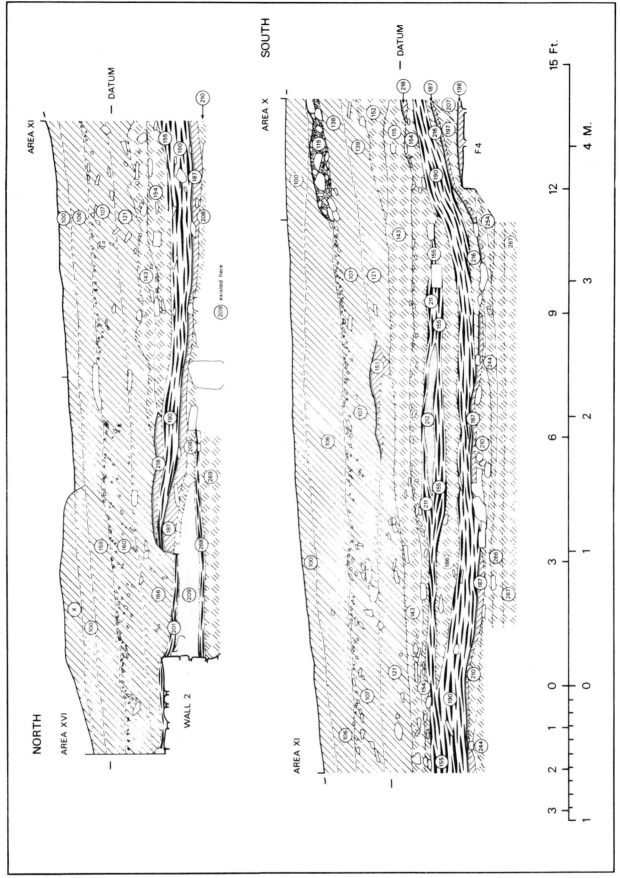

Fig. 27. CT 72–4 section A–C, north-south (see fig. 17)

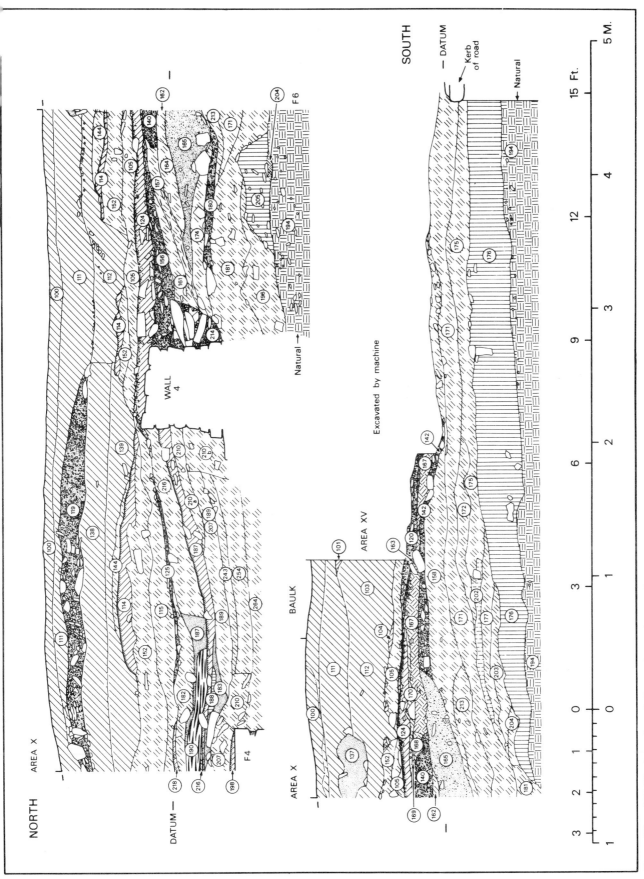

Fig. 28. CT 72–4 section C–E, north–south (see fig. 17)

9. Stone flooring inside building, looking south

excavation, where several changes of building method were seen, should be particularly noted. On the other hand it could be argued that details outlined above were all part of a single building phase which required a variety of techniques in its construction.

The building in its final form was rectangular, measuring internally 16 m. long by 7.5 m. wide at the south end and 7.0 m. wide at the north end. It was divided into two parts by an internal wall giving a room at the north end of about 7.0 m. by 4.0 m. and a larger area to the south of 7.5 m. by 11.5 m. The front, or southern, wall of the building (wall no. 4) may have been only a sleeper wall and never have risen higher than its surviving level, for the highest remaining course was heavily worn along most of its length.

Having been built around A.D. 280 the building did not survive long and may have been abandoned well before the cobbled surface was laid in c. A.D. 330; this accords with the evidence found from within the building where only one floor surface, made of flagstones, was noted, some of which were up to 1.40 m. long (layer 215). This floor only survived in the southern part of the large room and had sunk in places, pulling the slabs away from the walls (pl. 9). Despite its substantial nature little of it shows on the main section across the building (figs. 27–28). Small areas of mortar in the northern part of the building against wall 2 (layers 187 and 224) may have been an attempt to patch up a damaged floor or the remains of make-up for a floor of different material.

In the same area were a number of layers of burnt material containing much charcoal, pre-sumably associated with the use of the smithing hearth (F 19). Layer 201 is one such layer which, as can be seen from the section, (fig. 27), spread over wall 2, possibly indicating a doorway at this point. The building has the appearance of a workshop with perhaps simple living accommodation at the rear. The rough, hard nature of the main floor suggests that some craft or light-industrial activity was taking place and in the north-east corner of the main room was a possible smithing hearth, consisting of an almost circular chamber about 72 cm. in diameter at the top, tapering to 38 cm. at the bottom, and constructed from five courses of

10. Smithing hearth, F 19

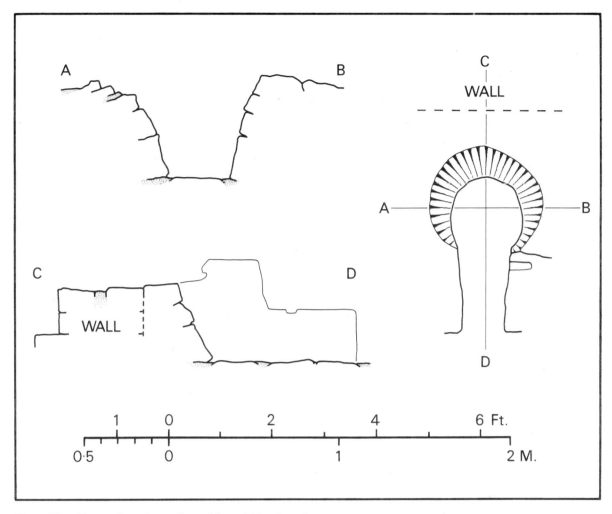

Fig. 29. Plan and sections of possible smithing hearth, F 19

stone giving an overall depth of about 64 cm. (fig. 29, and pl. 10). A well-built flue (made of 2–3 courses of well-cut stone) gave access to the chamber, the top course of which had two small grooves one on each side of the flue. The grooves were about 5–6 cm. wide and 1.5 cm. deep and presumably contained a metal object which regulated the supply of air to the hearth. Many of the stones used to pack around the hearth had been heavily burnt and wall 5, against which the hearth had been built, had also suffered from intense heat. Much of the surrounding area was covered with charcoal and ash and the stones used in the flooring in front of the hearth were heavily burnt. Samples taken from the hearth which were examined by Mr. L. Biek of the Ancient Monuments Laboratory included iron smithing residues and he thought that the hearth could have been used for this purpose. It is tempting to link the discovery of about 2235 hobnails from this site, many of them used, with activities which were taking place within the building and certainly such a large number requires some explanation. There is, however, a difficulty in using the evidence of the hobnails in determining what took place within the building as quite a number were found in layers which pre-date its construction. For example, they were found in the following period I layers:-

Table 1: Hobnails in period I layers

Period I layers	Number of hobnails	Period I layers	Number of hobnails
157	80	250	64
158	42	252	182
165	11	253	47
173	2	254	98
181	8	256	6
195	1	260	22
241	40	262	1
242	4	266	99
246	103	267	45
		271	1

The presence of so many nails in layers pre-dating the building suggests that they were not connected with what was taking place within it. However, they might have come from an earlier unidentified timber building of similar purpose. Hobnails were found in layers from all periods:-

Table 2: Hobnails in layers from all periods

Period	Number of nails
I	878
II	34
III	85
IV	c.1120
V	29
VI	89

Quite a number were found in association with the possible smithing hearth, F 19, but there is no evidence to show that it was used in their preparation. A study of their distribution shows that the majority found occurred in groups:-

Table 3: Hobnails by groups

Number of hobnails in group	Number of such groups
single nails	26
2–9	33
10–39	22
40+	22

This suggests that the hobnails were still attached to the leather when discarded and that the building was connected with the production of footwear and even possibly with the salvaging of material from used samples.

It is interesting to compare this building with one having similar features excavated by Mrs H.E. O'Neil at Bourton-on-the-Water, which she interpreted as a stable with its own forge and an oven (O'Neil, 1968, 35; McWhirr, 1981, 65). It was of a comparable width, but of unknown length and had a heavy flagged floor similar to the one in the Cirencester building; both were apparently workshops of some sort.

PERIOD IV

As so little datable material was found associated with the use of the building, the extent of its occupation has to be deduced from pre- and post-occupation levels and from the material associated with features contemporary with the flagged floor. Its eventual fate is not clear but, as no layers of debris were found on the floor surfaces, it is likely that the building was deliberately dismantled sometime before A.D. 330.

PERIOD V

Some time after the building had been taken down a cobbled surface was laid over most of the site although it was not encountered in the 1976 excavations. This was first revealed when a large area of the topsoil was cleared in order to examine the Fosse Way in detail. It appeared on the northern side of the road and overlay a considerable build-up of road silt. The surface covered a wide area and was traced over the whole of area XII to the east of the earlier building and in area XVII to the west. Although the surface was located in area XIII to the north of the site it was beginning to fade out here; it also extended into area XI, but was not continuous over the whole of that area.

PERIOD VI

Some nineteen skeletons were found between 1971–4 and a further group of 50 were uncovered by Dr. Leech in 1976 using different techniques. These skeletons and matters relating to the cemetery are dealt with elsewhere in this report, but one or two points are relevant to this section. Period VI followed the laying down of the cobbled surface which in turn sealed the remains of the building. The skeletons excavated in 1972–4 were found to have cut the cobbled surface where it existed and in view of the fact that the cobbled surface sealed the remains of the building there can be no doubt that, in the area of the 1972–4 excavations, graves were being dug without regard to the building which must have long since disappeared from view. They must therefore post-date the cobbled layer, and be later than c. A.D. 330.

An enigmatic feature which may belong to this period is 119. During the 1973 excavations it was considered to be post-Roman, although even then it was difficult to see when it was built since no other post-Roman stone walls have been noted in the vicinity. However, such walls have been found elsewhere in areas where they were not expected. One was found when the road linking the Querns Hospital with the new roundabout on the relief road was constructed. It was traced for about 60 m. and at first was thought to have been a road, as the earthmoving machinery had spread the stone over a fairly broad band, leaving only one edge of the wall intact which looked like the kerbing for a road. When this was investigated further by digging a trench in the adjacent field (site DW, fig. 3), it was found to be a 1.40 m. wide wall of post-Roman date.

On site CT feature 119 was traced across areas X, XII and XIII (see plan fig. 33, and sections figs. 19 and 27). It consisted of angular stones showing little sign of wear which were set in black earth. It was on average 0.8 m. wide, having fairly clearly-defined edges on both sides, although these do not show in the drawn sections. During the excavation of this feature it was described as a 'path', for want of a better description, and, because of its closeness to the surface, it was not considered at the time to be a wall. However, when the site was re-examined in 1976 a reappraisal suggested to the excavators that it was both a wall and Roman in date. It was certainly later than the stone building described above, but how it related to the burials is not clear. Dr. Leech draws attention to the fact that no burials were found south of the feature, that is between it and the Fosse Way, suggesting that the burials respected it and were contemporary with it. In the absence of any direct evidence its date must remain speculative as to some extent so must its function.

BATH GATE CEMETERY, 1969–1976
by
Linda Viner and Roger Leech

INTRODUCTION

In the summer of 1969, the principal aim of the Committee's excavation programme was to section the assumed line of the Roman road linking the town with the amphitheatre, a westward extension of the modern line of Lewis Lane and Querns Lane (figs. 1 and 2). This work was in progress when the tenant of the land, the late Mr. John Whyte, casually mentioned in conversation with the supervisor, his finding of human bones whilst double-digging his allotment during the war years. It has long been clear that a major cemetery lay on gently rising land to the west of the town, extending southwards from Tetbury Road for a distance of up to a quarter of a mile. Excavations by Richard Reece (1962, 51–52; Gazetteer burial nos. 1003–1056) in the grounds of Oakley Cottage produced evidence of an extensive cremation and inhumation cemetery. The confirmation of the line of the road to the amphitheatre, and the knowledge of Roman burial practice, bordering approach roads to the town, led to the supposition that a second cemetery might exist to the south-west of the town. This was further suggested by records of stone coffins found in the course of the construction and extension of the former railway yards (Gazetteer burial nos. 1086–7).

The area was under threat of development from the construction of the relief road, although at the time its exact course and nature of construction were still under discussion. The decision was taken in 1969, despite the small staff available, to open a number of limited-area trial trenches in the ground to the east of the allotment, which during the war years had extended to the railway boundary fence. Twenty-six burials were subsequently recovered concentrated in a very small area of trench CT 69(b). Excavations in 1970 to section further the line of the Fosse Way, were extended southwards to assess the relationship with the cemetery area as suggested by the concentration of burials in CT 69(b). The apparently piecemeal and haphazard layout of the trenches to the south of the road resulted from the uncertainty from year to year of whether and which parts of the site would be available for excavation in the following limited summer seasons to which finances and labour resources restricted the Committee. Without the knowledge in the early stages of excavation of the final route determined for the relief road, the choice of area investigated proved to be a representative sample of the land subsequently destroyed by the road. North of the Fosse further burials were recorded in the period 1972–76, with the result that a total of 453 Roman burials were archaeologically recorded from the Bath Gate Cemetery.

EXCAVATION AND RECORDING TECHNIQUES

Earth moving machinery was used in the initial stages of each season's work to clear the grassland vegetation and remove the topsoil to a depth of *c.* 23 cm.. The trench was then laid out, and arbitrary spits of earth were removed manually to a maximum depth of 15 cm. for each sweep across the trench. Time and the small labour force did not allow for trowelling at this stage by volunteers. This policy was endorsed by the nature of the soil with no stratigraphy evident in either texture or colour over ninety per cent of the area. High standards of precision were attainable with the use of the pick and identification of the bone uncovered allowed an estimate to be made of the orientation and extent of each burial. Further work of revealing the skeleton and any associated finds was completed with the aid of trowels, spatulae, spoons and brushes. The position of coffin nails, hobnails, and small finds was noted with markers, and the information transferred to the site record.

All burials were assigned a unique letter (1969) or number (1970–1976) and were cleaned to a state worthy of photography when a full record was made in black and white, and colour. A comprehensive drawn record was made of all burials to accompany a written description which included notes on orientation, three-dimensional recording, visible fractures and bone anomalies, grave goods where present, coffin fittings, and position in relation to other burials.

Burials thus recorded, were lifted, and the ground beneath trowelled to a depth of 10–15 cm. in case any pattern of the floor of the coffin should be evident in the pattern of surviving nails. The bones were carefully washed at the specific request of Calvin Wells, and packed for despatch. All site records, burials, pottery, and small finds have been retained, and deposited in the Corinium Museum, Cirencester.

Due to the difficulty of recognising grave cuts and other features in the homogeneous black loam covering the area both north and south of the Fosse, the opportunity was taken in the CT 76 excavations under the auspices of CRAAGS and directed by Roger Leech, to examine in greater detail an area 16 m. by 4.8 m.. All stones and bone fragments were planned at arbitrary 15 cm. intervals in depth. It was hoped that any evidence for former ground surfaces, spoil heaps of graves, mounds, disturbed graves and other ephemeral features might be revealed when graves were found and their shafts then projected in plan upwards through the already excavated and recorded levels.

Throughout the excavations the most memorable feature was the varying depth of black earth which covered the underlying bedrock of oolitic limestone, by depths ranging from 0.31 m. to 1.84 m. in CS 71–3 4 and CS 72–3 8 respectively. The homogeneous nature of the soil did not allow for strict stratigraphical excavation of the trenches, with burial cuts and features not apparent in the ubiquitous brown-black earth. For this reason many "layers" in trenches CT 69(b), CS 70–74 were purely arbitrary divisions for convenience of excavation.

In CS 72–3 8, layer 7 supplied a striking contrast to the 1.80 m. of black earth above it by representing the yellow-black silt junction between the black earth and the underlying yellow of the oolitic bedrock. Burials cut into it from an indiscernible higher level were the only ones to exhibit a clearly defined grave outline. The silty nature of the junction between earth and bedrock was less noticeable in the other trenches, and tended to be more loamy.

BURIAL ANALYSIS

The wealth of archaeological data available for each individual burial recovered from excavations in the period 1969–1976, north and south of the Fosse Way (site codes CT 69(b), CS 70–74, CT 72–76) has been condensed and tabulated, Table 4, mf. 2/5. The discussion which follows is a summary of the detail contained within the table and should be used in conjunction with figs. 30–33.

A full key to the information contained in the table is given below:-

General abbreviations:

N	=	North
S	=	South
E	=	East
W	=	West
I	=	indeterminate
p	=	prone
s	=	supine
l	=	left
r	=	right
i	=	indeterminate
x	=	both left and right elements/limbs

1. *Burial*
2. *Orientation (p. 76)*
    N/S head at north
    S/N head at south
    W/E head at west
    E/W head at east
3. *Attitude (p. 76)*
4. *Skull position (p. 82)*
    Skeletal survival (p. 83)
5.   complete
6.   nearly complete
7.   upper body only
8.   lower body only
9.   skull only
10.   legs only
11.   lower legs
12.   arms only
13.   fragments only
14.   trunk only
    Leg position (p. 83)
15.   straight
16.   crossed
17.   bent
18.   flexed
19.   indeterminate
    Arm position (p. 85)
20.   straight at side
21.   hands on pelvis
22.   crossed over chest
23.   at right angles
24.   indeterminate
25. *Site code*
26. *Depth* in metres, below modern ground level
27. *Grave Type*
    n - nails, number recovered and position (see p. 86)
    stone coffin, type (see p. 88)
    lead coffin (see p. 92)
    stone packing (see p. 92)
28. *Objects*
    A. Objects associated with burials (p. 128 and figs. 80–1)
    B. Objects from grave shafts (p. 132 and figs. 52–73)
    C. Objects from grave earth (p. 133 and figs. 52–73)
29. *Sex and age* based on analysis by Calvin Wells (mf. 3/4 and 4/5)
    M = male, F = female, ?M = probable male, ?F = probable female, ? = sex unknown.
    Relative chronology (p. 102)
30.   cuts
31.   is cut by
32.   seals
33.   is sealed by
34. *Burial*

BURIAL RECORDING SYSTEM

During the course of the excavation it was necessary to number for recording purposes all finds of human bone subsequently to be retained for examination. All skulls were automatically assigned a number (letter in CT 69(b)), as were articulated limbs and torsos. Because of the heavily disturbed character of the site, the problem of double-numbering of single skulls, arms or legs displaced from the rest of the body existed. In some cases, such as burials 759/765 and 731/732 individually numbered fragments of the same body have been united. This has been done in the most obvious cases, but it must be borne in mind that one or two fragments may have been assigned numbers that in effect belong to one individual

From an archaeological point of view, 453 recordings of human bodies were made within the area of the excavations. In effect the policy adopted is considered to have produced as close as possible a true representation of the minimum number of individuals buried in the area investigated by excavation, with the least duplication.

Anatomical analysis of 405 of the 453 'archaeological' burials has shown that in 15 cases, more than one individual is represented — burials 5, 19, 32, 36, 46, 49, 104, 175, 202, 210, 243, 251, 260, 278, and 721/22. This point is expanded p. 135. These 15 'archaeological' burials in fact represent a maximum of 34 individuals.

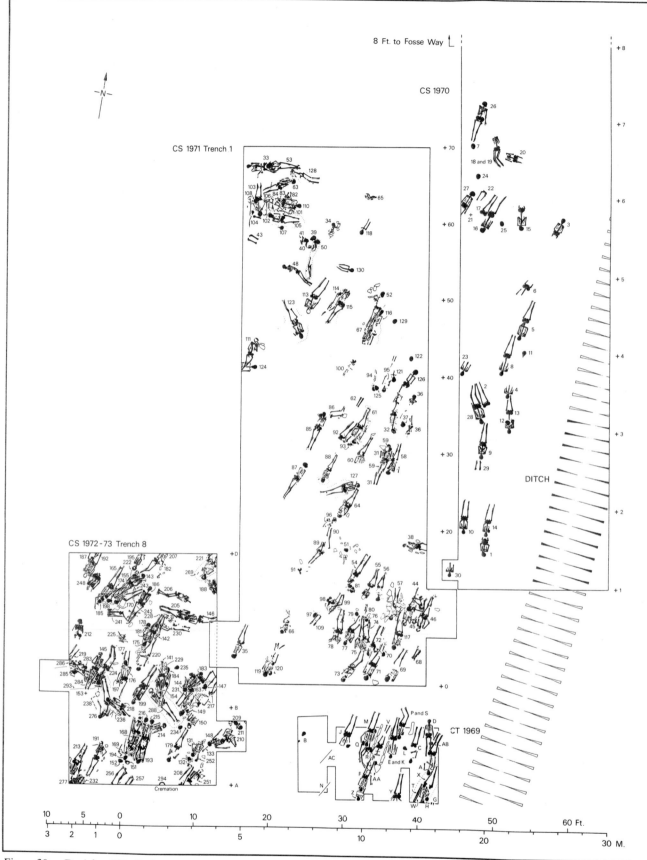

Fig. 30. Burials, CT 69 (b), CS 70, 71, 72–3 8

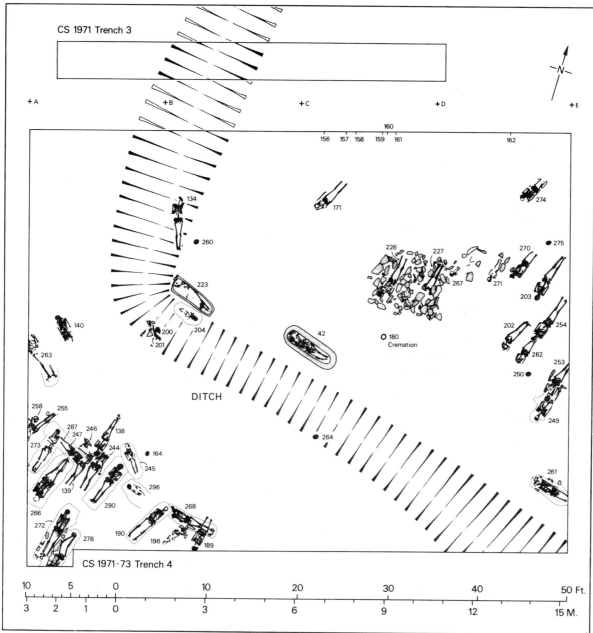

Fig. 31. CS 71–3 4 burials

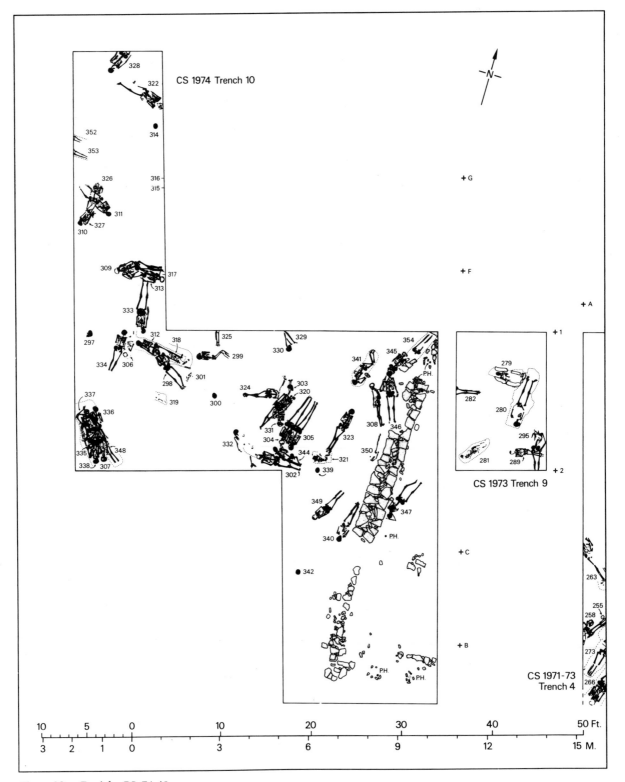

Fig. 32. Burials CS 74 10

Fig.   33.   Burials CT

ORIENTATION

Throughout this account the term orientation is used when the precise position of the skull in relation to the points of the compass is known — for example a burial with a north–south orientation signifies that the burial was lying with its head to the north on a north–south axis. A north–south orientation implies that the head was lying within 45° either side of compass north, with corresponding arcs for the remaining orientations around the compass. Alignment has been used to signify direction in more general instances.

Inhumations					*Cremations*
north–south	south–north	east–west	west–east	indeterminate	
104	181	30	67	68	3

As summarised above, within the Bath Gate cemetery the predominant alignment was on a north–south line, visually evident in figs. 30–33, and accounting for 285 of the burials recovered. For 68 burials skeletal survival was either too scant or disturbed for an accurate statement of orientation to be made, and it was decided that an indeterminate verdict should be given in these questionable circumstances. Anatomically it should always be possible to ascribe orientation with the proviso that degree of disturbance is taken into account, and it is justifiable to say that this figure could have been reduced in some cases if due attention had been paid to this point. In the case of the 15 burials where skeletal duplication of 34 individuals was observed by Dr. Wells, the orientation noted is that of the burial with the largest sample of bone. Following a detailed study of all records and photographs it has not been possible in retrospect to assess orientation for these 34 individuals.

Recent work, notably by Dr. Calvin Wells and Charles Green at Caistor-on-Sea, Norfolk, and Burgh Castle (Wells and Green, 1973, 435–443), and Sonia Hawkes at Fingelsham, Kent (Hawkes, 1976, 33–51), has explored the hypothesis that although apparently of random orientation, without a compass and consequently a fixed east point, the bearing of sunrise on the day the grave was dug might have guided the line of digging. Consequently this would be preserved in the orientation of the grave, and using a Nautical Almanac to give the sunrise times at the relevant latitude for the site, with a correction for the time of the Noon Transit of the sun for that day, the bearing and therefore, the date of burial can be worked out.

It was felt that detailed application of this technique was not within the scope of this present report. Exact compass bearings were not taken at the time of excavation, an action possibly necessary to reduce the errors in degrees which may arise from taking readings from a composite plan drawn after the completion of excavations. With the lack of distinctive grave cuts, a feature very common within the Bath Gate cemetery, a subjective decision would have been necessary to determine exactly the line to be drawn through the burial — possibly along the line of the vertebral column. In many cases this would not reflect the line of the grave cut but merely the position at rest of the body within the grave.

ATTITUDE

Inhumations					*Cremations*
Prone	Supine	Left Side	Right Side	Indeterminate	
33	330	3	7	77	3

The position of the body in the grave has formed a major part of the study of Romano-British burial practices and great importance has been placed on whether the burial is prone or supine, the position of the limbs, and in particular the position of the arms — those with arms crossed over the chest it has been suggested are indicative of Christianity particularly if they are also on

11. Burials 190 and 196 lying prone, 189 supine

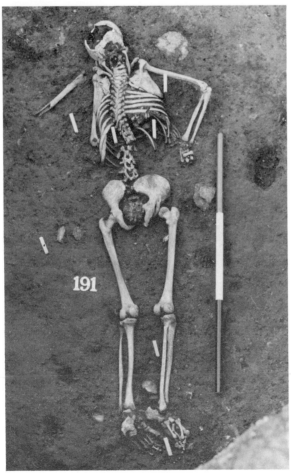

12. Prone attitude, burial 191

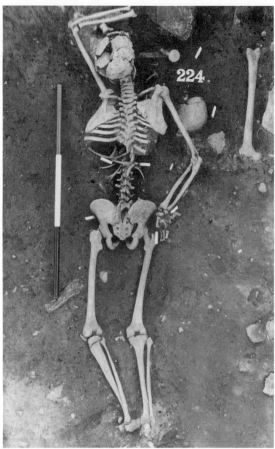

13.   Burial 224

an east–west orientation. Therefore, attitude of the body must be studied in conjunction with arm and leg positions, and orientation.

PRONE

Thirty-three burials were recovered in a prone attitude: W; 2; 9; 12; 40; 43; 59; 81; 100; 111; 114; 146; 186; 188; 190 (pl. 11); 191 (pl. 12); 196 (pl. 11); 219; 224; 238; 251; 252; 258; 273; 283; 295; 299; 307; 309; 313; 323; 345; and 701. These represented 14 female adults; 13 male adults; 1 unsexable adult; 3 children; and 2 burials which were not anatomically investigated. The question as to why these burials should have been buried face down is an intriguing one, and several explanations can be put forward — a defined burial practice with ritual, ceremonial, or religious significance, with either benevolent or malevolent intent; or a degree of irreverence, or neglect on the part of the grave diggers.

In a number of cases the burials have been well disposed with legs straight, and arms folded under the pelvis (burials 146, 186, 190, and 295); extended straight at sides (burial 59); folded at right angles under the stomach (burials 273, 307 and 323); or across the chest (burial 9). In the remaining cases where arms are present the position is haphazard (burials 224, 251, 283 (with legs crossed), 309, and 313). Burial 224 almost looks as though he put his arms out to prevent a fall, pl. 13. Burial 229, a probable female aged 14 with arms tucked under the shoulder blades and legs bent, may have died in her sleep in such a position. One might almost say in the interesting case of 309 and 313, two men aged 35–45 and 25–35 respectively, that they had been "tossed" into the same grave.

Sixteen prone burials exhibited nails, varying in quantity from 1 to 12. Those with less than 4 nails (2; 100; 186; 196; 219; 251; 258; 273; 307; 309; 323; and 345) do not show any other positive evidence to indicate a coffin. Burial 190 (female, aged 45–55) is of great interest with a clear coffin outline, and a distinctive grave shaft cut into the limestone quarry rubble, fig. 34 and pl.

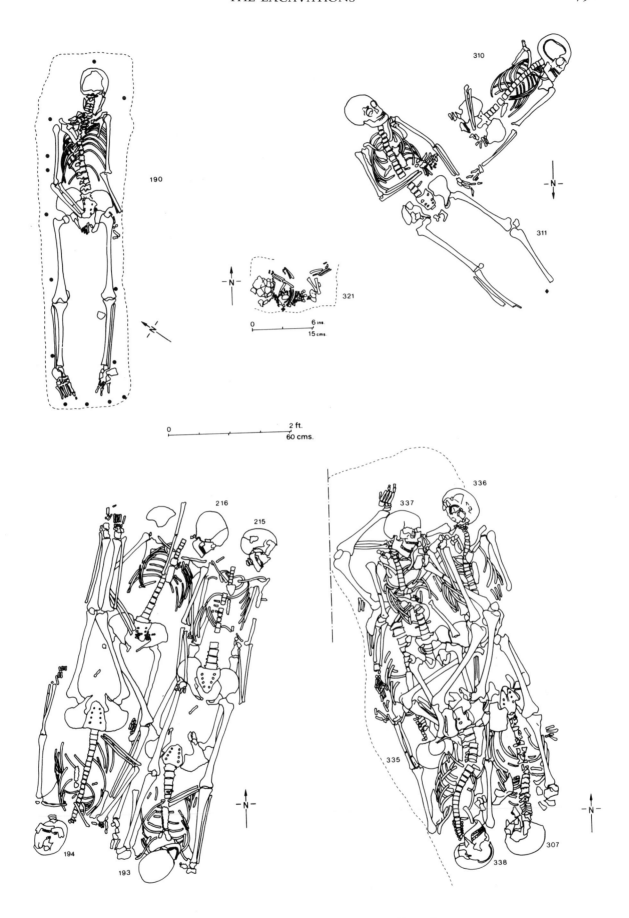

Fig. 34. Burials 190, 321, 310/11, 193/194/216/215, 307/335–8 (• coffin nails)

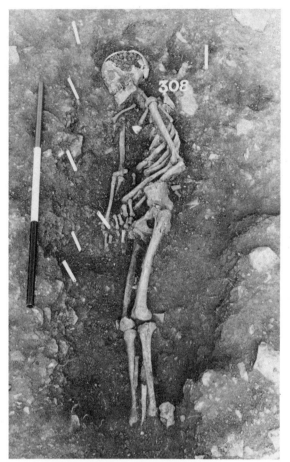

14. Burial 308 lying on right side

15. Burial 341 lying on right side

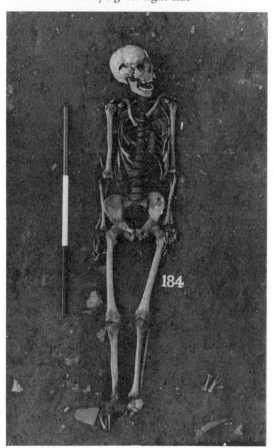

16. Burial 184 with arms extended at sides

11. The presence of a wooden coffin cannot be denied, and the question arises as to whether the body was deliberately placed face downwards in the coffin, or whether the coffin was accidentally placed upside down in the grave. One further point of interest is that the left arm of the woman was in effect lying behind her back, her hand lying over the base of the sacrum. Dr. Wells has speculated that perhaps her hands had been tied behind her back, as the shoulder blades certainly appear to have been pulled together.

Lying in close proximity to burial 190, was a small child, aged *c*. 3 years, burial 196, pl. 11, the only burial adorned with a necklace (fig. 43c) and bone bracelets (fig. 43, a, b). The paucity of associated objects elsewhere in the cemetery, and the comparative wealth in this one burial might argue that the child died wearing normal adornment and the jewellery was not removed before burial. The objects closely parallel examples found at Lankhills Cemetery, Winchester, but as the only examples to be recovered from Cirencester their presence cannot be said to provide conclusive evidence for the presence of intrusive Germanic elements (Clarke, 1979).

SUPINE

The supine position was the most favoured, with a total of 330 burials, lying on their backs, with arms and legs disposed in a number of positions, p. 83–5, figs. 30–33, pls. 16–18.

BURIALS ON SIDES

Ten burials were recovered lying on their left or right sides as distinct from a clearly prone or supine position — burials 34, 48, 50, 66, 82, 167, 206, 308 (pl. 14), 321, and 341. In three instances the burials were of children: burial 34 aged between 2½–3½ years; 66 a child of 7–8 years; and burial 321 of a newborn child, with most of the skeleton surviving in fairly good condition, fig. 34. In all ten burials death during sleep is the easiest explanation for the grave attitudes — and certainly understandable in the case of burial 321. Rigor mortis would have set the bones making the undertakers unwilling to move them to a supine position.

In the case of 206, illness may have prevented him from lying supine during life. This male, aged between 38 and 42, was affected by osteophytosis in at least 10 vertebrae. Gross osteoarthrosis had deformed the right talus and calcaneus, with extensive deformity of the base of the right hallucial proximal phalange also. The fifth lumbar vertebra lacked its neural arch, as a developmental defect, and the sacrum was sharply angled anteriorly, with much reduction in height and size of the third sacral segment. Radiography revealed no sign of a fracture and it was probably the result of a developmental defect due to an unusual posture in sitting on the sacrum for very long periods and starting in childhood; possibly occupational as a working posture.

Of the other adult burials, lying on their right or left sides, burial 341 (pl. 15), the only female, aged 50–60, exhibits the most representative sleeping attitude, her right hand near her mouth, left arm across the body and legs slightly bent. She also exhibited osteophytosis on at least twelve vertebrae at all levels of the spinal column, with advance osteoarthrosis on thirteen vertebrae. Arthrosis was also present on the left and right mandibular condyles; it was severe on both scapular glenoid fossae and the sigmoid notch of the right ulna; slight on both humeral heads; distally on both ulnae, with eburnation. Again arthrosis suffered in life may have dictated the posture in death.

Burial 48 was of an adult male, aged 40–50, with a fracture of the right sixth or seventh rib; burial 50 was male, 35–55; burial 82, adult male (only legs survived); burial 167, male aged 50–65, with osteophytosis and osteoarthrosis of the vertebrae and mild arthrosis of both humeri and ulnae at the elbow joints; burial 308, male 40–60, with osteophytosis and osteoarthrosis of the vertebrae, and mild arthrosis of both humeri and ulnae at the elbow joints; and burial 308, male 40–60, with osteophytosis and osteoarthrosis on the surviving fragments of 17 vertebrae at all levels of the column.

In only four instances were nails recovered from the area of the body — 34, 66, 308, and 341 — and the presence of 2 to 3 nails in the vicinity of the body cannot be taken as substantial evidence for confirmation of the presence of a coffin.

SKULL POSITION

Inhumations					*Cremations*
Prone	Supine	Left side	Right side	Indeterminate	
9	74	75	84	208	3

The survival of complete skulls for analysis archaeologically and anatomically was very small — hence in 208 cases it was not possible to give a firm identification of whether the medial line of the skull was prone, supine, to the left or to the right. Many skulls were discovered either broken or fragmentary due to collapse through earth pressure; or disturbance by Roman grave diggers. The lack of discernible grave cuts meant that often as not movement of volunteers over the excavated surfaces concurrently with the gradual lowering of the ground surface resulted in increased pressure over the empty cranial vault which then collapsed. Under the conditions it was understandable that so many unfortunately were damaged.

From those available for study, excluding 208 indeterminate examples, the following table has been drawn up correlating attitude and skull position.

Table 5: Correlation of Attitude and Skull Position

Inhumations

Attitude	Skull position	N-S	S-N	E-W	W-E	Indet	Total
prone	prone	4	2	1	1	1	9
prone	left side	5	1	1	2		9
prone	right side	4		1			5
prone	indeterminate	4	5		1		10
left side	supine			1			1
left side	left side	1					1
left side	indeterminate				1		1
right side	right side	2	3		1		6
right side	indeterminate	1					1
indeterminate	indeterminate	5	1	2	6	63	77
supine	supine	15	37	7	14		73
supine	left side	22	34	3	6		65
supine	right side	14	46	5	8		73
supine	indeterminate	27	52	9	27	4	119

Cremations							3
						Total:	453

Of especial interest amongst the 33 burials in the prone attitude, the skull position was prone in nine cases, with skull resting on the left cheek in nine cases compared to only five on the right cheek. (In the prone attitude, the skull position 'left' is taken to mean that the left cheek is in contact with the coffin base or ground surface, and vice versa for 'right'. Prone is therefore fully face down, and supine could only be represented in cases of grave disturbance, or a skull twisted through 180°. In the supine attitude, left side is to be interpreted as the left side resting on the coffin base or ground surface).

Seventy-three per cent of burials were in a supine attitude and this is reflected in the figures in the chart. Despite the high incidence where it was not possible to determine skull position accurately, the figures for the remaining three positions of supine, left side and right side, show an interesting equality, with no one position being especially favoured. These three skull positions represent 211 burials of 330 supine cases. From the sample available it can be inferred that if all had been available for study the probability exists that there would have been an equal distribution among the three positions.

One burial, with a left side attitude and left skull position, burial 34, would appear to be in a sleeping position, as would the six burials with a corresponding right side attitude and skull position — burials 48, 50, 66, 167, 308, and 341.

SKELETAL SURVIVAL

Complete skeletons, with all long bones, vertebral column elements, and skull surviving comprised 26.9% (excluding 3 cremations) of those recovered. Small bones of the hand and feet in some cases did not survive soil erosion or were not recovered because of inadequate excavation and identification. For those burials to be classified as 'nearly complete' obvious losses were noted such as long bones, or skulls, but the loss was not sufficient to allow the burial to be classed under one of the remaining categories.

However, 48% of inhumations recovered were far from complete, a reflection of the high level of disturbance to the cemetery caused by the Roman grave diggers and use over a long period. A degree of modern disturbance and destruction of parts of skeletons at the time of excavation under rescue conditions is not to be forgotten or forgiven, but close study of the burials points to the Romans as the greatest culprits of skeletal loss. Figs. 30–33 serve to illustrate the disturbance of Roman citizen by fellow Roman — the lower body of 310 has been destroyed by 311, fig. 34; and most of the left side of 230 has been destroyed by 228, fig. 36. Evidence where available of relative stratigraphy afforded by burials which have cut or sealed, or been cut by or sealed by other burials is given in table 4.

Table 6: Skeletal Survival

Inhumations

complete	122	26.9%
nearly complete	112	24.7%
upper body only	43	9.5%
lower body only	10	2.2%
skull only	42	9.3%
legs only	41	9.1%
lower legs	16	3.5%
arms only	4	0.7%
fragments	56	12.4%
trunk only	4	0.7%
Cremations	3	0.7%

Disturbance of earlier burials led to a large scatter of unarticulated human bone over the cemetery — fragments of arms, legs, ribs and feet tossed haphazardly and mingled with animal bone and pottery which had been dumped casually over the site prior to its use as a cemetery. It was not possible to re-assign in retrospect scattered bone to disturbed individuals. Planning of all bone scatters in CT 76 was a useful indicator of grave shafts cutting earlier burials, but anatomical study of the bone, often very fragmentary and mixed did not allow the bone to be assigned to the appropriate dissected grave. Sexing and ageing of the bone scatters was impossible in many cases because of the poor nature of the bone survival.

LEG POSITION

Five descriptive categories were considered adequate to allow all leg positions to be tabulated succinctly: straight; crossed, either at knee or ankle; bent (between 90° and 180° to the horizontal); flexed (less than 90°); and indeterminate where long bone and/or foot survival or loss did not allow for an accurate assessment.

In 209 cases both legs were extended, and in 18 further examples one of either legs was straight, the other leg being bent, flexed, or indeterminate. The leg position was indeterminate in 171 cases for both legs. Perhaps the most interesting cases were the 14 burials with both legs crossed; 26 both bent; and 9 both flexed.

Table 7: Leg position

Inhumations

Right leg	*Left leg*	
straight	straight	209
straight	crossed	1
straight	bent	1
straight	indeterminate	5
bent	straight	4
flexed	straight	1
indeterminate	straight	6
crossed	crossed	14
bent	bent	26
bent	flexed	1
indeterminate	bent	2
flexed	flexed	9
indeterminate	indeterminate	171
Cremations		3

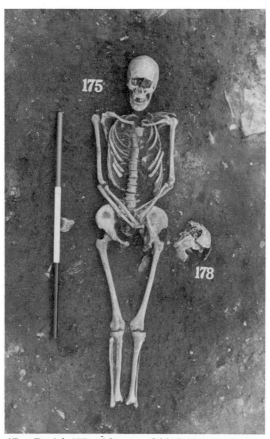

17. Burial 175 with arms folded across pelvis

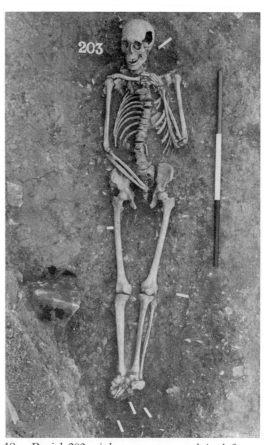

18. Burial 203, right arm across pelvis, left arm across chest.

ARM POSITION

As with leg position, five possible arm positions were classified: straight at side, pl. 16; radius and ulna lying across the lower abdomen and pelvis, pl. 17; radius and ulna resting diagonally across the chest; radius and ulna lying at right angles across the body; and an indeterminate position, often ascribed because although the humerus may survive, the radius, ulna and finger bones were absent.

All twenty-five permutations of position are represented, for example burial 203, pl. 18, with an additional category of 'orante' as exhibited by one burial only, burial 341, to be discussed later. Failure at the time of excavation to identify small hand bones has contributed towards the high figure of 214 cases in which it was not possible to determine lower arm position.

Table 8: Arm Position

Inhumations		
Right arm	*Left arm*	
straight	straight	31
straight	chest	4
straight	pelvis	10
straight	right angle	11
straight	indeterminate	10
chest	straight	8
pelvis	straight	12
right angle	straight	5
indeterminate	straight	14
chest	chest	13
chest	pelvis	4
chest	right angle	3
chest	indeterminate	4
pelvis	chest	6
right angle	chest	2
indeterminate	chest	1
pelvis	pelvis	45
pelvis	right angle	7
pelvis	indeterminate	7
right angle	pelvis	4
indeterminate	pelvis	6
right angle	right angle	23
right angle	indeterminate	3
indeterminate	right angle	2
indeterminate	indeterminate	214
orante		1
Cremations		3

GRAVE TYPE

SHROUDS

The presence of a shroud or sheet in archaeological contexts is very difficult to assess under the range of soil conditions present on any site. In specific cases textural impressions have been left in gypsum and lime covering bodies at York, and Poundbury, Dorset. Unfortunately none of these preservative factors existed at Cirencester, and only negative evidence can be advanced to postulate the presence of a shroud. The presupposition of its existence is based on our modern

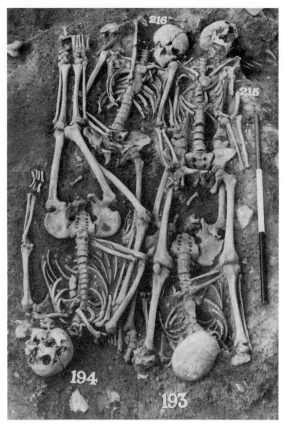

19. Burials 193, 194, 215 and 216

20. Burials 307 and 335–8

ideas of minimum decency — the dead at least being covered in a cloth, or winding-sheet, and not simply placed in everyday attire in the cold earth. Be that as it may, the absence of nails or other metallic coffin fittings in the ground immediately surrounding the burial might be taken to indicate the absence of a wooden coffin, but it should be borne in mind that coffins could have been held together with wooden pegs. Soil conditions have doubtless caused the corrosion and destruction of some iron objects, but the number of nails required to hold wooden planks together, and their relative abundance elsewhere on the site, would seem to indicate that specific burials had not been placed in wooden coffins.

Multiple graves, in particular burials 193, 194, 215 and 216 in CS 72–3 8 fig. 34, pl. 19; burials 335–8 and 307 in CS 74 10 fig. 34, pl. 20; and CT 76 burials 739, 720–2, 729–735, 737–8, would preclude the use of wooden coffins. The arrangement of the bones, their respect for and interlocking with adjacent limbs, suggests simultaneous burial without coffins, in a grave purposefully dug large enough to accommodate more than one burial. Equally the physical disposition of limbs of some burials would appear to preclude coffin burial, and suggest a shroud — for example burial 232 in CS 72 8; and certainly burial 741 in CT 76 in the orante position.

WOODEN COFFINS

Table 4, mf. 1/5, lists all those burials which were recovered with nails associated. For the purpose of this investigation it was considered necessary to set a minimum number of nails required before suggesting the existence of a wooden coffin. Wood and any other organic material used has not survived, either physically or as a stain, and therefore the only positive evidence for the presence of a wooden coffin has been the presence of nails and in the case of

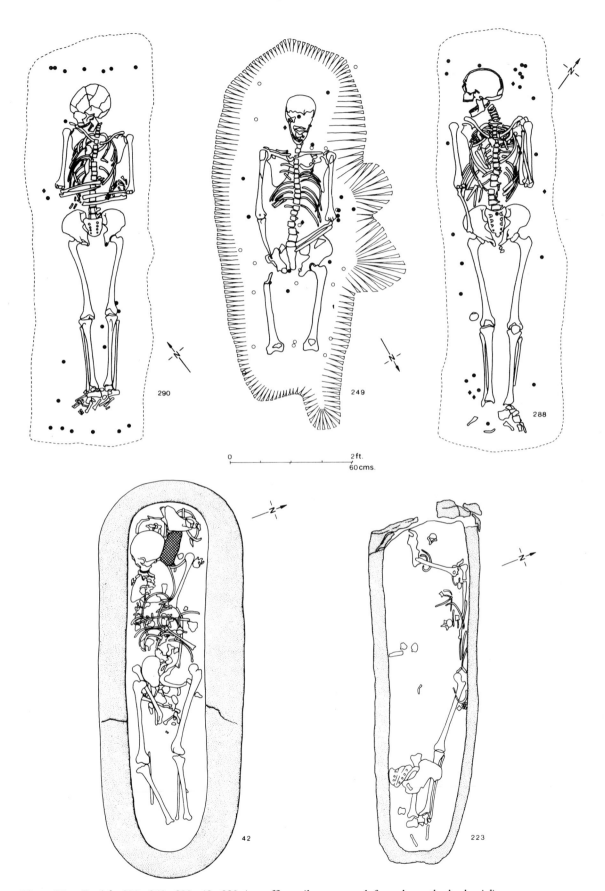

Fig.   35.   Burials 290, 249, 288, 42, 223 (o coffin nails recovered from beneath the burial)

only one burial, 228, additional hinge and bracket fittings. Burials with more than 3 nails surviving have been analysed for evidence of coffin construction.

The intensive 'use' of the site has resulted in the disturbance of many early burials by later ones, and nails from decomposed coffins would have been scattered in the fills and mounds of subsequent burials. For this reason haphazard arrangements of nails have to be treated with caution, but allowing for collapse and displacement of nails by earth pressure, it has been possible in a few noteworthy cases to be able to recognize the outline of the coffin.

The nail pattern around 72 burials can be categorised as follows:

a)　lines of nails observable at sides, head and feet, for three burials — 190, 226, and 290

b)　sides only — total of 30 burials

c)　head only — for 8 burials

d)　feet only — for 5 burials

e)　scatter in vicinity of burial, with no observable pattern, but more than three nails recovered — for 25 burials

f)　coffin fittings other than nails — for one burial.

Burial 290, CS 73 4, fig. 35, with a well-defined grave outline cut into the limestone rubble, clearly demonstrated lines of nails at sides, and both ends of the coffin. With burials 190 and 226, these three were the only instances where a complete outline of the wooden coffin was recovered. Burial 249, CS 73 4, fig. 35, produced parallel lines at sides and head, with an interesting pattern recovered beneath the burial suggesting parallel lines of short planks.

From the evidence obtainable at Cirencester, the coffin outlines would appear to be rectangular, compared to those in the Trentholme cemetery, York, which taper to a narrower foot compared to the head end (Wenham, 1968). Nail survival and soil conditions however would not preclude the presence of sub-rectangular coffins.

The nails used in coffin construction had circular domed heads and square-sectioned shanks, and varied in length from 10 mm to 80 mm. The number recovered from individual burials in many cases can only constitute a representative fraction required in the construction of substantial coffins. Many nails, even from those burials where more than six survive, may have gone unrecorded because of corrosion, disturbance by later burials, and selective collection of recognizable iron nails as opposed to amorphous lumps of corroded iron. For those burials where no nails were recovered, the possibility cannot be ruled out that wooden coffins had once existed, either bound by organic ties or held together with wooden pegs.

Burial 228, CS 72 8, an adolescent buried on an east-west orientation, fig. 36, seriously disturbed and destroyed the remains of the earlier burial 230. Burial 228 was the only burial to exhibit more substantial coffin fittings in the form of hinged brackets, fig. 36 a, b. Two brackets were recovered from positions to the left of the head and feet, respectively, suggesting their function to have been hinges for the lid. Wood impressions in the iron corrosion products, with the nail positions and configuration suggest that the wood comprising the coffin was *c*. 20 mm thick.

The decoration of coffins with bronze handles and fitments would seem to be a practice not widely used in the Bath Gate Cemetery. Finds of this kind are difficult to assess as having been used deliberately to ornament coffins. The large amount of 'rubbish material' dumped in the cemetery and subsequently incorporated into grave fillings has confused the issue in many cases.

STONE COFFINS

Five stone coffins were uncovered in the course of excavation and observation — burials 42, 223, 355–357 south of the Fosse; and burial 719 to the north of the road. All details of coffin shape, size, and construction have been summarized in table 9.

Based on detailed descriptions and measurements where they survive of 14 out of the 25 recorded stone coffins from Cirencester, it has been possible to group the outlines under the following seven types:

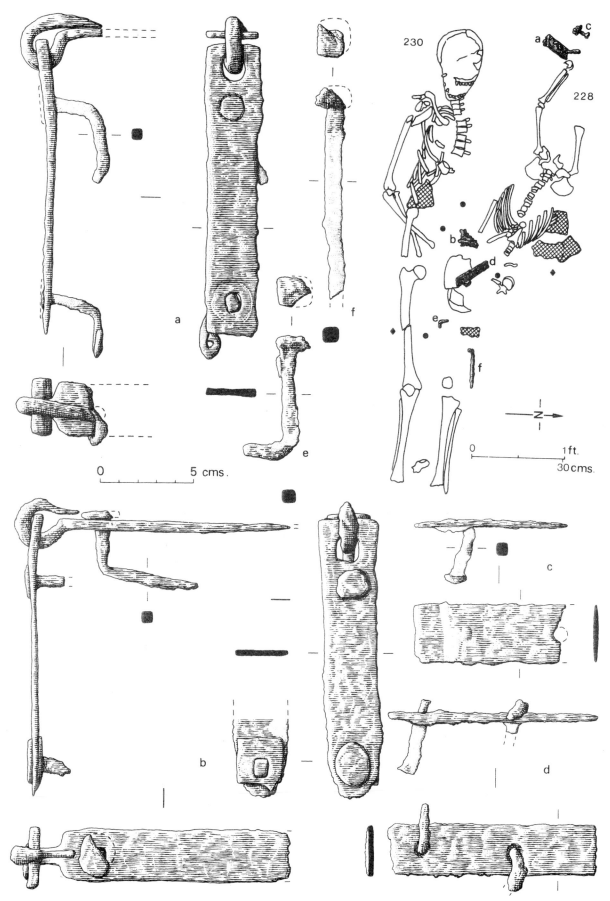

Fig. 36.   Burials 228, 230, coffin fittings

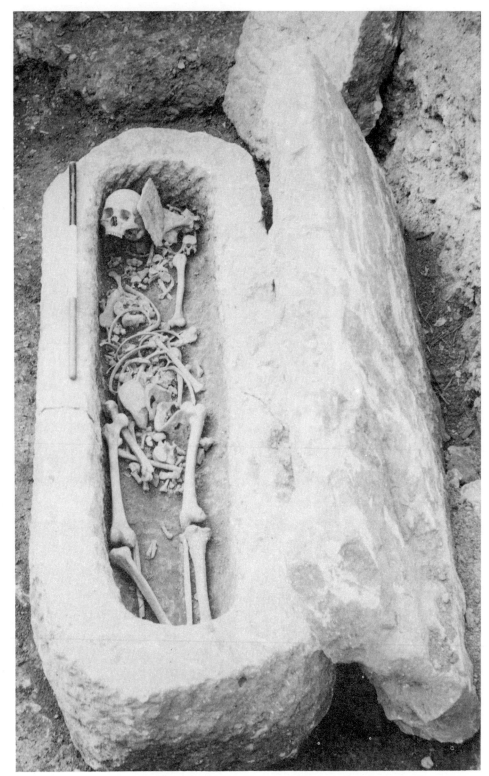

21.   Burial 42 in stone coffin

A. parallel-sided, both ends square
B. parallel-sided, one square end, opposite end semi-circular
C. parallel-sided, both ends semi-circular
D. tapering sides, square ends with internal head rest
E. tapering sides, square ends
F. tapering sides, with semi-circular ends
G. irregular-shaped stones placed to produce the outlines of A-F.

In most cases the external form mirrors the internal shape. Following from this the lid was made to give maximum cover to the base and also mirrors the base type, except in circumstances where irregular blocks of stone, Type G, were used to provide a cover to the burial. Type D closely resembles medieval coffins, but is included here on the evidence of notes by Professor Buckman in the Corinium Museum (Gazetteer burial no. 1061). The types as listed represent the outline of the receptacle used to house the burial in the ground. The majority of the stone coffin bases were monolithic, but Type A could be achieved in two parts, as for burial 719.

Of the coffins recovered from the Bath Gate cemetery, type A was represented by burial 719, type B by burial 356, type C by burials 42 (fig. 35, pl. 21), 355, and 357, and type F by burial 223 (fig. 35). Taking into consideration all stone coffins recorded in cemeteries around the town, type A is further represented by burial 1082, 1093, and 1098; type B by 1094 and 1097; type C by 1096 and 1100; type D by 1061; and type E by 1099.

The stone coffins recorded to date have been found to the west of the town, and close to the nearest limestone source. All were of oolitic limestone, and being of such a weight this would obviate against removal a great distance, and explain their close proximity to the quarry source, and concentration in the area of the Bath Gate Cemetery. However, the large inscribed and sculptured tombstones to Dannicus, Genialis and Philus outside the South Gate, indicate that transport problems could be overcome when necessary.

Economic and social conditions presumably controlled the choice of a stone coffin for the disposal of the dead, the more wealthy townspeople choosing stone for ostentation. Because of the difficulty of transportation it might be supposed that people desiring a stone coffin had to be buried to the west of the town close to the source of materials. Specific reasons for burying a person in a particular cemetery are unknown but presumably were very varied and numerous: proximity of cemetery to the deceased's home, place of work or place of death; burial club ground; family plot; administrative or 'parish' area; availability of ground.

One theory has suggested that stone was used for those individuals with contagious diseases. Anatomically this is difficult to either prove or disprove as few diseases leave any visible effect on the bones. Of the burials from stone coffins it is interesting to note that coffin 42 contained the remains of a middle-aged man suffering from gout. Of the other individuals, 355 was a child aged c. 9 months and no anomalies or pathological rarities were observable in such small bones. Burial 223, a female aged 27–33, suffered arthrosis on one rib facet, with well-healed fractures on at least seven ribs, and a six-segment sacrum. Burial 356, again of a female aged 40–50, had Schmorl's nodes on her 10th and 11th thoracic vertebrae; while burial 357, a female aged 23–29, had complete spina bifida of the sacrum, and a well-healed Pott's fracture on the right fibula.

Statistically the preponderance of females to males in stone coffins is the reverse of the general trend in the cemetery as a whole, where males outnumber females by 2 to 1, but in such a small sample it would be unwise to place any emphasis on these figures.

Table 9: Stone Coffins

Burial Number	Orientation	Type	Base External Measurements	Type	Base Internal Measurements	Type	Lid Measurements	Grave Goods	Anatomical Analysis	Disposal
42	W/E	C	w. 0.74m. l. 2.01m. d. 0.38m.	C	w. 0.38m. l. 1.65m. d. 0.28m.	C	w. 0.87m. l. 2.36m. d. 0.20m.		M 45–65	Left in situ. Later used for hardcore in road construction
223	W/E	F	w. 0.67m. 0.31m. l. 1.70m. d. ?	F	w. 0.30m. l. 1.45m. d. 0.25m.	G	to cover coffin		F 27–33	Private grounds, South Cerney
355	S/N	C	w. refer to l. photographic d. record, pl. 23	C	w. l. d.	C	w. l. d.	lead coffin, pl. 23	unsexable, c. 9 mths.	Unauthorised removal from site.
356	E/W	B	w. 0.79m. l. 2.16m. d. ?	B	w. 0.43m. l. 1.80m. d. 0.23m.	B	w. 0.81m. l. 2.19m. d.	glass carafe hobnails fig. 44	F 40–50	
357	N/S	C	w. 0.61m. l. 1.96m. d. ?	C	w. 0.41m. l. 1.68m. d. 1.55m.	G	w. 0.58m. 0.58m. l. 1.55m. 0.66m. d. 0.28m. 0.30m.	glass jar fig. 44	F 23–39	
719	W/E	A	w. 0.64m. l. 2.20m. d. 0.55m.		w. 0.44m. l. 1.98m. d. 0.34m.	G	to cover coffin	pot, fig. 44 chicken carcass		Christian Brann Ltd. display in forecourt

LEAD COFFIN

Burial 355 was of particular interest in producing only the second example of a lead coffin to be recovered from the town. A decorated fragment, unfortunately unprovenanced and discovered pre-1880, is discussed in the gazetteer, burial 6000, mf. 5/5.

Lying outside the area of controlled excavation, 355 was rescued during machine excavation for a storm-water drain at the side of the dual carriageway, fig. 2. The lid and base of the stone coffin, type C, pl. 22, were damaged, revealing an inner lead coffin, pl. 23, which had also suffered some damage, but was salvaged and taken complete with the inhumation to the Corinium Museum.

The lead base, 79 x 28 x 20 cm., was made from one rectangular piece of lead for the sides, base and ends, with the corners cut out and sides and ends bent up (Toller, 1977, 11, fig. 2, 2). Each side was slightly folded around the end, with one lead rivet in the upper corner of each end to secure the seam. The lid was larger than the body, 86 x 33 cm., and was folded over the sides and ends of the coffin base. The base and lid were plain except for a raised St. Andrew's Cross in the upper surface of the lid, the arms of the cross 33 cm. in length, the centre of the cross 41 cm. from one end. No analysis has yet been made of the lead. The double seal of lead and stone container had prevented infiltration of even the finest soil. With the assistance of the contractors the stone coffin was moved to the side of the dual carriageway on discovery and photographs taken without the lead coffin, pl. 23. Unfortunately before the coffin could be measured it was removed from the site by persons unknown and to an unknown destination, and the photograph is the only extant record of its size and shape. The lead coffin, although with square corners, fitted comfortably into the stone coffin with its semi-circular ends, and was orientated south-north.

GRAVES WITH STONE PACKING

Evidence for true stone burial chambers or stone cists, with mortared or dry-stone walls, roof and floor, was not found in the Bath Gate Cemetery. A total of 27 burials produced evidence of

22.   Burial 355 stone coffin

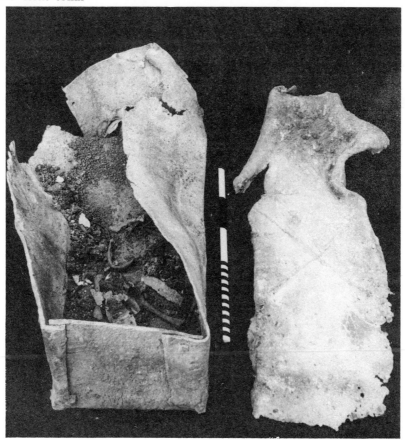

23.   Burial 355, inside lead coffin

24.   Burials 226 and 227

25.   Burial 279

26. Burial 274 with stone tile covering   27. Burial 274, covering removed

stone packing around the coffin or burial. To simplify the description of stone packing around burials the following categories can be considered:

a)   stone packing at sides, head and foot
b)   at sides only
c)   at head only
d)   at feet only
e)   covering the body
f)   stones near head

In all instances, except burials 253 and 274, the stone used was rough or semi-worked blocks of limestone, as shown in pl. 24 surrounding burials 226 and 227. Here the grave cuts were packed with stones on all sides of the wooden coffins and a pile of stone heaped on top.

Although the site of an earlier quarry there were few large blocks of stone in the black earth, and a large concentration of stone such as that around 226 and 227 was rare. Likewise stones placed around isolated burials, such as burial 279, pl. 25, were obviously deliberate placings.

Stone roofing tiles were given a secondary function as grave packing in the case of burials 253 and 274. The packing for burial 253 used limestone blocks around sides and head, and also incorporated a pennant sandstone roofing tile set on edge to the left of the left pelvis. The lower legs of burial 274, pls. 26, 27, were destroyed in machine excavation of the west–east section but excavation revealed three pennant sandstone roofing tiles standing on edge along the left side of the burial, with additional tiles placed herring-bone fashion to cover the burial. The tiles presumably covered the feet as well.

In 12 cases out of the 18 with stone packing, there was evidence in the form of nail survival to suggest that burials had been placed in coffins. The significance of the stones apart from packing or wedging the coffin in place is difficult to assess. In seven cases, large stones appeared to have been placed deliberately at the head of the burial. In the case of burial 198 the stones,

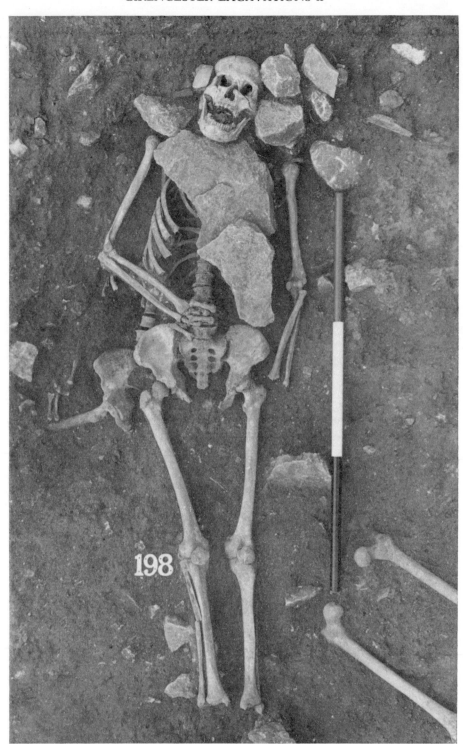

28. Burial 198

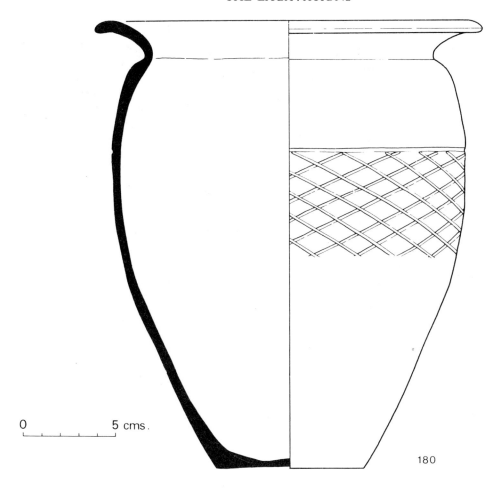

0 _____ 5 cms.

180

Fig. 37. Burial cremation 180

were placed around and under the chin, pl. 28. The skulls of burials J and 11 were found lying directly on top of unworked blocks of stone. None of the stones were worked or inscribed, their depth and proximity to the burial precluding their function as tombstones, or surface markers. In no instance was a tombstone or grave marker recognised for 453 burials. The only inscribed fragment found was a section of tombstone used as make-up for a wall footing in the roadside building and which could have originated from any one of the cemeteries around the town.

CREMATIONS

Within the area investigated two urned cremations were found, burials 180 and 294, with the remains of a third cremated body, contained in an inhumation-sized pit, burial 293. The two urned cremations will be considered first as being more typical examples of the method used for the deposition of cremated bones in the ground.

The cremated remains of burial 180, CS 71–3 4, were placed in an urn set upright in the ground. The pot, almost complete, was hand-made, Black-Burnished I (Fabric 74), with a wheel-finished rim, fig. 37. With a burnished rim top and shoulder and smoothed lower body, decoration consisted of a narrow band of burnished lattice, below a single shoulder groove. This would suggest a probable origin for the pot in Dorset, in the late third or early fourth century A.D..

A shallow circular depression, 0.46 m. in diameter, at a depth of 1.06 m. below the modern ground level, had been scooped out in the upper level of the limestone sub-strata to contain the urn. An oolitic limestone diamond-shaped roofing tile was used as a cover for the urn, and had

29. Cremation 294

very effectively prevented all earth from entering the pot. During excavation of the black earth no indication of the hole was discernible until trowelling had reached the top of the roofing tile. The filling around the pot was of the same black earth and it was therefore not possible to assess the level from which the hole had been cut. Earth pressure above the tile had caused the fracturing of the rim which in places had collapsed inwards. The remains of a bird were found in the fill of the hole lying outside the pot, and sheltered by the tile. These represented the only grave goods associated with the burial.

Examination of the calcined bones by Calvin Wells, showed them to be those of an adult male, of sturdy build, possibly less than thirty-five years of age. The remains had been well cremated with virtually no signs of under-firing present. Collection of the fragments had been carried out with thoroughness, including a few fragments of animal bone. The lack of burnt earth in the vicinity would suggest that the pyre was at some indiscernible distance from the place of deposition.

The second urned cremation, burial 294, CS 73 8 layer 7, was in an inverted pottery vessel, at the lowest level of the site, with a build-up of black earth above of 1.70 m. The stratigraphy of the site is very difficult to establish, and it was not possible to discern from what height the burial had been deposited. In digging a hole to take such a comparatively small receptacle, ease of excavation and safety factors would have limited the depth from which such an operation could have taken place, and suggest the level of the ground surface at the time of burial to have been considerably less than 1.70 m. A shallow circular scoop had been made into the yellow limestone sub-strata, the only level at which grave cuts for inhumations such as 288 and 269 could be easily discerned, and the pot containing the bones was inverted over the scoop. No lid was used to retain the bones and consequently many had spilled out and surrounded the pot in the process, pl. 29. A heavy concentration of charcoal, discolouring the original clean yellow rock surrounded the pot. Again there was no scorching of the surrounding area and this would suggest that the pyre was not in the immediate vicinity.

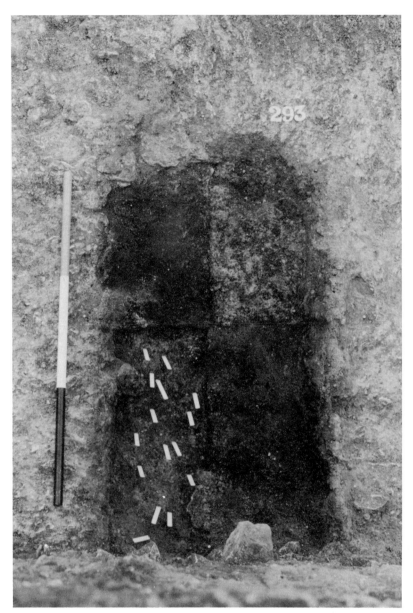

30. Cremation 293, quadrant excavation, white markers indicate nails

Anatomical study estimates this individual to have been an adult male, and the well fused cranial sutures suggest that he may have been more than 45–50 years of age. The condition of the bones indicates that firing had been moderately well carried out, with collection of the remains being efficient, many hundreds of small fragments from virtually all parts of the skeleton.

One of the most interesting features of the cemetery was the discovery of an inhumation-sized pit full of burnt matter, burial 293, CS 73 8, pl. 30. Doubt was raised that this constituted a human burial but analysis of the cremated bones showed them to be of an adult male.

Aligned east-west or west-east the first indications at the lowest level of excavation in the area was of a rectangular demarcation of burning showing dark in the yellow-black silt of layer 7 representing the junction between the black earth and limestone rubble sub-strata. A small extension was made on the western edge of the trench with the intention of demarcating the western end of the pit, fig. 30. The sides of the shallow scoop had been heavily scorched and in section showed a gradation from black through red to yellow outwards from the centre of burning. A thick layer of charcoal lined the depression with a mixture of black earth and limestone with charcoal flecks above. There is the possibility that the pit was left open for a while, the charcoal layer becoming compacted by rain and the elements before the earth layer was thrown over.

The section in the western edge of the trench unfortunately does not give any indication of the depth from which the pit was cut. When the extension was cut to locate the western end it was found that a diagonal cut NW-SE had destroyed the end. Excavation of this later fill of silty yellow-black earth failed to produce evidence of any burial. The cremation pit was effectively sealed by later burials, 283–6 and 145, fig. 30.

The condition of the calcined bones suggests that the pyre was a small one which had been badly stoked as the fragments showed much underfiring. This conclusion was reached independently by Dr. Calvin Wells without prior knowledge of the method of disposal of the bones. In excavating the pit by the quadrant method, all fragments of calcined bone from within the pit were bagged and despatched to him simply numbered as cremation 293. "Collection [by the Roman undertakers] of the surviving fragments was carried out in a very incomplete and perfunctory manner, although those examined included scraps of cranial vault, vertebrae, splinters of long bone shafts, including humerus, ulna, femur, and tibia and a clavicle fragment". This would seem to suggest that the body placed on a pile of wood or possibly in a coffin (?) was burnt in the pit, and the larger pieces of bones picked out of the ashes and placed somwhere else in a pot, or scattered. The remains found in the pit represented the insignificant scraps not felt worthy of collection.

A pattern in the scatter of nails found within the fill of the pit was not discernible and unfortunately no charred fragmentary pieces of wood survived for identification. It is not possible to say definitely whether the burial was encoffined before cremation, or whether old timbers with nails attached were used as fuel for the pyre to produce the great number of nails. The coffin-shaped depression might be used to substantiate a belief in the presence of a wooden coffin, but then a pyre would of necessity be rectangular or sub-rectangular for the disposal of a body by cremation.

A sample of charred material from the pit was sent to Harwell for C14 analysis, with rather surprising results, entailing a re-examination of the sample. Results of 3300. bc and 3180. bc (expressed as bp-1950) were obtained, and the proviso given that the cremated bone contained within the sample may have contained mineral carbon giving a falsely old date. Bone samples from three inhumations analysed by the same methods gave dates of A.D. 220 (burial 57); A.D. 270 (burial 28); and A.D. 310 (burial F), (expressed as bp-1950).

At the end of the seasons excavations in 1973, a small experimental firing was conducted in a shallow rectangular pit scooped into the limestone rubble. After burning wood for two hours the fire was allowed to die down. The following day, after overnight rain, it was found that charcoal filled the pit to a depth of 5–8 cm. The sides of the scoop when examined showed a colour gradation from black-red-yellow — similar to that in the pit for 293.

CEMETERY ORGANISATION

The physical methods observed in the Bath Gate cemetery for the disposing of the body in the ground have been described: shrouds; coffins of wood, stone or lead; and cremations in urns and pits (Grave types, p. 85). To a limited extent the rationale for such physical acts of respect can be conjectured from a study of the physical layout and organisation of the burial area. Points of interest for study include orientation of the burials, should there be a consistent, or more favoured alignment; and groupings according to particular grave types, sex, age or object associations.

ALIGNMENT AND ORIENTATION

The majority of the burials recovered were on a north-south alignment — consistently placed as to suggest that within the organisation of the cemetery either physical features of the Roman landscape or religious beliefs guided the grave diggers. Although many burials had destroyed or been destroyed by others — suggesting use over a long period of time, with few surface indications to mark earlier burials — the predominance of north-south burials would appear to indicate this to be the consistent burial rite.

Alignment on topographical features has been evidenced in cemeteries at Lankhills, Winchester (Clarke, 1979), and Poundbury Camp, Dorchester. At Cirencester, from the evidence recovered from within the excavated area it can be suggested that several features may have been used as guides, either positively or negatively, towards the establishment of a semi-ordered policy of lay-out. This lay-out appears now to be very haphazard, perhaps an indication that control was not entirely strict throughout all or part of the period of the cemetery's use.

In the area to the south of the Fosse, burials on a north-south alignment closely parallel the ditch running down the slope into the quarry. Burials at right angles to this feature may also of course have been influenced by its presence. In the later stages of the cemetery's use the ditch must have been an insignificant feature as several burials were recovered from its upper levels — burials 134 and 264 — or were actually cut into its banks, as in the case of 204. In CS 70 burials respected the lip of the ditch, and there is a quite noticeable area with no burials to the west of it. In CS 71–3 4, apart from those burials along its length already quoted, and the two stone coffins, 42 and 223, a similar unused area borders the ditch.

On the evidence of the few coins found associated with burials, there does not appear to be a chronological significance for burials east or west of the ditch. Apart from the two stone coffins and one cremation east of the ditch, similar burial practices, orientations and associations were followed either side of the feature. Archaeologically there is no evidence to suggest that the ditch acted as a delimiting boundary, although it is very probable that it may have fulfilled this function in the early stages of the areas use as a cemetery. The ditch might initially have served as drainage and/or boundary demarcation in the quarry area. A possible early military use should not be overlooked.

The line of the Fosse Way appears to have guided the orientation of graves north and south of the road. Many of the east-west graves were located in the north of trench CS 71 for example just to the south of the road. Here a concentrated overlap of east-west and north-south burials occurs in an area equidistant from the Fosse Way and the ditch, moving southwards away from the road — the east-west graves aligned parallel to the Fosse Way, and the north-south graves lying parallel to the ditch, with neither orientation chronologically earlier than the other. This would suggest that access to the site, and the line of the ditch and Fosse may have been the deciding factors governing grave alignment. Conversely, the east-west graves can be described as lying at right angles to the Fosse. The axial nature of the Fosse and ditch, if these physical features were the guideposts suggesting lay-out for the Roman grave digger, would as a matter of course produce such a pattern of overlap and lay-out.

A series of rows of north-south burials are observable in CS 70, CS 71, and CS 72–3 8, lying at right angles to and to the west of the ditch, the burials themselves being parallel to the ditch. Although less distinct, similar rows can be seen in CS 72–3 4 and CS 74 10. A guide to the rows may be obtained by taking a line at right angles to burials 89, 54, 55, 56, 57, and 46; and burials 98, 78, 77, 75, 74, 72, and 68 in CS 71. When this line and approximate interval is projected as a rough grid over the whole site, the rows can be visualized. It must be stressed that the lines are very arbitrary, with many burials overlapping the guide lines, the rows also being irregularly spaced.

The complexity of factors governing grave orientation has recently been emphasized by Rahtz (1978). The interpretation of orientation patterns must take into account many factors, and be founded on sound data. Having provided the data the scope for interpretation is enormous and varied.

BURIAL CHRONOLOGY

The build-up of great depths of mixed burial earth over a long period of time did not allow for

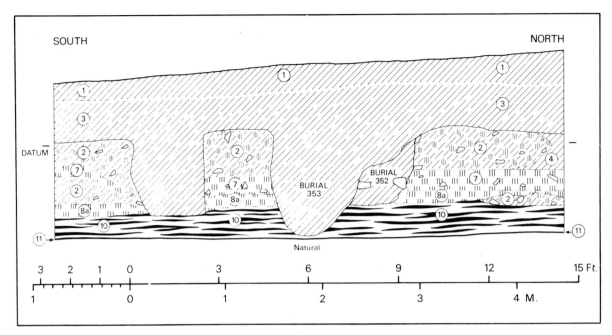

Fig.   38.   CS 74 10 south-north section

excavation according to strict stratigraphical principles with the removal of the latest graves first. The recognition of grave cuts in such uniformly coloured earth was extremely difficult. Only in section, such as CS 71–3 4, fig. 15, and CS 74 10, fig. 38, was it at all possible to record the vertical grave cuts where graves were cut through road make-up and repair, and accumulated silts.

The burial of one individual relative to another chronologically could only be studied in those areas where a later burial either cut or sealed an earlier one. Table 4, columns 30–33, mf.1/5, lists those burials for which a relative chronology can be established. This information is of course represented graphically in figs. 30–33; and is summarised in Table 10. For example, on 4 occasions a north-south burial cut a north-south burial; and on 16 occasions a south-north burial cut a north-south orientated burial.

Table 10: Burial chronology

Data group	Cuts				Cut by				Seals					Sealed by				
	N/S	S/N	E/W	W/E	N/S	S/N	E/W	W/E	N/S	S/N	E/W	W/E	i	N/S	S/N	E/W	W/E	i
north-south burial (67)	4	2	2	4	4	16	2	2	17	24	7	11	4	17	28			
south-north burial (106)	16	19	3	4	2	19	4	4	28	40	8	12	2	25	40	5	4	5
east-west burial (18)	2	4	1	3	2	3	1	1	1	5		2	2	7	7		8	2
west-east burial (44)	2	4	1	5	4	4	3	5		4	8	12	7	11	12	3	12	2
indeterminate										5	2	2		4	2	3	6	

The relationship between two burials is quite often a simple one — for example in the case of burial D, on a north-south orientation, table 4 shows it as being sealed by the south-north burial A. The extent of horizontal sealing can be assessed by a study of figs. 30–33. In many cases the degree of cutting or sealing by another burial can range in degree from minimal to complete. In this case the left foot of D at 0.86 m. depth is covered by the lower left leg of burial A at 0.53 m. Chronologically therefore burial A is later than burial D. This method can only give a relative rather than absolute chronology. In this instance 0.33 m. of earth separates the two burials, which could chronologically represent anything from one year to two hundred years. A burial can both cut and seal an earlier one, as in the case of AA, which has been partially destroyed by Z, but also sealed by it in the same act of cutting the grave.

Within the cemetery evidence exists to suggest that groups of burials were placed in the grave cut at the same time — the most notable being the groups 193, 194, 215 and 216, pl. 19; 307 335–338, pl. 20; and 720–722, 729–735, 737–738, fig. 33. Groups of two burials buried simultaneously can be illustrated by 309 and 313; and 304 and 305.

Those burials which cut or seal others but which are neither cut by or sealed by others, can be said to be the latest in terms of the relative burial chronology of the cemetery where this can be established. They are: A, E, F, H, M, T, 12, 14, 17, 18, 31, 32, 37, 45, 52, 53, 54, 57, 61, 63, 71, 73, 76, 85, 88, 90, 97, 99, 105, 108, 109, 111, 115, 120, 131, 138, 141, 143, 144, 145, 146, 148, 165, 168, 175, 176, 182, 186, 187, 189, 190, 199, 208, 213, 215, 217, 218, 219, 221, 232, 253, 254, 258, 272, 273, 295, 298, 302, 303, 304, 309, 311, 320, 329, 338, 346, 353, 700, 701, 702, 711, 724, 729, 740, 741, 744, 750, 754, 757, 759/765, and 761 — a total of 91 burials of which 29 were orientated north-south, 42 south-north, 2 east-west, 15 west-east and 5 were indeterminate.

In those instances where it has been argued that group burial occurred, the uppermost burial can be said to seal the group, and has therefore been included in the list, for example 215, 338, and 309, thus emphasising that time is relative. A spatial differentiation or concentration of burials based on criteria of relative burial position alone cannot be expected to give an absolute chronological development for the cemetery.

With the aid of pottery and coin evidence it was hoped that a more securely dated sequence could be established. In only three cases was it possible to give a *terminus post quem* based on the evidence of coins found directly associated with individual burials. Burials B and 1 were found with coins in their mouths, but corrosion and wear did not allow a more specific identification to be made than to say they were both of fourth century date. Burial 214 had a coin on each eye — Helena, A.D. 337–345, on the right, and Constans, A.D. 345-8, on the left. Taking into account relative burial stratigraphy, burial 1 can be said to provide a *terminus post quem* of the fourth century for burial 14 which had cut it. Burial 214 was cut by burials 193, 194, 215 and 216 and sealed by burial 168, and so has provided them with a *terminus post quem* of A.D. 348.

The study was then extended to the 58 graves with coins recovered from the grave shafts, see table 11.

Table 11: Coins in grave shafts

Burial	Coin in grave shaft	Coin provides t.p.q. for burial	Coin provides t.a.q. for burial
A	Constantius II, A.D. in356–61		X, D
D	Constantine II, A.D. 330–5	A	AB
F	Honorius, A.D. 395–406		R, V, AA, Z
G	H. of Constantine, A.D. 330–5		
J	Claudius II, A.D. 268–70		
L	Constantius II, A.D. 330–5		
M	Illegible, C3/4		R, Q
3	H. of Constantine, A.D. 330–45 Barbarous Radiate, A.D. 270–90		

Burial	Coin in grave shaft	Coin provides *t.p.q.* for burial	Coin provides *t.a.q.* for burial
16	Valerian, A.D. 253–9	17	
19	Constantine I, A.D. 313	18	
28	H. of Constantine, A.D. 330–45		
32	Constantine I, A.D. 310–17		126
33	Claudius II, A.D. 268–70	53	
37	H. of Constantine, A.D. 330–45		
38	Barbarous Radiate, A.D. 270–90		
44	Urbs Roma, A.D. 330–45	45	117
47	Gallienus, A.D. 253–9		
59	Constantius II, A.D. 337–41	31	58
66	Constans, A.D. 348–50		
117	Salonina, A.D. 253–59	44, 57	
142	Magnentius, A.D. 350–3	175	230, 220, 228
143	Constantine I, A.D. 310–7		222, 198, 155,
	H. of Constantine, A.D. 330–45		170
146	Constantine I, A.D. 310–7		205
	Barbarous Radiate, A.D. 270–90		
155	H. of Constantine, A.D. 330–45	143	170, 222
170	H. of Constantine, A.D. 350–60	155, 143	198, 222
174	Constans, A.D. 337–41	165	185, 198
186	Constantine I, A.D. 322–3		241
	Constantine II, A.D. 320–4		
193	Magnentius, A.D. 350–3		214
198	H. of Constantine, A.D. 330–5	174, 143, 170	222, 241
	Constantine I, A.D. 310–17		
	Valens, A.D. 364–78		
217	Constantinopolis, A.D. 330–45		149, 150
226	Constantius II, A.D. 330–5		
293	Vespasian, A.D. 69–76	283, 284, 285, 286, 145	
302	H. of Constantine, A.D. 330–45		344
	Barbarous Radiate, A.D. 270–90		
304/5	Gallienus, A.D. 260–8		344
	Constantinopolis, A.D. 330–48		
308	Caracalla, A.D. 196–211		
309	Barbarous Radiate, A.D. 270–90		313
328	Helena, A.D. 337–41		
	H. of Constantine, A.D. 350–60		
332	Tetricus, A.D. 270–3		
340	Constantine I, A.D. 320–4		
344	Tetricus I, A.D. 270–3	304/5, 302	
345	Constantine I, A.D. 320–4	346	
703	Illegible, C4	700, 701, 702	704, 705
704	Constantine I, A.D. 330–5	701, 703	
706	Constantine I, A.D. 307–37	711	
709	Tetricus I, A.D. 270–3	711	715
713	Valerian, A.D. 253–6		
741	Constantinopolis, A.D. 330–5		748
	Barbarous Radiates (x4), A.D. 270–90		

Burial	Coin in grave shaft	Coin provides t.p.q. for burial	Coin provides t.a.q. for burial
743	Constantinopolis, A.D. 330–5		
	Illegible, C3/4		
748	Valens, A.D. 364–75	741	
755	Constans, A.D. 345–8	745	747, 769, 770
756	Constantine I, A.D. 313–7		
758	Radiate, A.D. 260–90	744	763, 767
	Carausius, A.D. 286–93		
	Barbarous Radiate, A.D. 270–90		
763	Tetricus II, A.D. 270–3	758	
764	Tetricus I, A.D. 270–3		
768	Claudius II, A.D. 270		
	Barbarous Radiate, A.D. 270–90		
	Aurelian, A.D. 270–5		
	Gallienus, A.D. 260–8		
769	Tetricus I, A.D. 270–3	755	
771	Claudius II, A.D. 270	759/765	
	Barbarous Radiate, A.D. 270–90		
772	Carausius, A.D. 286–93		

South of the Fosse Way, 27 burials provided *termini post quos* for 22 burials, and *termini ante quos* for 26 burials, when the configuration of related burials was taken into consideration, see Table 4, columns 30–33. North of the Fosse Way 11 burials provided *termini post quos* for 11 burials and *termini ante quos* for 9 burials.

In instances such as burial 44 with its associated coin of A.D. 330–45 providing a *t.p.q.* for burial 45, and a *t.a.q.* for burial 117, the coin of A.D. 253–9 associated with 117 corroborates the stratigraphic sequence of burial 44 sealing 117, and thus being later in date. In contrast, coins of A.D. 330–45 in the grave shafts of burials 143 and 155 illustrate the degree of caution needed in assessing relative chronology based on coin evidence in such a disturbed site. Burials 143 and 155 seal burial 170 which has a coin of A.D. 350–60 associated with it, thus 143 and 155 have to date to after A.D. 360. Similarly burial 741 with an associated coin of A.D. 335, must in effect date to after A.D. 375 on the evidence of the coin associated with burial 748 which 741 cuts.

The distribution of these coins across the cemetery does not show any 'blocking' of early or late issues in specific areas. Only one coin was found in a grave shaft to the east of the ditch and taking into account the small area examined and the proportionally fewer burials recovered, no evidence can be put forward to corroborate or refute the theory that the ditch was a demarcation boundary, and of chronological importance within the history of the cemetery. The majority of the coins date to the period A.D. 310–360, with the greatest number falling within the 340's. The earliest was of Vespasian, A.D. 69–76, found amongst the ashes of burial 293, while the latest was of Honorius, A.D. 395–406, recovered from beneath the vertebrae of burial F. This latter coin would seem to imply a degree of 'activity' on the site into the fifth century. The coin of Vespasian, the earliest recovered from the site, certainly provides a *terminus post quem* for burials 145 and 283–6 which seal it, but it cannot be taken to indicate that burial was taking place as early as the first century.

North of the Fosse Way, the graves with dated coins show a similar date range and distributional pattern, with no obvious chronologically early areas. Burial appears to have taken place simultaneously either side of the road from the fourth century onwards.

The depth at which a burial was recovered cannot be taken to indicate a phase within the chronology of the cemetery. Many shallow graves were cut by later, deeper ones, and conversely primary deep graves were sealed by shallower, later ones. The limestone sub-strata would certainly appear to have influenced burial siting indirectly in this respect, imposing a shallow depth for most graves in trenches CS 71–3 4 and CS 74 10. Experience over the years would have provided the grave diggers with a knowledge of those areas with the easily dug burial earth, thus concentrating burials in specific areas such as CS 72–3 8, and further augmenting the depth of earth in the process of burial and subsequent decomposition.

An interim statement (McWhirr, 1973, 198) after excavation of CS 69, CS 70, CS 71, and CS 72–3 4 upper levels only, suggested three phases of burial — the earliest phase on a north-south alignment; with an intermediate phase on a different alignment, nearer east-west than north-south; and a final phase again north-south. Where superimposition of two burials only exists alignment is predominantly north-south, but this would be statistically weighted towards such a result considering the fact that 285 burials were on a north-south alignment as compared to 97 on an east-west line.

Following excavation of CS 72–3 8 to natural and the recovery of all burials, the interim phasing must be revised, and probably discarded altogether. East-west burials in some cases are the earliest burials within relatively-dated groups, for example 185 in CS 72–3 8, and 304, 305, 302 and 344 in CS 74 10. Alignment would not appear to reflect either a chronological phasing or a specific religious belief in the layout of the cemetery. It would appear to reflect in effect chance, and directional access and availability within the burial ground, with topographical features exerting some influence.

Orientation groupings of N-S, S-N, E-W, W-E and indeterminate were compared at intervals of 25 cm. depth below ground level. It was found that relative proportions by orientation remained fairly constant within the depth groupings. No one orientation was dominant at a particular depth.

Table 12: Correlation of depth and orientation

Depth	N-S	S-N	E-W	W-E	Indet	Total
0 - 25 cm	5	2		1	1	9
26 - 50	12	15	2	10	6	45
51 - 75	30	52	7	23	13	125
76 - 100	31	72	8	13	23	147
101 - 125	16	21	3	7	8	55
126 - 150	5	5	6	4	5	25
151 - 175	3	6	1	5	2	17
176 - 200	1			1		2
201 - 225			1			1
Indeterminate					27	27

453

Key: 3 cremations classified as indeterminate at the appropriate depths
       Indet.-Indet. = orientation may be known but depth was not recorded at the time of excavation

CEMETERY AREA

Combined with information supplied from the gazetteer (mf. 5/5) the evidence would suggest that the Bath Gate cemetery covered a considerable area, extending at least 60 m. north and south of the Fosse Way. The lateral extent was at least 120 m. based on the recorded positions of burials 719 and 1086.

To the north, the precise limits of the cemetery are unknown. Observations and field-walking along the line of the dual carriageway in May 1975 produced no evidence to the north of burial 719. Topsoil was removed by grading to produce a firm foundation base for the rubble make-up along the line of the road. In the area to the south of burial 719 and north of the Fosse, shattered fragments of human bone were noticed, but under the circumstances it was not possible to estimate the number of individuals exposed, but sufficient to show that burial activity extended to the west of the building.

South of the Fosse Way no positive evidence was found in the form of vacant spaces or ditches to indicate that the spatial limits of the burial area had been reached, although there was evidence to show that density of interments was declining southwards and westwards. To the east, the railway embankment has masked all availability for investigation, and gazetteer entries for burials 1085–7 represent the only evidence to suggest burial eastwards towards the line of the town wall. The nature of the area and its previous use as a quarry may well have unconsciously produced limits for the cemetery. The decline in density in burials south and east of CS 72–3 8 may have been influenced by the inadequate depth of topsoil. Trial trenches in 1970 certainly produced evidence for further burials within the quarry hollow. Time and the rescue nature of the work did not allow for full investigation of the area, and the total number of burials cannot be estimated. However, a westward boundary of the cemetery must have existed in the walls and banks of the amphitheatre itself. During road construction, grading and removal of topsoil south of burial 356 produced only a small number of human bones. The density of bone in trench 8 was not reflected in any of the sweeps made by the grader, either north or south of the Fosse Way along the line of the relief road.

From a study of figs. 2 and 87 two concentrations of burials are discernible — north and south of the Fosse Way between the amphitheatre and Bath Gate, and a linear strip south of the former Tetbury Road in the grounds of Querns House, the Cattle Market, and Oakley Cottage (formerly Earl Bathurst's kitchen garden).

If the road found at the Querns Hospital, see p. 49, is a continuation of the Fosse Way leading from the Bath Gate, then burials 1099, 1100, 1093–1095, 1082 and 1083 would appear to border it also, half a mile outside the town. In grading operations along the line of the modern road adjacent to the Querns Hospital no human bones were observed in the black topsoil or underlying limestone rubble, and the only burial evidence came in the form of either stone coffins or cremations placed within stone receptacles. The immediate area is again one of irregular humps and hollows representing old stone workings, and the stone coffins and cremation stones may have originated from here, rather than from the quarry to the south-east. The discovery of stone coffins suggests this to be an exclusive area reserved for the more wealthy members of the town, although positioned some way from the town — perhaps for pre-eminence, or merely because of the quarry source.

The density of burials south of the former Tetbury Road might argue for the line of an unknown road approaching the town and perhaps a gate somewhere in the vicinity of the junction of Tetbury Road, Castle Street, and Sheep Street. Archaeological evidence for this gate does not exist, although the course of the town wall south of Lord Bathurst's grounds in the area of the former G.W.R. town station is known (Brown and McWhirr, 1969, 225–9). The density of cremations particularly in the area of the Cattle Market may indicate an early course for the line of the Fosse.

EVIDENCE FOR GNAWED BONES

Anatomical analysis by Dr. Calvin Wells revealed that at least 5% of the skeletons studied had been gnawed by rodents and other small animals, p. 194. This evidence was not noted during the course of excavation, but retrospectively is of interest, and a study within their archaeological context has been made of those burials affected.

The table below forms a representative sample of those bones affected, and is by no means a complete list — full details can be obtained by a study of the individual inhumation notes, mf. 3/4 and 4/5.

Table 13: Evidence for gnawed bones

Burial	Bone affected	Animal	Depth below ground level
P	r. clavicle		0.69 m.
S	r. tibia	rodent	
16	r. tibia	rodents or small animals	

Burial	Bone affected	Animal	Depth below ground level
22	forearms, legs	rodent	0.92 m.
55	l. humerus		0.81 m.
133	l. tibia	fox/dog, and mouse	0.74 m.
141	r. ulna & radius	small dog/ fox	0.76 m.
168	l. scapula		0.84 m.
170	r. tibia & fibula	mouse-like	0.99 m.
176	r. radius	fox/dog and mouse	1.17 m.
203	r. femur	fox/dog	0.76 m.
208	r. tibia	small rodent	0.99 m.

Dr. Wells has suggested that many interments were placed in shallow graves which were not firmly compacted, p. 195. The bones then could be easily reached by burrowing predators as large as dogs, which further suggests that the graves were neglected 'soon' after burial (less that five years is likely, while up to fifty years is possible.) Presumably there must have been some flesh or moisture on the bones to attract the scavangers. There was no evidence of post-inhumation erosion of the bones by coleoptera, although this is often very difficult to identify. Rodent gnawing was not present on any of the skulls, a common area of activity being around the borders of the orbits, of the zygomata and of the mandibular rami and body.

A study by Clare Thawley of the animal bones recovered from CS and CT, produced evidence of gnawing by dogs, mf. 2/5 on ox, sheep, pig and fowl bones. This would indicate that the dogs had access to domestic waste in the homes, or scavenged in the area of the cemetery after the rubbish had been dumped. The animal bone recovered did not indicate the presence on the site of small rodents, but this is merely a reflection of the collecting methods — small bones being overlooked in the absence of sieving techniques. The gnawed human bones would certainly corroborate the presence of small rodents in the area.

There is uncertainty about the date of introduction of black rats into the British Isles, but there is the suggestion that the rodent gnawing exhibited on burials F, S, 16 and 133 is very similar to that of black rats. This raises the interesting question of whether black rats were present in Roman times, or whether the rodent gnawing is a medieval/post-medieval disturbance of the site.

The greatest depth recorded for gnawed bones is 1.17 m. for burial 176, but from modern ground level the average depth was c. 0.76 m., and must represent the shallowest grave it would have been feasible to dig to ensure the minimum cover for the body, with or without a coffin. Allowing for soil degradation and removal of topsoil, depth does not appear to have impeded access to the bones. As Dr. Calvin Wells has suggested many of the graves may not have been firmly compacted, and with collapse of the coffin through decay access would have been possible. One instance, burial 208, had cut an earlier grave, burial 252, and in the process and nature of the disturbance cavities may have been left, allowing access by burrowing animals into the relatively softer ground.

DECAPITATED BURIALS

Anatomical investigation revealed that six individuals had been decapitated — burials R, 123, 215, 216, 304 and 305. In all six cases the skull had been carefully repositioned in the grave at the top of the spine. Archaeological evidence failed to suggest anything unusual for any of the burials and decapitation was not implied by positioning of the skull at the feet or the sides of the legs as has been recorded in other cemeteries, for example at Lankhills, Winchester (Clarke, 1979, 372–375, and Table 40).

The comments below on the nature of the individual decapitations are taken from Calvin Wells analysis of burial anomalies and pathology, mf. 3/4 and 4/5.

Burial R had been decapitated by a sharp weapon from back to front between the atlas and axis vertebrae. This had presumably been inflicted with a sharp sword or a very narrow axe, but it is difficult to say whether it was the cause of death or inflicted very soon afterwards. Burial 123, although missing the axis and atlas vertebrae, retained sufficient evidence to show that he had been decapitated from back to front. Burials 215 and 216, lying in the same grave (pl. 19), had both been decapitated through the fourth cervical vertebrae from front to back, during life or immediately after death. The fifth cervical vertebra of burial 304 had been cut through cleanly, and again unfortunately there was no indication whether the action was carried out before or after death. Burial 305 was decapitated from behind forwards, with the third cervical vertebra and the tip of the axis cut by the weapon. Burials 304 and 305 were similarly found occupying the same grave.

DISTRIBUTION OF SEXED BURIALS

Anatomical investigation by Dr. Wells suggests that at least 241 males, 96 females, and 62 unsexed (children and adults) were interred in the Bath Gate Cemetery. As noted by Dr. Wells the defective condition of most of the skeletons made it difficult to assess the sex in a number of cases, and the unsexed individuals are of all ages — from newborn infants and adolescents to whom gender cannot be attributed, to mature individuals for whom the poor survival rate of diagnostic skeletal features prevented accurate gendering.

The sex ratios as estimated by Dr. Wells are as follows: for burials north of the Fosse 38 males or probable males to ?7 females; and south of the Fosse 207 males or probable males to 93 females or probable females. Such a high proportion of males to females, Dr. Wells suggests, should be accounted for on either biological or cultural terms. He considered that there was no evidence to suggest a biological cause for the imbalance in the sample. Tests by Dr. Waldron (p. 203) show an abnormally high lead content in the bone tissue but this would be a phenomenon experienced equally by men and women and equally could not explain the higher ratio of men to women.

As a cultural explanation Dr. Wells has suggested that Cirencester, like York, was given over to retired legionaries and various Roman officials 'many of whom lacked regular wives, and whose sexual partners, if any, were probably drawn from the professional prostitutes who were no doubt an abundant and pleasant amenity of the town'. The age distribution of male and female adults, fig. 82, shows female deaths to be fairly evenly distributed over the eight lustra from 18–58 years, whereas those of the males mount steadily from the mid-twenties to 53. The males do not 'block' at an early age which might be explained as death in combat. The range, for both males and females, is representative of a normal, civilian population, unless as Dr. Wells has suggested the males are retired legionaries, material and archaeological evidence for which is not evident from the excavations.

A study of the spatial distribution of male and female burials in the cemetery was made to see if there were significant groupings or distributions bearing in mind the unusually high ratio of males to females. However, female burials were found to be scattered evenly throughout the area of the cemetery sampled by excavation and there would appear to be no demarcation of the cemetery with specific areas set aside for females. If burial groupings were obviously sexual, with no mixing of the sexes permissable, the high proportion of men might have been explicable — the corresponding female area lying outside the bounds of the area excavated or in some other, as yet unsampled, cemetery area around the town.

It is interesting to note that of the three obvious multiple burials south of the Fosse, all were male:

Burial group a)   Inhumations 283, age 25–30; 284, age 30–40; 285, age 30–50; and 286, age 30–40

Burial group b)   Inhumations 193, age 43–47; 194, age 23–25; 215, age 24–28; and 216, age 38–46

Burial group c)   Inhumations 307, age 45–55; 335, age 45–50; 336, age 50–55; 337, age 26–32; and 338, age 35–40.

Each group exhibited a wide range of age at death:

a) 25–50; b) 23–47; and c) 26–55 years.

Anatomically there is little of note in the first group — 285 had a well healed fracture on the proximal third of the right fifth metatarsal. In the second group both burials 215 and 216 had been decapitated. In life burial 215 had received a number of fractures — to the left third or fourth rib; the left ulna exhibited a firmly healed 'parry' fracture; the shaft of the right second metacarpal bore evidence of a well healed fracture; and the right talus and calcaneus had both sustained a compression fracture which Dr. Wells suggests was almost certainly due to falling on the heel from a great height. The fourth cervical vertebra had been cleanly cut through the middle of its body in a horizontal plane, either during life or immediately after death. The wound to the vertebra was according to Dr. Wells undoubtedly inflicted from front to back, probably with a narrow bladed sword or sharp dagger, almost certainly not with a thicker axe. Dr. Wells further imagined that 'it may have been caused by an assailant standing behind the victim and drawing a dagger across his throat, into and through the bone'. Whether this was done as a murderous attack or as a post-mortem procedure cannot be solved by either anatomical or archaeological evidence. Burial 216 was similarly decapitated through the fourth cervical vertebra, and lay parallel to 215.

In the third group the anomalies and pathology of 307 consisted of a sacrum with six segments; an asymmetrical atlas; osteoarthrosis on the left and right scapular glenoid fossae and acetabula; a well healed fracture of a proximal phalange of a finger; and ?seven well healed fractures of bodies of middle ribs. A small remodelled area at the distal extremity of the sustentaculum tali of the right calcaneus and another on the right navicular are probably due to organisation of a small blood clot consequent on a torn ligament. Burial 335 suffered slight osteoarthrosis after fracturing the distal end of the left tibia. A six segment sacrum was found in burial 336; with osteoarthrosis on both clavicles, and humeral and femoral heads; and a 'flange' lesion of the left acetabulum. A firmly healed fracture of the left clavicle of burial 337 resulted in only moderate deformity but the bone was 7.8 mm. shorter than the right clavicle. Burial 338 suffered ankylosis of a middle and distal phalange of a toe. As a group the burials contribute a wide variety of fractures and anomalies. Buried so close to the amphitheatre it is tempting to think they had participated in combat in the arena.

The concentration of newborn infants in CS 74 10 is of particular interest. As Dr. Wells has stated, the figure for juvenile deaths as a whole in the cemetery is low compared with other sites. Of 63 juveniles found south of the Fosse, 30.2% died before their second birthday. Soil conditions (untested scientifically) did not appear to vary dramatically over the site, the survival of adult skeletal material was uniform over the entire area, and therefore, it can be assumed that taking into account the more frail nature of children's bone and the expectation that of all skeletal material they would be the first to deteriorate, the retrieval of so many newborn infants in CS 74 10 was either because of greater awareness and recognition of the problem, or the fact that there was a proportionally higher concentration of children in that area. Burial 243, in CS 72–3 8, was in fact found to be the remains of two newborn infants. It was not possible in the anatomical study to confidently allocate bones between the two babies, as equally archaeologically it had not been recognised that the bones represented two infants. Dr. Wells believed that if the two infants were siblings then they must have been twins.

An interesting pattern emerged whereby several of the infants were found near the feet of adults, and at the time of excavation it was thought that this might represent a mother–child bond, the mother perhaps unfortunately dying in child-birth. However, after anatomical study it was found that if there was any family grouping, with one exception it was with the father or a male sibling/relative. The exception was burial 318, a newborn infant found at the feet of 312, a woman with an estimated age at death of between 48 and 54 years. Osteoarthrosis and osteophytosis were severe in the vertebral column at all levels of 312, with widespread arthrotic changes affecting both bones of the sacro-coccygeal joint; the glenoid fossa of the right scapula; both acetabula and both femoral heads; and all three bones of the left knee joint. The right sacro-iliac joint surfaces were very much smaller than those of the left and were abnormal in shape. The bones of the left arm were not only shorter but also very much lighter than those of the right, with consistently weaker muscle markings also. In the absence of the clinical history of the case, Dr. Wells, however, thought that a very high probability must be given to poliomyelitis as the cause of these anomalies, either a moderately benign attack in early childhood or a later, perhaps less benign occurrence near the end of the growing period resulting in the changes found in the skeleton. Parity for many of the other female skeletons found in the cemetery has been estimated by Dr. Wells, but in this case no positive evidence was available, and a mother–child bond for 312 and 318 would not appear feasible.

THE POTTERY
by
Valery Rigby

INTRODUCTION

Throughout the processing, the pottery has been dealt with in its stratigraphical groups, and this is continued in the report. The report on the samian has been arranged separately, and is limited to the potters' stamps and those decorated pieces which are of special interest since the whole collection is residual, mf. 1/5, and fig. 39. The report on the mortaria has been fully integrated into the pottery groups, and the discussion into the fabric classification.

The vessel-forms have not been classified; but to aid the recording of small and indeterminate body sherds which could not usefully be drawn, as well as to reduce repetition in the descriptions, the fabrics have been classified, mf. 1/5. The classification was based on the superficial characteristics of the ware and the inclusions — the grain-size and texture of the ware, the presence of visible mica and quartz, the size, colour, type and density of inclusions, and finally the colour, the combined result of the presence of impurities, particularly iron compounds, and the firing conditions. When such methods of classification have been used, it is essential to realise that fabrics which are superficially identical, need not be from the same source, while dissimilar fabrics need not be from different potteries. Only a long-term and intensive programme of analysis may be able to settle some of the questions raised by the fabric classification, but this is beyond the resources available at present.

Hand-made vessels are specified as such in the report, while in the descriptions of the remaining vessels, it is understood that they were wheel-thrown.

The parallels quoted are limited to those which, if not identical, are very similar in both form and fabric so could be considered to be of the same date and even from the same, or closely related sources to the Cirencester pottery. All the relevant sherds have been examined. In some cases, although the parallels quoted are from published sites, they could not be identified in the relevant report.

THE POTTERY GROUPS

It was decided to publish in full the pottery from the following groups from sites CS and CT despite various reservations because of the date and quality of the assemblages.

The evidence from sites CS and CT has to be used with caution since the finds from the lowest layers were almost certainly not derived from occupation in the immediate area, rather were introduced from elsewhere, probably from somewhere in the town centre, during rubbish disposal or area clearance. The time lag between the use of the pottery, its initial discarding and final dumping outside the town defences, and the erection of the building (CT) and the cutting of the first burials in areas of CS, could be greater than the pottery and coins suggest. The lack of previous occupation in the areas CS and CT has had the advantage of limiting the date range of the residual pottery, while the absence of extensive re-building operations during the short period of occupation, coupled with the fact that there were no post-Roman building and antiquarian activities has resulted in unusually undisturbed stratification for a site in Cirencester. Very few sites excavated to date within the area of the Roman town can offer either of these conditions, never mind both, and they off-set the initial disadvantages of CS and CT.

The assemblages are of particular interest because they include ranges of forms and fabrics which are poorly represented in stratified groups from sites in the town centre, and are not even numerous amongst the unstratified material. If evidence from town sites alone had been available, what were in fact standard products, would have been considered as comparatively rare 'imports', e.g. mortaria like nos. 3, 49–51, flagons like nos. 8 and 63–4, and tankards like nos. 13 and 72–4. Typical Severn Valley ware wide-mouthed necked jars, with characteristic hooked rims, like nos. 89 and 140, would appear to be extremely rare, and the Alice Holt potteries would have been left with even fewer rims to its name. The most numerous and complete examples of colour-coated wares imported from Central Gaul and the Rhineland, including "motto" beakers, are those found on sites CS and CT. Clearly the sources of all these types, whether local or not, were more important to the life and economy of Cirencester than the previous evidence from the town centre sites suggested. The finds imply the existence somewhere in the region of at least one major pottery specialising in flagons and mortaria, and possibly both, in the third century. (See Fabrics 88 and 97).

Building CT, with its fairly extensive groups from below and above the building, has provided some internal evidence for filling-out the scope and chronology of pottery reaching the town in the third and early fourth centuries by providing the widest range of fabric and form associations for the period found to date. There are smaller and more limited comparable groups from stratified contexts within the town, in particular site AH and Parsonage Field 1959, and also from unstratified contexts on the site of the Beeches town house (sites CQ, CX, CY and DE; see McWhirr, 1973), and from Parsonage Field, Insula IV (sites AH and AX excavated by J.S. Wacher, and areas excavated 1958–9, Rennie, 1971, and Richardson, 1962 Fig. 3, 11–30). The additional groups support the associations and dating evidence indicated by sites CS and CT. Supporting negative evidence is provided by the absence of parallels from the very large groups of pottery from make-up layers of second century date which occur extensively in the town centre, from the first phase of the town rampart, and also from the late fourth or fifth century deposits.

Considering the stratigraphically earliest groups, the layers lying on natural sub-soil, CS 72–3 8 layer 7 and those pre-dating building CT, the earliest pottery could be late Antonine in date, with little or nothing which needs to be earlier than A.D. 180, while most, with the exception of the samian, could be of third century date. The mortaria span the late second-early third century period but with the addition of pieces from the Oxford potteries which should post-date A.D. 270 (see mf. 1/5). Amongst the products of the regional potteries, there is one type which has not yet been identified from any site in the town centre, no. 51 in Fabric 88. Taking the sites in turn, the group from site CS 72–3 8 layer 7, appears to have accumulated after A.D. 180 according to the samian, but more particularly after A.D. 200, until c. A.D. 250. There are some sherds, including the sherd of Oxford red-slipped ware (Fabric 83) and the flanged dish in B.B.1, which post-date A.D. 250. The scarcity of types of later third century date, suggests that these pieces could have been intruded when the rubbish accumulation was being moved to its final dumping ground on site CS. Although there are flagons and mortaria in white slipped ware, Fabric 88, there are no flagons and mortaria in white slipped ware, Fabric 88, there are no flagons in the closely related orange-brown burnished ware, Fabric 97, possibly indicating a considerable difference in the date of their introduction — Fabric 88 in the late second century, Fabric 97 in the mid-third century. The probable products of the White Hill Farm kiln complex, Wanborough, do not figure particularly largely in a rim count, but clearly this production centre was already a significant supplier to Cirencester.

The layers immediately above layer 7, layers 5 and 6, became contaminated with later material. However, excluding the obviously modern sherds, they produced basically the same assemblages, covering the same period. The next successive layer, layer 4, while also producing very similar groups, included sherds from six vessels in Oxford red-slipped wares, two bowls of samian form 31, one samian form 38, one carinated bowl and two beakers. The earliest burials in this particular area of the cemetery, site CS 72–3 8, are cut into layer 7, and once the area had been officially taken over as a burial ground, it can scarcely have been available for the disposal of rubbish in any quantity, the possibility exists therefore, that at least some of the apparently later pottery typified by the Oxford products from layer 4, had been disturbed from layers 5–7, when the graves were being dug. In such a case, it becomes more likely that later pieces were not intruded, and that the original accumulation of the rubbish later to turn up in layers 5–7, was still accumulating after c. A.D. 270, which effects the dating of the first burials in the area of CS 72–3 8, moving it to considerably later than A.D. 270.

Although the groups from below the building are similar to that from CS 72–3 8 layer 7, the proportion of material dated to after A.D. 250 or 270, is greater, this being typified by the greater number of Oxford products, both cream and red-slipped wares (Fabrics 83 and 84). As with site CS, either the rubbish was still accumulating until after A.D. 270, or else the later pottery was intruded at the time of final dumping or when the building was being erected. Despite the unresolved problems, the earliest groups from sites CS and CT illustrate the range of pottery reaching Cirencester in the middle period of the third century.

The mortaria are from quite different sources to those from early-to-mid-second century contexts elsewhere in the town, but they show marked continuity with those found in late-second century deposits, and represent a much more varied range of sources than were available later, in the fourth and fifth centuries A.D.. There are imports from the Rhineland, while the south-east is represented by wall-sided mortaria from either Kent of Colchester. Three centres shared evenly the major part of the market — the south-west, the exact location being unknown, but possibly local to Cirencester; the Mancetter-Hartshill potteries (65/70 miles); and the Oxfordshire potteries (40/5 miles). In the earlier groups the Oxfordshire products are almost exclusively cream wares, but some wall-sided vessels in red-slipped wares appear in the second half of the third century. All three sources are represented here by products of the late second as well as the third century.

The specialised colour-coated wares also show a diversity of sources different to those from early and mid-second century contexts. Imports from the Rhineland and Central Gaul account for almost half of the recorded finds, but the biggest group of sherds are of 'Castor' ware fabrics within the range of the lower Nene Valley and New Forest potteries, although they are not all necessarily from these sources. Other sources include more possible imporst from Gaul or the Rhineland (Fabric 80), the New Forest, Oxford and a local one, probably in the Swindon area. The proportions must have been affected by the "family heirloom principle" which appears to distort the discarding of fine, specialised and imported wares to a greater or lesser extent. Allowing for this, the assemblages do indicate the sources for colour-coated wares in the earlier part of the third century. The vast majority of vessel-forms represented are beakers, with just one open bowl and one closed form, probably a flagon.

The sources for the flasks and flagons appear to be more limited than those for mortaria and colour-coated wares, being firmly orientated to local and regional sources in the south-west, in particular Fabrics 88, 97, 95 and 96. With the exception of vessels in Fabric 95, the flasks and flagons are neatly made and well finished with burnished surfaces, whether slipped or self-coloured, and include some rare variants, like nos. 58, 63 and 127. The potters making flagons in Fabrics 88, 97 and 96, were obviously skilled and specialised, and if the dating of their products at Cirencester is correct, they could be considered as innovators rather than mere copyists of products of the colour-coated ware factories. They could have been producing flagons with cordoned and flanged necks at least as early, and possibly earlier than potters in the New Forest and Oxford.

Black-burnished wares constitute more than half of the groups by volume, excluding samian. They account for almost all the identified platters, and dishes; the largest group of jar rims and bases, and the most complete profiles. Dishes with flanged rims are only just represented, suggesting that they were not common until the second half of the third century. Those with grooved pie-dish rims, like no. 136, are much more common, indicating an introduction earlier in the third century, if not the late second. But pie-dishes are by far the most common dish-type, the numbers probably being inflated by the presence of doubly residual second century examples.

Local wares, of which Fabric 98 is numerically by far the most important, appear in forms which would not compete directly with B.B.1 products, a trend first apparent in second century contexts, but which is much more obvious in later groups, despite some attempts at 'copies'. The fabrics include both oxidised and reduced versions of the same wares, the latter being more numerous, and the finish is usually matt, for the use of the burnishing tool was limited. The range of forms includes types which are considered characteristic of the Severn Valley potteries — flanged bowls and tankards, as well as necked jars and wide-mouthed necked jars, with or without a cordon at the base of the neck. Vessels which on the grounds of both form and fabric are typical of the Severn Valley ware products are only just represented, being limited to bowls with applied handles at the rim, and necked jars with hooked rims. The significance of the trade in pottery from sources to the north, in the Severn Valley, depends to some extent on how widely the definition is interpreted owing to the extent of the overlap of forms with the local potteries in north Wiltshire, near Swindon.

The later groups from above the abandoned building, although not sealed, are sufficiently undisturbed to indicate the trends of pottery supply in the early fourth century. There are considerable differences from the groups which pre-date the building.

The specialised wares, mortaria and colour-coated wares, are dominated by Oxford products almost to the exclusion of all else, although there are still sherds from Castor ware beakers, probably from the lower Nene Valley. From a simple sherd count, it appears that the source of flagons in Fabric 95 dried-up sometime in the mid-third century, for the majority in the later groups are in Fabrics 88 and 97. Locally produced coarse wares are still limited to non-B.B.1 forms, with the exception of the occasional copy, like nos. 148 and 167. The shallow dish, no. 167 is in a micaceous grey-black ware with a highly burnished finish, and it may be the fore-runner from a production centre which made wheel-made copies of B.B.1 forms which begin to show up in groups from mid-fourth century contexts. Severn Valley ware products are more frequent than in the earlier group, so would appear to have been more plentiful in the early fourth century. No bowls or tankards could be identified in the later groups, so that trade may have been limited to the necked jars, like nos. 89 and 140, which suggests that it was the contents rather than the vessels which were being traded.

The B.B.1 producers were still dominating trade in cooking-pots, dishes and platters, but a comparison of the early and late groups would appear to illustrate major changes. Flanged dishes now outnumber the other two basic types, while the number of narrow-shouldered jars, with wide flaring rim, similar to Gillam 147, and decorated with a narrow band of markedly obtuse-angled lattice, has increased, apparently at the expense of the more hybrid intermediate jar types, like no. 31 (see mf. 1/5). The apparent simple progression suggested by the quantities of each dish type is complicated by the presence in groups from various sites in the town, of deep, carinated and chamfered bowls, with grooved pie-dish or flanged rims, in typical B.B.1, but in contexts dating from the late first to the mid-second century. Unless the almost complete wall depth is extant, the classification of the form cannot be absolutely definite in all cases, and in addition, the dating of so-called local copies of B.B.1 forms is rendered even more obscure.

Datable pieces from the group sealing the building, suggest that the pottery was accumulating in the first half of the fourth century, possibly before A.D. 330. The quantity and range of products from the Oxford potteries in red-slipped wares are notably limited to beakers, several of which are Hunt Cups, and the bowls which were directly influenced by samian forms 31, 38 and 45. There are no identified examples of the forms thought to be characteristic of the period after A.D. 320 — necked jars, necked bowls and dimpled bowls — nor of the decoration common in the later period — scroll patterns in white slip, rouletted patterns or stamps. (See Young, 1977, for the full discussion of the dating of the fabrics, forms and decoration). Possibly of significance only to the Cirencester region is the rate and scope of the introduction of Oxford products in the later third and fourth centuries.

No examples of the cream slipped Fabric 84 were found below the building. They frequently shared the same matrices as the red slipped Fabric 83, as well as sharing the forms of the self-coloured cream Fabric 90, both of which are well represented. On the grounds that they shared the same forms and matrices, all three wares have conventionally been dated to the same period. Also absent from below the building, are the red-slipped wares which are considered by Young (1977) to have been made in Gloucestershire because their provenances are concentrated in the north of the county (e.g. Fabric 105). Their absence may indicate that their production followed the major expansion of the Oxfordshire potteries in the early decades of the fourth century. The forms and fabrics which appear to have replaced B.B.1 products in the mid-fourth century onwards, since they dominate the latest groups within the town, are totally absent even from the layers sealing the building.

Just as there is no pottery dating to the late fourth or early fifth centuries sealing the dismantled building, there is none even in the uppermost layers of sites CT and CS generally, except in the vicinity of the ditch, CT 366, and the graves 720–1 and 729–35. Here there are a few examples of the later wares, in particular, wheel-made necked jars in shell-tempered fabrics, Fabric 115. The amount is small, as are the sherds themselves, and their condition generally suggests the usual weathered and abraided sherds found in ploughsoil. Post-Roman pottery is equally as scarce as late Roman, there are nine small rim sherds from gritted jars of thirteenth- or fourteenth-century date, and the occasional modern sherd. None of the later material occurs in any of the grave fillings. Their presence is probably as a result of manuring once the area had reverted to agricultural use.

It is relevant here to compare the dating evidence provided by the pottery with that from the coins. The coins suggested that the material in the layers pre-dating the building began accumulating after A.D. 145/61, and that the building cannot have been erected before A.D. 270. The number of Radiates found below the building is very small, which may indicate that the construction took place comparatively soon after A.D. 270. Occupation could have extended into the early fourth century, but the absence of actual occupation layers means that there is no evidence. At least one of the so-called cobbled surfaces which overlay the collapsed building, was not laid down until after A.D. 310. Ignoring the very large group of Radiates from the layers above the patches of cobbles, the first group of coins is dated to after A.D. 330. The absence of these normally common Constantinian issues from below the cobbles probably indicates that the layers which they post-date had developed between A.D. 310 and 330, at the latest. The coins present an unexpectedly similar chronological framework to the pottery.

Reservations remain about the date of the use of the area of Trench 8 on site CS for burials, using only the pottery in CS 72–3 8 layer 7. Burials were already taking place in certain areas of CS and CT not long after the mid-third century judging by the typology of the B.B.1 jar which accompanied burial 719. One problem so far barely hinted at, is that of the very large quantities of samian which were found during the excavations of both sites, most usefully in CS 72–3 8 layer 7 and the layers below the building, but generally in all layers but topsoil. The sherds are large and in fairly good condition, with some wear but no signs of weathering. The vast majority are Central Gaulish plain forms and are dated to after A.D. 160, they have the appearance of a selected group of homogeneous sherds, with a negligible amount of intrusive earlier material and only a slight admixture of East Gaulish sherds, most of which have been dated as late second or early third century. All of the 46 stamps found fall into the date range A.D. 135–220, while 19 post-date 160, and all the remaining unidentified stamps, 14, are of Antonine or late Antonine date. The minimum number of vessels from CS 72–3 8 layer 7 is 49, and from below the building 139. The samian far outweighs in volume, quality and condition, all the other fine wares together, i.e. seven vessels from CS 72–3 8 layer 7, and 31 from below the building. There is no group of coarse wares of comparable date and size to the samian from the same contexts, although some of the coarse wares could be of late second century date. As it stands, the collection suggests that there could be a systematic, but as yet unknown factor at work during the time when samian was discarded and its final deposition in the location from which it is excavated, which resulted in the accumulation of large amounts of samian of limited date range, in good condition, in contexts alongside pottery in use considerably after the date of manufacture of the samian itself.

When tracing parallels in groups from sites within the town centre for the 'new' forms and fabrics which occur in the groups from sites CS and CT, it became apparent that they were very specific in their findspots, even when they occurred in topsoil. The results of this work are shown in the graphs, fig. 40, mf. 1/5. Figure 2 in Wacher and McWhirr 1982 shows the location of all the sites excavated to date in Cirencester. They cover most of the accessible areas of the Roman town, with most *Insulae* having been investigated at least once. As controls, the mortaria from the Oxford potteries were chosen, because of the quantity and the ease of identification. They were divided into two categories, first, forms made in the second century in cream ware (Fabric 90), secondly, the versions made in the third and fourth century in cream, red- and cream-slipped wares (Fabrics 90, 83 and 84). Only sherds where the forms could be definitely identified were used. The remaining mortaria for the study were in Fabrics 88 and 91, and the products of the unknown centre in the south-west and the Mancetter-

Hartshill potteries. The graphs mf. 1/5, fig. 40 give the results of the investigation.

The Oxford products of second century date were more specific in their distribution than the later products. Not only that, they are markedly concentrated, (41%), in a group of layers traced across the northern end of *Insula* VI, and used to level-up the site prior to re-development with the construction of a major colonnaded building.

The south-western and Mancetter-Hartshill products have very similar distributions, which is not surprising since they frequently occur together in groups, whether stratified or not. They too favour only a limited number of *Insulae*, in particular IV, V, VI and XII, in which some areas have been excavated to natural. It is possible that the distribution indicates similar contemporary events taking place in widely different areas of the town. It also shows that while much third century rubbish was being dumped outside the town, a lot was being finally discarded within the town. While the distribution of the second century Oxford products coincides with sites which were excavated to very low levels, if not natural, the coincidence is less marked in the case of the essentially third century mortaria. The later Oxford mortaria have by far the widest distribution which coincides with that of sites excavated, regardless of the depth achieved. It is the concentrations which are of interest, particularly those in the vicinity of the Verulamium Gate, which scarcely figures in the other distributions.

Distributions of this sort can be of great assistance in building-up a framework for the development of the Roman town in general, and of specific areas within it, but they also emphasise some of the major problems encountered when dealing with finds from a town. Whether or not the sites were excavated to natural, the range of finds from an *Insula* cannot be assumed automatically to provide a representative cross-section for the town as a whole, nor even the next *Insula*. Where thick deposits rich in finds occur it cannot be assumed that they were derived from the occupation in the immediate area, and so be used to indicate the nature, density and length of occupation there. In many cases the reverse is the case, and the major deposits mark the use of the derelict area for rubbish dumping, or else they were brought in to level up the site prior to re-development, possibly following a period of dereliction.

A full and comprehensive catalogue with illustrations and discussion of all pottery recovered from CS and CT is contained in microfiche, mf. 1/5, figs 41–51. The group of coarse wares from layers pre-dating the building, Period I, nos. 42–123, figs. 43–46, has been extracted from the full report and is published here in conventional format. Fabric classification is discussed mf. 1/5.

PERIOD I — PRE-DATING THE BUILDING

COLOUR-COATED WARES

Imports
42. **CT 242.** Fabric 80A. Decoration — rouletted band. Late second or early third century. In addition, a plain body sherd possibly from the same beaker. Central Gaul.
43. **CT 158.** Fabric 80A — iridescent brown slip. At least one strap handle. Decoration — routletting. Probably a cup with two handles. Central Gaul. Late second or early third century. In addition, three body sherds, probably from the same beaker, with white barbotine decoration, like no. 152. (CT 253; CT 207; CT 267).
Rhenish Imports (not illustrated) — rim and two body sherds from beakers. Fabric 80B. (CT 242).
44. **CT 354.** Fabric 80A — highly iridescent brown slip. Decoration — at least two bands of rouletting. Central Gaul. Late second-early third century.
Local products
45. **CT 251.** Fabric 85 — rough coral slip. Decoration — coarse, pecked rouletting. The fabric closely resembles self-coloured wares from local sources suggesting that it too is local, although it cannot be paralleled.
New Forest
46. **CT 354.** Fabric 82 — metallic purple slip. No evidence of whether decorated or left plain.

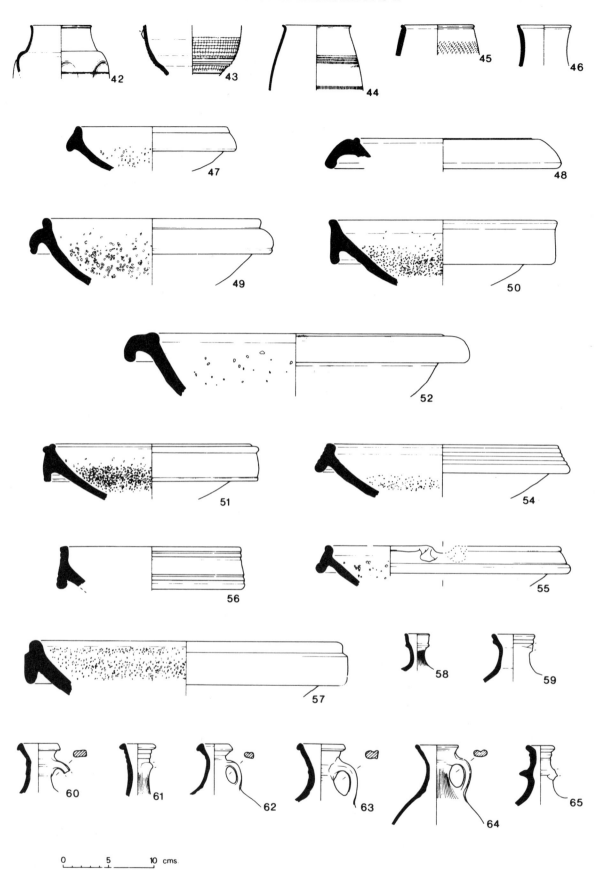

Fig. 43. Coarse pottery, nos. 42–65

Fulford type 39 or 42, Fulford Fabric (F.F.)1a, (Fulford, 1975, 24).

In addition, sherds from one folded beaker in F.F.1a (CT 371). After *c.* A.D. 280. The remaining vessels were represented by body sherds (not illustrated):-

'Castor' wares, Fabric 81 — sherd from 16 different beakers as Gillam 79, dark green slip (1) (CT 354); Hunt Cup, red-brown slip (1) (CT 354); Hunt Cup or barbotine scroll (2) (CT 315); folded, with rouletted bands (2) (CT 375; CT 376); base from a large beaker, with a rouletted band (CT 315); roughcast, brown slip (2); beaker bases (4); body sherds (3) (all CT 354). Red-brown slip wares, Fabric 86 — roughcast beakers, grog roughcasting (2); folded beaker (1). Possibly imported since identical examples occur in France. Oxford red-slipped ware, Fabric 83 — body sherd from a flanged bowl as Young form C 51, (1977, 160, fig. 59), base from a bowl, and rouletted sherds from two beakers (CT 354; CT 315; CT 242). After *c.* A.D. 270.

MORTARIA

47. **CT 354.** Fabric 88 — matt cream slip. Typical trituration grit.

In addition, a flange fragment from a mortarium like no. 4 (CT 371).

48. **CT 251.** Fabric 88 — cream slip, burnished on the rim. Translucent white, grey and brown trituration grit, with the addition of some opaque grits. Very worn and burnt. Antonine.

Other examples — CT 371 (1); BC I 8, with an illiterate Mark; DB I (2); Parsonage Field 1959, CW2, A/B I 3, E5 3; AH I 34, AH I 42 — with illiterate Mark, AH I 43; AL III 8; AK II 9; AM III 9; CQ XIV 8/9.

49. **CT 315.** Fabric 88 — matt cream slip. Typical trituration grit.

50. **CT 253.** Fabric 88 — thick matt cream slip. Typical trituration grits. Worn. Possibly late second or first half of the third century.

Other examples — 1971 CY u.s.; DB III 1.

51. **CT 246.** Fabric 88 — rough matt cream slip. Typical trituration grits. Shows moderate wear. First half of the third century.

In addition, rim from another identical, very worn (CT 251).

Mancetter-Hartshill potteries

52. **CT 315.** Fabric 91 — black grog trituration grit. Broken at the edge of a stamp since the end of a splodge of brown slip survives. Second century.

53. **CT 304.** Fabric 91 — mixed black and red grog trituration grit. Not illustrated.

54. **CT 242.** Fabric 91 — fairly fine red and black grog trituration grit. Well worn. Made later than A.D. 240, probably A.D. 240–300.

Not very common in Cirencester, other examples AS I 6; CY XVI 8; CR V 3; DH XL 168; Parsonage Field 1958, CW/58/385.

55. **CT 315.** Fabric 91 — occasional red-brown grits. Black grog trituration grit. In addition, rims from two others similar, with mixed red and black grog trituration grit (CT 309; CT 354).

Other examples — CQ VIII 9/10; AH I 42; DB VI 1; Parsonage Field, 1958, CW/58/325.

There are flange fragments from two mortaria with deep curved flanges, (CT 315; CT 354), and a base sherd from another, with mixed red and black trituration grit (CT 375).

Colchester potteries (or possibly Kent)

56. **CT 304.** Fabric 92 — cream ware. No trituration grit. Identified examples are rare in Cirencester; other examples — Parsonage Field 1958, CW/58/54; 1959, CW 2 E5.

Oxfordshire potteries

Rim sherd from a mortarium like no. 5, in cream ware, Fabric 90. (CT 304). (Not illustrated).

?Imported mortaria

57. **CT 354.** Fabric 94 — cream ware. White and pale brown crystalline trituration grit, with concentric scoring. Probably first half of the third century.

In addition, a rim fragment from a large mortarium identical to no. 213, Fabric 93, probably the work of Verecundus (CT 376).

AMPHORAE (not illustrated)

a.   A handle from a Dressel type 20. Fabric 40. South Spanish. An incomplete two–line stamp along the handle reads EPMACO/ILFRAR, or]ERACO]ILFRAR? The reading is uncertain, and the stamp is not included in Callender, 1965.

b.   Sherds, Dressel type 20. Fabric 40. (CT 209).

c.-e.   Body sherds and bases, Dressel, type 30. Fabric 35. (CT 315; CT 354 (2)).

f.   Sherds, probably from North Africa. (CT 254).

FLASKS AND FLAGONS

58.   **CT 241.**   Fabric 96 — well-finished matt rim, vertically burnished neck, horizontally burnished shoulder.
Other examples — AW I 48.

59.   **CT 354.**   Fabric 95 — thin and patchy white slip. The handle was fixed into the body of the flagon by a tang, a feature of (probably) local products in the second century and cream slipped wares in the later second and third century.

60.   **CT 260.**   Fabric 88 — thick cream matt slip.
Other examples — DK II 4; Parsonage Field, 1959, CW2 A4 5; AF I 4; DL I 13; DL I 11; DB IV 1.

61.   **CT 371.**   Fabric 96 — matt rim, vertically burnished neck. The rings are well executed and are reminiscent of much earlier products of the late first and early second century. It is clearly from the same source as the small flask no. 58.

62.   **CT 260.**   Fabric 88 — thick matt cream slip.
Other examples — DL VI 9.

63.   **CT 266.**   Fabric 88 — thick cream slip, matt rim and handle, vertically burnished neck. The neck was made separately and luted into the body.
Other examples — Parsonage Field 1958, CW/58/347.
In addition, body sherds from three vessels with a burnished finish (CT 246; 269; 270), and one vessel with a matt finish (CT 253).

64.   **CT 181.**   Fabric 97 — well-finished matt rim and handle, vertically burnished neck and shoulder.
Other examples — Parsonage Field 1959, CW2 A9 3.

65.   **CT 315.**   Fabric 97 — grey core; orange-buff surfaces. Matt rim and flange; vertical burnishing on the neck.
In addition, necks from two other examples and a base (CT 315; CT 354).

BOWLS, DISHES AND JARS

66.   **CT 242.**   Fabric 111 — dark grey core; orange-brown surfaces, worn and vesicular, but with traces of a burnished finish. The fabric and form fall within the definition of Severn Valley ware.

67.   **CT 239.**   Fabric 98 — originally orange ware, heavily burnt and discoloured.
In addition, sherds from five other bowls in Fabric 98. (CT 315 (3); CT 354 (2)).
Other examples — CS burial 319, from the filling of the grave; Parsonage Field, 1959, CW2/ D1/2.
There are body sherds from a large bowl with at least one handle applied below the pie dish rim, a typical Severn Valley ware form, Webster type 45, (1976, fig. 8). Fabric 106 — orange-brown micaceous ware.

68.   **CT 315.**   Fabric 109 — occasional red grog grits, presumably accidental. Very worn. Possibly a product of one of the Severn Valley ware potteries.
In addition, sherds from two tankards, like no. 73, in orange Fabric 98.

69.   **CT 252.**   Fabric 30 — micaceous. Faceted interior and rim top, smoothly burnished exterior.

70.   **CT 260.**   Fabric 5 — faceted burnished exterior finish and worn interior.

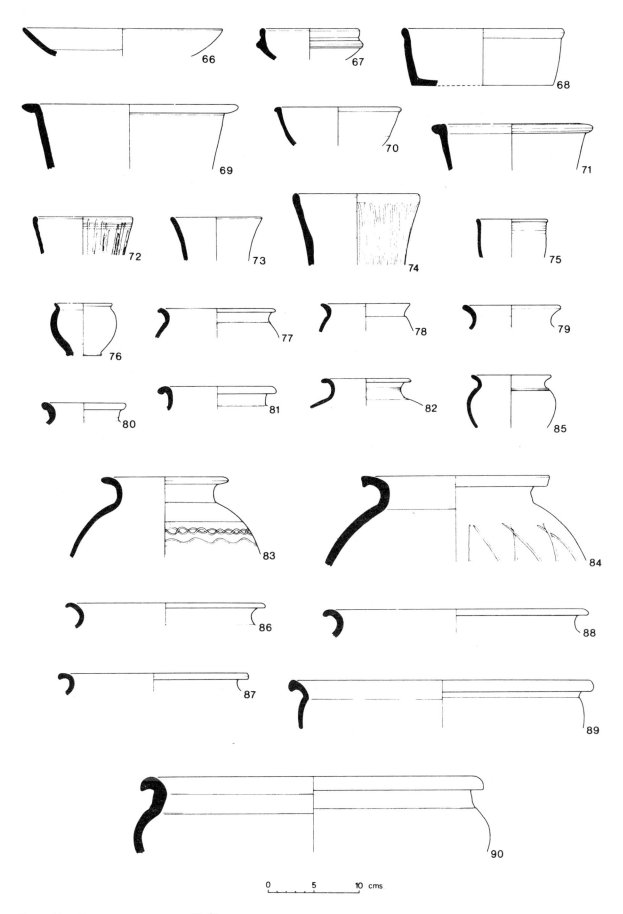

Fig. 44. Coarse pottery, nos. 66–90

71.   **CT 260.**   Fabric 30 — burnished rim top and interior, faceted exterior. Very slight groove on the top of the rim. Very worn and weathered. Probably local.

72.   **CT 256.**   Fabric 98 — blue-grey core; orange surfaces, streaked with grey on the outside, where burnished, horizontal burnishing at the lip, vertical burnished stripes below.

73.   **CT 260.**   Fabric 98 — matt surfaces.

74.   **CT 304.**   Fabric 110 — dense ware. Blue core; orange surfaces, with vertical burnishing on the outside.

In addition, sherds from a tankard in oxidised Fabric 98, (CT 269) and one in reduced Fabric 98 (CT 304).

Other examples — CT 354, identical.

75.   **CT 304.**   Fabric 98 — orange ware; rilled matt finish.

76.   **CT 304.**   Fabric 20 — with sparse grey grog grits. Roughly smoothed finish. Probably local, from the potteries near Swindon.

77.   **CT 252.**   Fabric 17 — burnished rim top and shoulder, matt neck. A slight cordon at the base of the rim. A local product. Late second-early third century.

78.   **CT 253.**   Fabric 17 — burnished rim top and shoulder. Decoration — probably either burnished lattice or combed stripes. Second century.

In addition, body sherds from three jars in Fabric 98, decorated with right-angled burnished lattice.

79.   **CT 267.**   Fabric 95 — matt white slip.

In addition, similar rim in Fabric 98, blue-grey (CT 304).

80.   **CT 239.**   Fabric 98 — blue-grey ware; burnished rim top, matt neck.

81.   **CT 260.**   Fabric 98 — blue-grey ware; burnished rim top and band on the neck.

82.   **CT 158.**   Fabric 98 — dark orange core; light orange surfaces, matt finish. Third century

In addition, rim sherds from similar jars in Fabric 98, blue-grey; Fabric 17, blue-grey; body sherds from two jars decorated with acute burnished lattice, Fabric 17.

83.   **CT 315.**   Fabric 98 — brown core; dark blue-grey surfaces. Burnished rim and shoulder.

84.   **CT 354.**   Fabric 6B — dark blue-grey core; pale grey cortex; dark blue-grey surfaces. Burnished rim top and shoulder. Decoration — burnished lines on matt rilled ground.

In addition, a rim sherd from another similar (CT 354), and rims from five other necked jars in Fabric 6 (CT 195; CT 315 (3); CT 371).

85.   **CT 253.**   Fabric 17 — burnished rim top and shoulder.

In addition, rims from three similar, larger jars, in oxidised Fabric 98 (CT 252; CT 254; CT 256; CT 262; CT 266; CT 304 (8)).

86.   **CT 266.**   Fabric 98 — orange core; blue-grey surfaces, matt ground with narrow burnished bands.

In addition, rim sherds from two other similar jars (CT 266; CT 304).

87.   **CT 251.**   Fabric 17 — burnished rim top.

Other examples — CT 300, in Fabric 98; CT 315.

88.   **CT 260.**   Fabric 6E — grey burnished rim top, lumpy matt neck. Third century rather than earlier.

In addition, rim sherd from a similar jar, Fabric 6 (CT 249).

Other examples — Parsonage Field, CW 2, G5. 2.

89.   **CT 354.**   Fabric 108 — very worn, no finish survives.

In addition, a rim from a second example. Possibly by-products of the potteries south of Cirencester, near Swindon.

In addition, rim sherds from at least seven necked jars in oxidised versions of Fabric 98 (CT 315 (3); CT 354 (3)), and 11 necked jars in reduced versions of Fabric 98 (CT 354 (9); CT 371).

90.   **CT 354.**   Fabric 6E — grey core; brownish buff surfaces, with grey patches. Burnished rim top, neck and shoulder.

91.   **CT 239.**   Fabric 30 — matt finish. Decoration — two interlocking burnished scrolls.

92.   **CT 252.**   Fabric 41 — grey core; brown with dark grey-black surfaces, rilled matt interior and lip, exterior smoothed with matt band at the lip edge.

93.   **CT 256.**   Fabric 20 — matt finish.

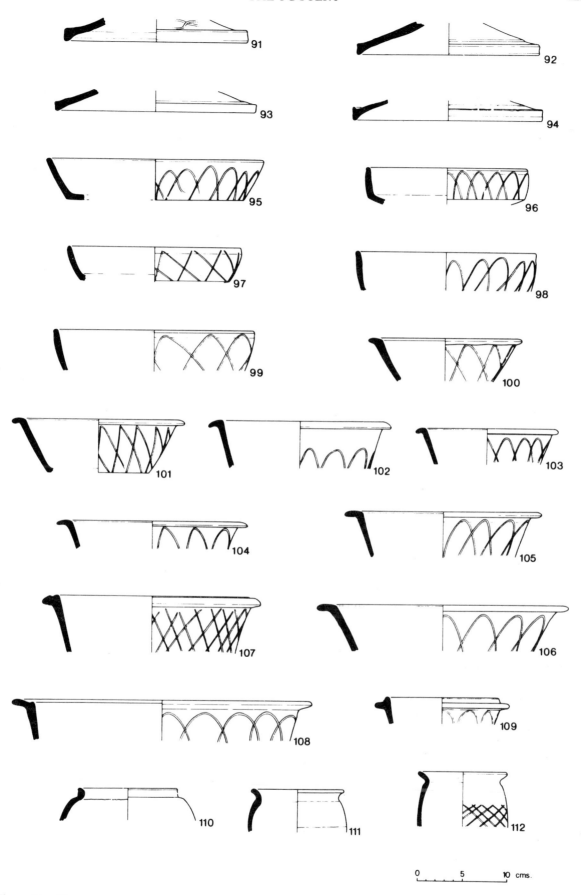

Fig. 45. Coarse pottery, nos. 91–112

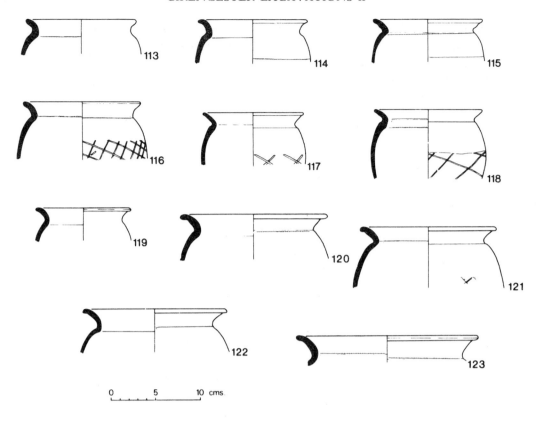

Fig. 46. Coarse pottery, nos. 113–123

94. **CT 251 & 253.** Fabric 98 — hard ware. Grey core at the lip; dark orange-brown ware, with a matt rilled finish.

In addition, knobs from two other lids in orange-brown Fabric 98. (CT 251; CT 304).

Black Burnished Ware — B.B.1 (Fabric 74 — hand-made, unless stated otherwise)

95. **CT 271.** Burnished interior and lip. Decoration — burnished interlocking arcs on matt ground.

96. **CT 239.** Burnished interior. Decoration — smoothed exterior with burnished interlocking arcs and scribble burnishing on the underside.

97–99. **CT 251; CT 267; CT 253.** Burnished interior. Decoration — smoothed exterior with burnished interlocking arcs.

In addition, rims from 34 other platters (CT 165; CT 158; CT 242 (2); CT 246; CT 251 (2); CT 252 (2); CT 260 (4); CT 266; CT 269; CT 271; CT 304 (10); CT 354 (5); CT 371 (3)).

100–106. **CT 251; CT 262; CT 252; CT 267; CT 251; CT 253; CT 267.** Burnished rim top and interior. Decoration — faceted exterior with burnished interlocking arcs.

In addition, rim sherds from 29 different dishes (CT 158; CT 172; CT 195; CT 242; CT 249; CT 251 (3); CT 252 (2); CT 253 (3); CT 254; CT 256; CT 260; CT 266 (2); CT 304; CT 315 (2); CT 354 (6); CT 371 (2)).

107. **CT 253.** Burnished rim top and interior. Decoration — smoothed exterior, burnished lattice.

108. **CT 260.** Burnished rim top and interior. Decoration — crudely smoothed exterior with interlocking burnished arcs. The angle of the rim suggests that it could be from a carinated bowl.

In addition, rims from three other dishes (CT 197; CT 242; CT 315).

109. **CT 242.** Burnished rim, very worn interior. Decoration — smoothed exterior with interlocking burnished arcs.

In addition, rims from six dishes (CT 242 (3); CT 253; CT 315; CT 354).

110. **CT 252.** Highly burnished inside and outside rim, and shoulder.

In addition, rim from a second example. (CT 253).

111. **CT 253.** Light blue-grey.

112. **CT 260.** Decoration — right-angled burnished lattice on a rough matt ground. Rim from another (CT 254).

113. **CT 256.**

In addition, rims from 8 jars similar to Gillam 124, (CT 250; CT 252; CT 253; CT 256; CT 267; CT 315 (2); CT 254); three similar to Gillam 127 (CT 241; CT 260; CT 354); 15 jars like Gillam 119 (CT 158; CT 195 (2); CT 197; CT 251; CT 253 (3); CT 315; CT 354 (4); CT 371 (2)); 11 jars similar to Gillam 135 (CT 315 (2); CT 354 (9)); two jars similar to Gillam 36 (CT 315 (2)).

114–115. **CT 250; CT 246.**

In addition, at least 16 other similar jars (CT 171; CT 181; CT 246; CT 252 (2); CT 260; CT 266 (2); CT 267; CT 271; CT 304 (6)).

116. **CT 266.** Decoration — lightly burnished lattice on rough matt ground.

117. **CT 252 & 232.** Decoration — obtuse burnished lattice on rough matt ground.

118. **CT 252.** Decoration — burnished right-angled lattice on rough ground.

119–120. **CT 241; CT 239.**

121. **CT 251.** Decoration — burnished obtuse lattice.

122–123. **CT 242; CT 252.** Hand-made.

In addition, rims from 16 similar jars (CT 181; CT 158; CT 165; CT 242 (3); CT 250 (2); CT 251 (3); CT 267; CT 271; CT 304 (3)). Excluding the illustrated examples, there are sherds from 11 jars decorated with obtuse burnished lattice (CT 158; CT 181; CT 242 (2); CT 260; CT 262; CT 266; CT 267; CT 304; CT 315; CT 371); Sherds from 10 jars decorated with right-angled lattice (CT 181; CT 250 (2); CT 252 (4); CT 253; CT 256 (2); CT 260; CT 267); sherds from two jars decorated with acute lattice (CT 250; CT 253).

THE FINDS

INTRODUCTION

All small finds recovered from the excavation of sites CS and CT are described and illustrated by function within the material categories of copper alloy, iron, bone, shale, jet etc. in mf. 2/5, figs. 52–79. The decision was taken to group all objects of the same material from all sites rather than treat each site as an individual unit. Archives held by the Corinium Museum are available for consultation on prior application, and provide detailed listings of all objects for each specific stratigraphic unit.

THE COINS
by
Richard Reece

As so few of the coins are actually associated directly with the bones of the various burials they are all listed in chronological order within stratigraphical groups mf. 2/5. This is not the place to deal in detail with some of the interesting numismatic points which the coins raise for many details depend on coins from other sites in the town and these will be much better dealt with as a whole at a later date. Numismatic comment has therefore been kept to a minimum. One coin, which is, I think, foreign to British experience is the Sestertius of Septimius Severus formed from two copper plates over an iron core. This class of forgery has recently been studied in the Danube frontier area in Austria by Dembski and was the subject of a paper by him to the International Numismatic Congress in Berne, 1979. It is hoped that his findings will be published in due course in the Acta of that Congress.

With the listing of these coins in stratigraphical deposits it is no longer possible to see all the coins in this report as one single group. The coins which are associated with the building have little in common with those which accumulated later during the life of the cemetery, and the coins in the grave earth are doubtfully related to the other groups. This therefore gives us several fairly small groups of coins none of which permit detailed numerical comparison and the commentary will therefore be qualitative, not quantitative.

The first point for discussion is the dating of the building on site CT and its subsequent disuse, purely from the evidence of the coins. The latest coin in the pre-building group is a barbarous radiate if the coin of the House of Constantine is regarded as intrusive, which from the later coins seems likely. This suggests that the building belongs to the very end of the third century. From the coins alone there is no obvious difference in the date of the construction of the building, its use, and its disuse, because all of these deposits contain coins which could go up to about the year 300. All three of the deposits contain coins of the period up to 230, and this argues for a date nearer 270 than 300, for, by the end of the century, the earlier Denarii and Sestertii had virtually disappeared from use and circulation.

The coins from the cobbled layer suggest a date of about 310 to 320; although this depends on only two coins they do agree together, they follow deposits which seem to end by 300, and coins of the 320's and 330's, often the most commonly found coins are absent. On site CT, therefore, the coin evidence suggests that the cemetery may spread in the first quarter of the fourth century.

Only four coins are recorded as part of the grave-goods — Period VI(a). Two of those are not legible but the other two belong to the years 335–345. This shows that the cemetery was in use perhaps in the 340's and 350's, after which such coins would be unusual, but not unknown.

126

The other coin which has actual dating value is the siliqua of Honorius, for which a round date of 400 may be suggested. Since this lay physically under the lumbar vertebrae of burial F it is possible to say that burial continued after 400.

This leaves us with the large number of coins which were either associated with the burials in a general sense, or part of the earth into which the burials were dug. Coins in grave fills on site CT begin with Valerian I around 255 and conclude with the coin of Valens. On site CS the list is similar but starts earlier, with the coin of Vespasian associated with the cremation 293, ends later with the siliqua of Honorius, and has a greater concentration of coins of the House of Constantine in the middle of the fourth century. The coins in the grave earth form the greater numbers of coins found, but are unfortunately less well associated with use, disuse or reuse of the building or the cemetery. On site CT there is a good collection (comparatively speaking) of coins of the middle of the third century, a peak of radiates at the end of the century, and less fourth century coins than might be expected from the general picture of coin finds in Cirencester. On site CS there is again the excellent representation of coins from 220 to 260, the expected radiate peak, but then a more usual number of coins of the fourth century continuing strongly up to the House of Theodosius. In all these deposits there is a good number of coins of 317 to 330, probably above normal. The topsoil shows simply a mixture of coins commented on elsewhere.

No clear cut divisions are obvious in this description. Dated graves tell us that the cemetery was in use in the fourth century; the general run of coins cannot add to this. Site CT has few late coins associated with burials, but site CS has the greater number of late coins loose in the grave earth. Two unusual concentrations of coins are obvious throughout the different deposits, the first containing coins of c. 200 to 260, the second, coins of c. 310 to 330. It seems likely that these two groups are of different origins for the base silver denarii and radiates of the first half of the third century are presumably too early in the building and cemetery sequence to represent a major phase of burial. Their origin is presumably to be found in the general rubbish levels which formed the sub-soil of the later cemetery and they have therefore a bearing on rubbish removal from the town, rather than intensity of burial on this site. It is all the more remarkable that these coins are, in general, rare in deposits inside the town, or, for that matter, inside any of the towns of southern Britain. The only other deposit in which similar numbers of these coins have been found is the Balkerne Lane deposit at Colchester where Philip Crummy and the Colchester Archaeological Trust excavated outside the walls of the town in advance of ring-road construction, and were able to empty considerable stretches of the city ditch. I have already used these two deposits of what I take to be third century town refuse dumped outside the walls to argue that this shows considerable organisation and some prosperity inside the towns in the first half of the third century, and this argument need not be repeated here (Reece 1982 forthcoming).

The coins of 310 to 330 must come from a different source if the cemetery was in use at the beginning of the fourth century, since that would have precluded the tipping of rubbish. These coins would then suggest a phase of cemetery use, and, presumabley, the deposition of coins with the burials, or in the grave fills. Whether or not the beginning of this putative burial phase can be pinned down is interesting. The coins which occur in unusual numbers are coins which normally occur on any site in Britain; what is unusual is their number compared, say to the coins of the preceeding and following decades. The earlier coins which I picked out as unusual are not in this class for they are distinctly uncommon even in large groups of site finds from inside towns. The second peak is therefore an intensification of coin deposition of the normal pattern rather than an abnormal pattern.

If we look, for a moment at earlier coins, struck and used before 310 then different patterns emerge. The coins of 260 to 275 are so commonly found everywhere that their presence can say little. Coins from mints in Italy struck between 270 and 294 are unusual as site finds anywhere in Britain, and again, their absence from this site is simply a conformation to the general pattern. The larger silvered bronze coins struck after Diocletian's reform of 294 do occur all over Britain, but always in small numbers. As these large coins gradually fall in weight so they are more commonly found on sites, until by 330 a final reduction makes them a very commonly lost coin. If we apply this to the cemetery coins the absence of coins of the first Tetrarchy (Diocletian, Maximian *et al.* 294 to 305) is strange; one or two might well be expected for they occur rarely but consistently as site finds. Their absence is the more remarkable when the larger numbers of coins after 310 are remembered. In general summary this would seem to suggest an absence of use of the site for any purpose, whether as rubbish dump or as cemetery, in the two decades around 300, and a fairly sudden rise in burials involving coins soon after 310. These points are, of course, subjective, for they could equally be replaced with a theory of non-coin burial from 290 to 310, and then a change of fashion around 310 involving the deposition of coins; at least an attempt has been made to interpret this coin pattern.

FINDS FROM THE ROADSIDE BUILDING (CT)

Material recovered from the roadside building CT is of interest in its reflection of a craft-agricultural function for a probable non-domestic building. Items of a personal nature such as brooches, rings and toilet articles are noticeably fewer in number than from cemetery levels. Craft and working tools, particularly in iron, dominate — styli, ox-goads, knives — with the on-site manufacture of small items of iron such as hobnails, and nails suggested by the presence of slag and the smithing hearth, p. 64. Structural items are represented by the nails, clamps, brackets, hinges, hooks and keys, with lighting provided by iron candlesticks. Re-use of material in the construction of the building is shown by the fragment of a tombstone from the footings of one of the walls, and the fragment of a statue of the *Deae Matres*. Worked objects in bone, shale and jet — materials used predominantly for objects of a personal character — are rare in comparison with levels post-dating the building. Of two intaglios recovered, one came from a context within the building.

FINDS FROM THE CEMETERY

A. OBJECTS ASSOCIATED WITH BURIALS

In accordance with the Roman practice of furnishing graves with objects to aid passage into, or for use in the after-life, a number of categories of objects might be expected to be present: coins; personal ornaments such as brooches, pins, combs, beads, necklaces, bracelets, rings; clothing requisites such as buckles, hobnails from shoes or boots; cosmetic necessities; and representations of the deceased's occupation or trade. Pottery or glass vessels may have contained food and drink, with joints of meat represented by finds of non-human bones. Fruits and berries may also have been deposited but archaeological techniques have failed to reflect these. Such grave goods were either left intact or for some unknown reason were deliberately mutilated.

For an object to be said to be associated with a burial a number of parameters have been considered essential; firstly, the object or objects, whether complete or broken, should be found on the skeleton in a corresponding position to that expected during life; and secondly if this is not the case, the position of the objects should reflect a consistent and deliberate placing out of context within the grave cut or coffin outline. Objects which constitute the physical encasement of the body in the ground — nails, hinges, decorative fittings — have been discussed on p. 86.

The paucity of burials with accompanying objects, is very obvious. Burial 196, a child of about three years of age, was by far the 'richest' burial buried within a wooden coffin, with a silver-clasped bead necklace, and two bone bracelets, one on each wrist. Two burials B (M, adult) and 1 (F, 35–50) had coins placed in the mouth, and burial 214 (F, 27–33) had coins covering each eye. An iron ring was recovered from the region of the left hand of burial 5 (M,

35–50; ?M, adult; F, adult; F, adult — the duplicity of individuals on anatomical investigation makes this association rather dubious); and copper alloy bracelets were worn by 179 (M, 45–55) and 228 (child, *c.* 3). In the context of personal toiletry, a double-sided bone comb was found above the sternum of burial 175 (F, 50–60; ?, 6–7). Five burials produced clusters of hobnails indicative of the presence of shoes or boots within the grave — 117 (F, 22–24); 252 (?F, 40–60); 280 (M, 18); 302 (M, 40–50); and 356 (F, 40–50).

Within three stone coffins, burial 719 was accompanied by a pottery cooking vessel containing the carcass of a domestic chicken; and burials 356 (F, 40–50) and 357 (F, 23–29) by a glass carafe, and a 'pickle' jar respectively.

Obvious joints of meat placed with burials were not noticeable in association with individual skeletons. However, following detailed anatomical study by Dr. Wells, animal bone fragments were segregated from the human, and were studied by Clare Thawley, mf. 2/5. By studying burial drawings and photographs in retrospect, it has been possible to differentiate between the two classes of bone in only one instance, burial 322, where two fragments of animal bone were found near the mouth. The fragments were of such an inconsequential size that they were not obviously alien to the burial during excavation, and probably represent rubbish introduced into the grave shaft during burial in rubbish-dumped levels, rather than a deliberate offering. The scattering of animal bone refuse through all levels of the grave earth as a result of domestic rubbish clearance from the town has led to problems in differentiating between deliberately placed offerings, and mixing of earth in the process of grave digging.

Those burials with an accompanying object or objects which can be said to be associated directly with the burial as a result of obvious deliberate positioning in relation to the body are listed below.

Burial B
A coin of third-fourth century A.D. was found in the mouth of the burial. Unfortunately the reverse was illegible and it is not possible to assign a more precise date to the coin.

Burial 1
Similarly a coin of third-fourth century date was recovered from the mouth of burial 1. The reverse was illegible.

Burial 5
An iron ring was recorded as being on the left hand of this burial. Corrosion has removed much of the outline, but the ring would appear to be a simple band of rectangular section, widening to give a flat oval bezel.

Burial 117
Clusters of hobnails were recovered from around both feet of this burial. No discernible pattern of nails was visible to suggest the pattern of the shoes.

Burial 175
Composite double-sided bone comb, one end decorated with a stylised representation of an owl, found lying across the sternum of burial 175. Examples of combs with very similar decoration have been found at Lankhills, Winchester, associated with Graves 297 and 381 for example, dated A.D. 390–410, (Clarke, 1979, fig. 84, 323; fig. 96, 479).

Burial 179
Flat bracelet of copper alloy decorated with alternating V-shaped notches, the ends hooked to form a simple interlocking fastening, was found on the left wrist of this burial.

Burial 196 (N.B. burial lying prone)
a. Bone bracelet of rectangular section, with decoration on the upper surface consisting of parallel grooves. A thin wrapping of sheet copper alloy joins two segments together, with other similar bindings presumably holding other sections to make up the complete circumference. Found on the left wrist.
b. Fragment of a bone bracelet of rounded D cross-section. Undecorated, the two surviving lengths overlap and are held together by two small iron studs. Worn on the right wrist of the child.

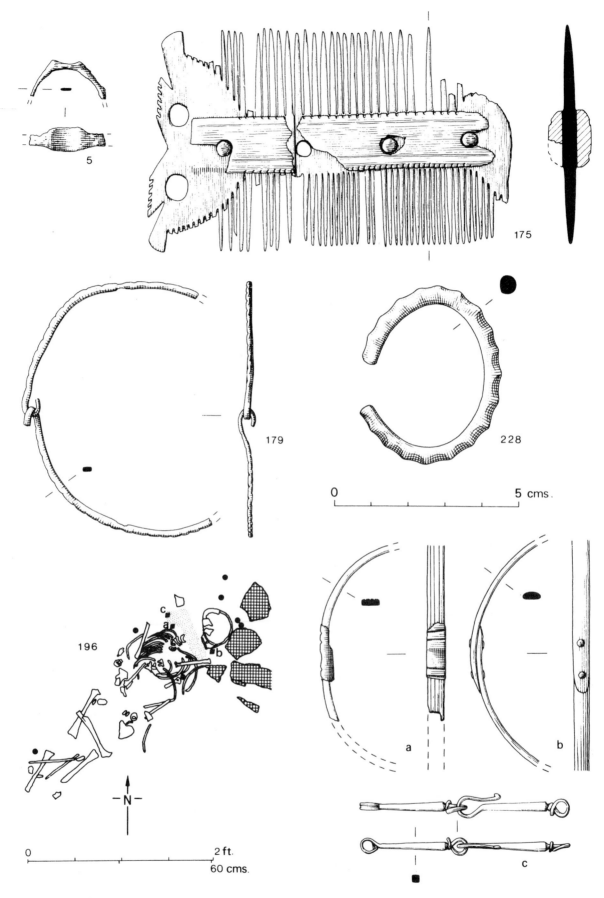

Fig. 80. Objects associated with burials 5, 175, 179, 228 and 196

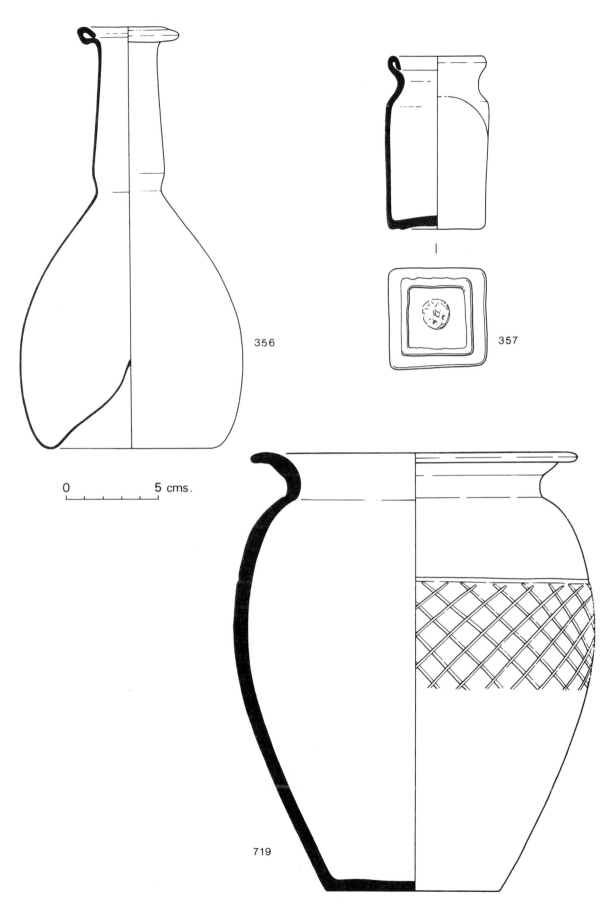

356

357

0   5 cms.

719

Fig. 81. Objects associated with burials 356, 357, 719

c. Silver clasp for a necklace of which 150 beads were recovered from around the neck of the burial. The clasp can be paralleled in copper alloy from two graves at Lankhills, Grave 117, dated A.D. 350–70, and Grave 183, dated A.D. 360–90, (Clarke, 1979, fig. 75, 140; and fig. 79, 182).

The beads have been analysed by Mrs. M. Guido who has supplied the following information:

The necklace comprised about 16 small tubular coral beads; 56 slightly graduated opaque emerald green short tubular beads; 86 tiny annular or sometimes slightly biconical beads of the same green glass; 3 small irregular beads of crystal; and one bright translucent blue bead of square section with a diamond facet on each face.

The character of the necklace is unusual and reflects 'intrusive' beads which appear to become commoner in late Roman times. As described above the clasp is of late fourth century date when compared with examples from Lankhills. The necklace also includes coral beads (?of Mediterranean or Black Sea origin) not very commonly found, crystal beads (more frequently associated with Anglo-Saxon necklaces), and a faceted bead of a type particularly common in Roumania and other East European countries. Bone bracelets associated with this burial are abnormal in Roman contexts, and can be similarly paralleled in the Lankhills Cemetery.

Burial 214

Two coins had been placed over the eyes of this burial: a coin of Helena, A.D. 337–345 (as HK 182;) was found covering the right eye; and a coin of Constans, A.D. 345–8, (HK 155), on the left eye.

Burial 228

A copper alloy penannular bracelet decorated with faceted knobs was found near the right elbow of this small child.

This burial is particularly noteworthy for the coffin fittings illustrated fig. 36.

Burials 252 and 280

Hobnails were recovered from the feet of both burials, suggesting burial with shoes on the feet.

Burial 302

Hobnails were found around the left foot only.

Burial 356

Lying in fragments at the feet of the burial within the stone coffin were the remains of a flask in thin greenish glass, with a flat infolded rim, bulbous body, and concave base with high 'kick' and pontil mark.

Hobnails were recovered from the remains of two shoes either side of the feet.

Burial 357

Small 'pickle' jar in green glass with an infolded rim. (Isings form 62). The square-bodied jar can be dated to the second century. Its base marking is a line round the edge with a St. Andrew's cross in the centre, largely obscured by the pontil mark.

Burial 719

Black-burnished cooking pot (Fabric 74) with right-angled or obtuse lattice, *c.* A.D. 240–290. Found at the feet of the burial within the stone coffin, with a chicken carcass inside, mf. 2/5.

B. OBJECTS FROM GRAVE SHAFTS

Table 4 lists all those objects not obviously closely associated with a burial but found within 15 cm. of the skeleton. The disturbed nature of the site and continuous use over a long period of time may have displaced objects once deliberately interred with an individual, in particular personal objects and jewellery. Objects in the list which have a less obvious burial association may have originated in the dumped rubbish material from the town, scattered over the site, which became incorporated in the grave shaft by digging through rubbish contaminated layers.

Objects of intrinsic interest from within the grave shafts have been illustrated and described, and will be found incorporated in the small finds catalogue, mf. figs. 52–79.

C. OBJECTS FROM GRAVE EARTH

Objects recovered from the grave earth are in a very fragmentary condition, and as has been argued for the pottery p. 112 so here also the objects may have been introduced in to the area after disposal in the town, rather than as casual loss of possessions or personal ornament carried or worn by individuals visiting the area. The cemetery grave earth contains a higher proportion of personal objects such as beads, bracelets, rings and toilet articles and in many cases disturbance of burials by later graves may have caused the dispersal of personal objects either worn by or intentionally placed with the burials.

Objects of intrinsic interest from the grave earth have been illustrated and incorporated into the catalogue, mf. figs. 52–79.

THE HUMAN BURIALS

Editorial Note

The skeletal material recovered from the Bath Gate Cemetery has for the purposes of this report been separated into two groups, divided geographically by the Fosse Way. South of the road burials were numbered alphabetically A–AC and numerically 1–357; with the second group, north of the Fosse, being numbered 700–770.

Anatomical reports for individual inhumations and cremations within the two groups are available in microfiche, mf. 3/4 and 4/5. The detailed summary and discussion of all the evidence completed by Calvin Wells shortly before his death is printed in full, with only minor textual alterations to standardise references to site codes and archaeological references.

Several of the graves included substantial parts of more than one person, with the result that the overall 405 burials examined by Calvin Wells represented a total of 421 individuals. Whenever an inhumation was found to be multiple its component skeletons have been recorded as 260 (a), 260 (b), 260 (c), insofar as it has been possible to disentangle them. This merely indicates what the osteological evidence reveals: it is not to be taken as archaeological comment indicating a deliberately contrived multiple interment. It reflects nothing more than the inadvertent mingling of bodies as a result of later burials having been placed where an original one had left no trace.

The summary which follows deals only with inhumation burials. Three cremations were found — nos. 180, 293 and 294 — and discussion of them can be found in microfiche.

All skeletal material recovered since 1969 is stored at the Corinium Museum, Cirencester.

THE HUMAN BURIALS
by
Calvin Wells

SOUTH OF FOSSE WAY

THE MATERIAL AND ITS CONDITION

The overall condition of this material is not good. A few of the skeletons are very well preserved; most are what can be described as poor to medium; a substantial number are in a very
poor state as a result of soil erosion and other post-inhumation hazards. It is especially noteworthy that very few skulls survive in a good enough condition to be measured without
extensive reconstruction. Because any such reconstruction and restoration would not only have
demanded much time but would almost certainly have been inaccurate it was decided to
measure only those skulls which were intact or nearly so.

SEX AND AGE

The defective condition of most of these skeletons made it difficult to assess the sex in a number
of cases. The pelvic bones are often much damaged in early burials and this is especially unfor-
tunate when, as in the present series, the crania are also in bad condition.

Owing to multiple burials the 347 inhumations examined from south of the Fosse represented
362 persons, of whom 207 were diagnosed as males or probable males, 93 as females or
probable females; the remaining 62 were unsexable. Of the 300 sexed persons 5 were juvenile
males, 2 were juvenile females, i.e. 293 sexed adults. Thirty-five males and 18 females were
assessed as "Adult" with no greater precision. An age estimate of variable reliability was
achieved for 239 adults of whom 167 were males, with a mean age at death of 40.8 years, and
72 were females, with a mean age of 37.8 years. This sexual difference, with males outliving
females by 3 years, is a very common one in early societies.

Burials to the south of the Fosse consisted of 207 males or probable males to only 93 females
or probables. A sex ratio such as this demands some explanation in biological or cultural terms
— usually the latter. In the present instance there is no evidence to suggest a biological cause
and the most likely reason is that Cirencester, like York, was largely given over to retired
legionaries and to various Roman officials, many of whom lacked regular wives and whose
sexual partners, if any, were probably drawn from the professional prostitutes who were no
doubt an abundant and pleasant amenity of the town.

The age distribution of male and female adults is shown in figure 82. A distinctive feature of
this histogram is that the female deaths are distributed fairly evenly over the eight lustra from
18–58 years, whereas those of the males mount steadily from the mid-twenties to 53.

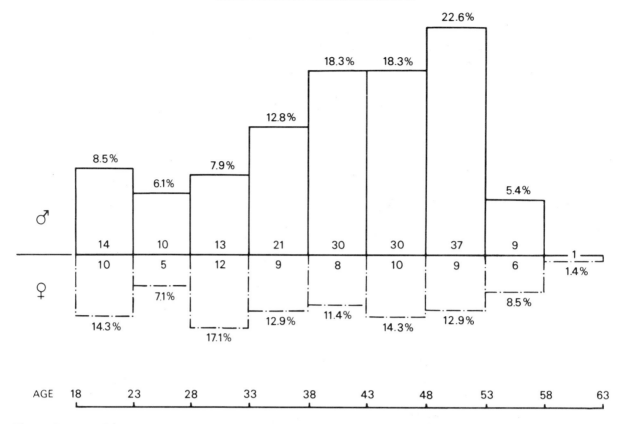

Fig. 82. Distribution of deaths at Cirencester

Of the overall 405 individuals 65 (16.5%) were juveniles under 18 years of age. Of the 362 burials 63 (17.4%) were juveniles. This is a low figure, as can be seen by comparing it with that of a few other populations shown in Table 32.

Table 32: Percentage of juvenile deaths

Site	Date	Burials	Juveniles	%
Cirencester: South of Fosse	R-B	362	63	17.4
Owslebury	IA — R-B	50	29	58.0
Caerwent	R-B — A-S	121	27	22.3
Kingsworthy	Early A-S	96	25	26.0
North Elmham Park	Late A-S	206	39	18.9
Thetford	Late A-S	85	24	28.2
Jarrow	A-S — Med	261	109	41.8
Monkwearmouth	A-S — Med	206	79	38.3

(IA = Iron Age; R-B = Romano-British; A-S = Anglo-Saxon; Med = Medieval)

The reasons for the seemingly low mortality of juveniles at Cirencester must remain uncertain. It may be a true biological phenomenon due to competent child rearing or to an above average health ambience; or it may be illusory and consequent on some social factor such as the infrequent interment of children and infants away from adult cemeteries. It may be partly due to the fact that children's bones were more vulnerable to post-inhumation deterioration and destruction than those of adults, although there is no clear evidence that this was so.

More intereting than the percentage of juvenile deaths is their distribution throughout child-hood. This is shown in Table 33.

Table 33: Age distribution of juvenile deaths

Age	Site											
	Cir.		Ow.		K.		N.E.P.		Ja.		Mk.	
	n	%	n	%	n	%	n	%	n	%	n	%
< 2	19	30.2	25	86.2	4	16.0	3	7.7	21	19.3	37	46.8
2–< 4	11	17.4	1	3.4	5	20.0	10	25.6	26	23.9	14	17.7
4–< 6	4	6.3	0	0.0	2	8.0	6	15.4	8	7.3	2	2.6
6–< 8	6	9.6	0	0.0	6	24.0	7	17.9	14	12.8	8	10.1
8–<10	4	6.3	0	0.0	1	4.0	1	2.6	8	7.3	5	6.3
10–<12	5	7.9	0	0.0	4	16.0	1	2.6	11	10.1	3	3.8
12–<14	8	12.7	0	0.0	1	4.0	6	15.4	9	8.3	6	7.6
14–<16	5	7.9	2	6.9	1	4.0	1	2.6	4	3.7	3	3.8
16–<18	1	1.6	1	3.4	1	4.0	3	7.7	8	7.3	1	1.3
?	0	0.0	0	0.0	0	0.0	1	2.6	0	0.0	0	0.0
% Juv	63	17.4	29	58.0	25	26.0	39	18.9	109	41.8	79	38.3

(Cir. = Cirencester, south of Fosse; Ow. = Owslebury; K. = Kingsworthy; N.E.P. = North Elmham Park; Ja. = Jarrow; Mk. = Monkwearmouth).

Of the 19 deaths less than 2 years old, 16 (84.2%) were newborn infants, i.e. 25.4% of the total 63 juveniles.

PHYSICAL TYPE

The poor, often totally fragmented, condition of many of the skulls prevents the measuring of all but a small sample of this group unless very extensive reconstructions were to be undertaken. To do this would have been a prohibitively enormous task and the rewards would not have been commensurate with the effort expended. Only rarely can a badly smashed and defective skull be reconstructed with impeccable precision. Any measurements taken from it, if dependent on the parts which have been restored, must therefore be inaccurate to some extent, however slight, compared with what they would have been in life or on the undamaged cranium.

These skulls are not palaeolithic rarities and it would be pretentious to treat them as though they were. In recording their craniometric data the policy adopted here has been to note only measurements on skulls or parts of skulls which have needed no reconstruction. Even this entails its own hazards because many calvae or calvariae, though still firmly united at their sutures, may have been slightly distorted by soil pressure or eroded to an unknowable (though doubtless small) extent.

The result of this policy of caution has been that, of the 293 adult burials south of the Fosse, only 66 (22.4%) — 45 males and 21 females — have had some of their measurements recorded in tables 34–37, mf. 3/4. Many of the commonly taken measurements were absent on even these privileged skulls.

This leaves a woefully small amount of material on which to base a statistical analysis and no such analysis has been attempted here. A brief gathering of a few distributions of Indices is recorded in Tables 38–47.

Individual cranial measurements are given in Tables 34–37, microfiche 3/4. Tables 38–42 briefly summarize a few proportions of the cranial architecture of the measured male skulls.

Table 38: 100B/L (Cranial Index)

Class	Range	Number	%
Dolichocranial	x–74.9	19	47.5
Mesocranial	75–79.9	17	42.5
Brachycranial	80–x	4	10.0

Table 39: 100H'/L (Height–Length Index)

Class	Range	Number	%
Chamaecranial	x–69.9	13	40.6
Orthocranial	70–74.9	15	46.9
Hypsicranial	75–x	4	12.5

Table 40: 100H'/B (Height–Breadth Index)

Class	Range	Number	%
Tapeinocranial	x–91.9	15	46.9
Metriocranial	92–97.9	9	28.1
Akrocranial	98–x	8	25.0

Table 41: $1000_2/0_1$ (Orbital Index)

Class	Range	Number	%
Chamaeconch	x–75.9	4	14.3
Mesoconch	76–84.9	22	78.6
Hypsiconch	85–x	2	7.1

Table 42: 100NB/NH (Nasal Index)

Class	Range	Number	%
Leptorrhine	x–46.9	12	54.5
Mesorrhine	47–50.9	8	36.4
Platyrrhine	51–x	2	9.1

The equivalent figures for female crania are shown in Tables 43–47.

Table 43: 100B/L (Cranial Index)

Class	Range	Number	%
Dolichocranial	x–74.9	5	27.8
Mesocranial	75–79.9	10	55.6
Brachycranial	80–x	3	16.6

Table 44: 100H'/L (Height-Length Index)

Class	Range	Number	%
Chamaecranial	x–69.9	9	52.9
Orthocranial	70–74.9	8	47.1
Hypsicranial	75–x	0	0.0

Table 45: 100H'/B (Height-Breadth Index)

Class	Range	Number	%
Tapeinocranial	x–91.9	12	63.1
Metriocranial	92–97.9	6	31.7
Akrocranial	98–x	1	5.2

Table 46: $100O_2/O_1$ (Orbital Index)

Class	Range	Number	%
Chamaeconch	x–75.9	2	20.0
Mesoconch	76–84.9	7	70.0
Hypsiconch	85–x	1	10.0

Table 47: 100NB/NH (Nasal Index)

Class	Range	Number	%
Leptorrhine	x–46.9	3	37.5
Mesorhine	47–50.9	4	50.0
Platyrrhine	51–x	1	12.5

It will be seen that the population as a whole was just dolichocranial for the men, and mesocranial for the women. Most males were orthocranial, tapeinocranial, mesoconch and leptorrhine; the women chamaecranial, tapeinocranial, mesoconch and mesorrhine.

STATURE

The estimation of the stature of early populations is normally achieved by measuring their long bones and using conversion formulae of various kinds.

The Cirencester results have been calculated from the tables of Trotter and Gleser (1952, for women; 1958, for men). With these formulae it has been found, on modern groups, that the most accurate reconstructions are obtained by using measurements of the lower limb. All the Cirencester data are based, therefore, on femoral or tibial lengths — tables 48–49, male and female long bone measurements, mf. 3/5. Table 50 shows the means and ranges for both sexes.

Table 50: Stature, means and ranges

Sex	n	Mean	Range
♂	107	1691 mm (5ft 6½in)	1598 mm (5ft 3in) — 1817 mm (5ft 11½in)
♀	44	1579 mm (5ft 2in)	1475 mm (4ft 10in) — 1698 mm (5ft 6¾in)

From this it will be seen that they were of medium height and that both sexes had a range close to 220 mm. The difference between male and female means is 112 mm. These figures are not especially remarkable and can be closely approximated by many early groups.

It is, therefore, useful to show on a histogram the distribution of stature among these men and women. Figure 83 does this in gradations of 20 mm.

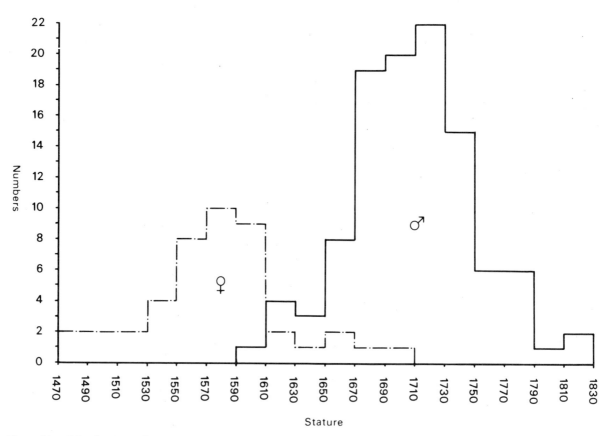

Fig. 83. Distribution of male and female statures

NON-METRICAL VARIANTS

For the purposes of this study non-metrical variants may be defined as anatomical features which can best be recorded on a "present or absent" basis. Metopism is a well known example so, too, is that perforation of the olecranon fossa known as septal aperture. Many such traits are found but very few of them have been studied in detail. They are mostly due to genetic variations, it seems, and for this reason they have great potential for revealing racial or family affinities. They can be considered as "normal" features in that their presence or absence appear to be unassociated with benefit or harm to the individual in the great majority of instances.

Few of these characters are sex linked, as far as is known, and so it is justifiable to combine males and females for statistical purposes. Unsexed adults and juveniles may also be included.

Although these traits are referred to as "non-metrical" they can, of course, all be measured in some way. The presence of a parietal foramen may be noted but its position and size can also be measured. Many of these features, however, are difficult to measure with accuracy either because of their small size (post-condylar canal of the occipital bone), their uncertain boundaries (malar tuberosity, supra-orbital grooves, blurred sub-nasal margin) or some other cause. Even when easily measurable (e.g. metopic suture) it seems to be the existence of the feature which is important, rather than its size. Therefore, all have been recorded here on a simple "present or absent" notation.

Table 51 shows the frequency of 35 non-metrical variants for males, females and unsexed persons combined, together with the rates from four other sites for comparison.

Few significant differences were found at Cirencester between the frequencies for men and women, which were calculated separately before being combined. The few notable differences between the sexes are for the following variants:

Variant	Male			Female		
	n	+	%	n	+	%
Malar tuberosity	116	53	45.7	54	5	9.3
Zygomaxillary tubercle	112	30	26.8	52	5	9.6
Gonial eversion	196	111	56.1	85	28	32.9
Infero-lateral mental tubercle	138	55	39.8	58	3	5.2

These are probably all secondary sexual characters which are normally more developed in males than females, just as supra-orbital ridges are, because not only do they have a lower frequency in women but, if present, they are usually smaller and less obtrusive.

MERIC AND CNEMIC INDICES

These features may conveniently be considered together although they are not necessarily functionally related. The Meric Index is a measure of the antero-posterior flattening of the subtrochanteric part of the femoral shaft; the Cnemic Index expresses the side to side flattening of the tibia at the level of the nutrient foramen.

The significance of these conditions is uncertain. They have been interpreted as a response to the habit of squatting, to the result of mechanical stresses on the bone, as a physiological device to economize in the use of minerals for bone formation, and as the result of various pathological conditions. None of these suggestions is wholly satisfactory. But much variation in both indices is found and many records are available for comparative purposes. For this reason it is perhaps worth recording what was found at Cirencester.

Table 51: Frequency of non-metrical variants (♂ + ♀ pooled + unsexed)

Variant	Cirencester			Caerwent			Kingsworthy			Jarrow			Monkwearmouth		
	n	+	%	n	+	%	n	+	%	n	+	%	n	+	%
Metopism	194	16	8.2	32	1	3.1	56	5	8.9	96	4	4.2	32	0	0.0
Bregma bone	150	2	1.3	8	1	12.5	43	2	4.7	45	0	0.0	27	0	0.0
Coronal wormian	227	13	5.6	6	4	66.7	79	1	1.3	66	2	3.0	37	0	0.0
Sagittal wormian	131	10	7.6	8	0	0.0	38	0	0.0	45	0	0.0	23	1	4.3
Lambdoid wormian	239	149	62.3	6	4	66.7	70	30	47.1	73	15	20.5	23	83	4.8
Asterionic ossicle	92	8	8.7	-	-	-	65	7	10.7	38	4	10.5	-	-	-
Epipteric ossicle	171	10	5.8	-	-	-	58	3	5.2	41	0	0.0	36	0	0.0
Inca bone	158	10	6.3	8	0	0.0	46	0	0.0	56	2	3.6	24	1	4.2
Supra-orbital notch	301	176	58.5	49	28	57.1	93	61	65.6	111	60	54.1	56	37	66.1
Double supra-orbital foramen	288	44	15.3	47	6	12.8	86	13	14.6	96	21	21.9	56	11	19.6
Supra-orbital grooves	252	102	40.5	26	15	57.7	81	39	48.1	90	56	62.2	43	21	48.4
Double infra-orbital foramen	97	9	9.3	17	3	17.6	28	0	0.0	63	8	12.7	-	-	-
Paramastoid process	59	2	3.4	-	-	-	26	6	23.0	28	10	35.7	21	2	10.0
Foramen of Huschke	270	10	3.7	66	1	1.5	83	5	6.0	154	15	9.7	-	-	-
Double or hourglass occipital condyle	146	2	1.4	-	-	-	50	1	2.0	76	1	1.3	-	-	-
Pre-condylar tubercles	137	10	7.3	12	0	0.0	55	3	5.2	100	4	4.0	24	0	0.0
Postcondylar canal	102	33	32.4	-	-	-	23	6	26.1	55	30	54.5	25	4	16.0
Double hypoglossal canal	230	35	15.2	11	3	27.3	51	10	19.6	110	15	13.6	23	3	13.0
Sagittal sinus turns left	180	32(+6)	17.8	38	4	10.5	44	3	11.4	80	6	7.5	30	9	30.0
Pterygoid spurs	28	12	42.9	-	-	-	4	2	50.0	14	10	71.4	-	-	-
Blurred sub-nasal margin	242	36	14.9	28	2	7.1	61	8	13.1	109	14	12.8	34	4	11.7
Sub-nasal fossiculae	211	15	7.9	28	0	0.0	58	2	3.4	104	3	2.9	-	-	-
Malar tuberosity	174	58	33.3	37	5	13.5	68	22	32.4	83	16	19.3	25	1	4.0
Malar marginal tubercle	175	15	8.6	34	3	8.8	59	9	15.3	52	12	23.1	21	1	4.7
Zygomaxillary tubercle	168	39	23.2	27	4	14.8	54	8	14.8	80	4	5.0	21	2	9.5
Gonial eversion	288	145	50.3	62	29	46.8	86	54	62.8	119	41	34.5	45	14	31.1
Multiple mental foramen	316	14	4.4	77	3	3.9	91	1	1.1	161	4	2.5	52	1	1.9
Infero-lateral mental tubercle	204	64	31.6	58	17	29.3	97	21	21.6	120	22	18.3	32	3	9.4
Atlas bridge	225	32	14.2	36	5	13.9	52	4	7.7	103	10	9.7	39	4	10.2
Ossified dens	97	15	15.5	-	-	-	26	1	3.8	50	6	12.0	-	-	-
Acetabular crease	229	60	26.2	35	17	48.6	69	28	40.6	95	20	21.1	41	12	29.5
Septal aperture of humerus	264	12	4.5	81	9	11.1	94	7	7.4	174	15	8.6	55	5	9.1
Femoral third trochanter	240	21	8.7	43	13	30.2	85	6	7.1	145	43	29.7	42	10	23.8
Vastus notch	169	20	11.8	32	2	6.2	56	6	10.7	85	10	11.8	22	0	0.0

Table 52: Meric Index: means and range.

Sex	Means			Range
	L	R	L+R	
♂	76.6(92)	77.4(95)	77.0(187)	61.3–92.9
♀	74.4(32)	72.6(39)	73.5 (77)	62.6–86.7

Table 53: Meric Index: distribution

Sex	x–74.9 (Hyperplatymeric)		75.0–84.9 (Platymeric)		85.0–x (Eumeric)	
	n	%	n	%	n	%
♂	72	38.5	96	51.3	19	10.2
♀	40	51.9	36	46.8	1	1.3

Table 54: Cnemic Index: means and range

Sex	Means			Range
	L	R	L+R	
♂	69.5(86)	69.8(87)	69.7(173)	56.7–89.1
♀	67.5(37)	70.1(35)	68.8 (72)	58.9–78.6

Table 55: Cnemic Index: distribution

Sex	x–54.9 (Hyperplatycnemic)		55.0–62.9 (Platycnemic)		63.0–69.9 (Mesocnemic)		70–x (Eurycnemic)	
	n	%	n	%	n	%	n	%
♂	0	0.0	17	9.8	64	36.9	92	53.2
♀	0	0.0	7	9.7	26	36.1	39	54.2

CONGENITAL DEFECTS

A number of congenital or developmental anomalies and defects have been sporadically noted in some of the other sections. A more ample record of them is presented here. But there is often uncertainty about whether to call these features congenital defects or to include them with the normal non-metrical variations as recorded in Table 51. In the case of some traits it seems little more than a matter of convenience where they are placed.

Anatomical or physiological developments and adaptations which are recently acquired (in an evolutionary sense) are often unstable and likely to show a wide range of variation or pathology. The mechanism of tooth eruption in elephants and mammoths illustrates this principle. In man, the erect posture of the vertebral column is a new evolutionary development and as a consequence a vast amount of pathology and anomalies affects this structure.

One of the commonest variations in the human spine is in the number of its segments. Departures from the normal seven cervical vertebrae are exceedingly rare and none were found among the Cirencester skeletons. Variation from the normal twelve thoracic vertebrae is somewhat uncommon and, again, none occur at Cirencester. But six lumbar segments are not rare and were found here in three persons: Inh. 74 (♂), Inh. 191 (♀) and Inh. 304 (♂). When this happens adjacent segments often show abnormalities. In the case of Inh. 74 there is an anomalous facet on the left ala of the sacrum which articulates with the L6. By far the commonest of numerical variations is found in the sacrum. At least 13 persons (11♂, 2♀) have sacra with six segments. The males are Inhs. 61, 72, 145, 171, 174, 288, 305, 307, 324/334, 333 and 336; the females are Inhs. Z and 223. When six segments are present in the sacrum it sometimes happens that a vertebra is dropped from the lumbar or thoracic series so that the supra-sacral column has only twenty-three segments. In many of the Cirencester skeletons the vertebrae are too deficient to reveal the full picture but in Inhs. Z, 145, 288, 305 and 333 a complete cervical, thoracic and lumbar series of twenty-four segments has survived as well as the six-piece sacrum. In Inhs. 72 and 174 the thoracic and lumbar series survive intact and it is unlikely that a vertebra would have been dropped at the cervical level. In 61, 171, 324/334 and 223 the normal five lumbars survive together with at least the T12. So it is probable that in the large majority of these Cirencester six-piece sacra no numerical anomaly was present at a higher level.

What, in effect, amounts to a functional diminution of the column to twenty-three vertebrae is found in Inh. 190 (♀). In this case the C2/3 are reduced to a single segment by what appears to be a congenital synostosis. But although this represents a functional curtailment, the morphological presence of twenty-four vertebrae is not altered.

Another common vertebral defect is spina bifida. Five persons (4♂, 1♀) have this anomaly and in every case the condition is limited to the sacrum with no involvement of lumbar vertebrae. Inh. 184 (♂), 280, (♂) and 357 (♀) have the whole length of the sacrum affected. In Inh. 222 (♂) only the S1 segment is involved and in Inh. 347 (♂) only S3/5.

In addition to this common form of spina bifida, which is situated in the lower segments of the column, a somewhat similar defect is caused by non-fusion or incomplete development of the two sides of the posterior vertebral arches. It may occur in any segment but is often in the upper levels of the column. Four persons had this anomaly. In Inh. 152 (♂) the T1 vertebra has a complete spinous process springing from each pedicle but the two processes are not fused. They are pressed closely against each other with the tip of the right one lying superior to that of the left. Inh. 186 (♂) has an incomplete posterior arch of the atlas. A hiatus 3 mm wide is present just medial to the right inferior articular facet. Inh. 214 (♀) has a similar defect of the atlas but its full extent is masked by post-mortem damage. However, the smooth stump of the left side clearly shows that this condition was present. Finally, in Inh. 297 (♂) the neural arches of C2 have not fused and it has a mid-line gap of 2–3 mm.

Superficially similar to spina bifida are the cases of detached neural arch. But in the former the common situation is that the posterior vertebral arches fail to develop fully and leave a gap in the mid-line which may be filled by fibrous tissue or even remain unfilled by any overlying structure. In that case the spinal cord or its terminal branches are left exposed — a condition incompatible with life. By contrast, in detached neural arch the arch is fully formed, or nearly so, and fused in the mid-line but the antero-lateral extremity of each side fails to unite with the pedicle of its vertebra. In life it is joined to it by fibrous or sometimes cartilaginous tissue so that after death and decomposition the vertebra is found to be two separate pieces of bone. In this Cirencester group seven persons (6♂, 1♀) had detached neural arches. It is usually a lower lumbar vertebra which is affected and here Inhs. 114 (♂), 171 (♂), 206 (♂), 337 (♂) and Z (♀) had detachment of the L5 arch. In 320 (♂) both L4 and L5 were affected and in Inh. J (♂) it is the L3 and L4 which are defective.

A few other miscellaneous vertebral anomalies remain to be noted. Inh. M (♂) has a complex articulation between the L5, the left ala of the sacrum, and the left ilium. The additional articular surface on the sacrum measures 24 x 21 mm, that on the ilium 13 x 11 mm. In Inh. Q (♂) there is an accessory articulation between the left transverse process of the L5 and the left sacral ala. A similar left accessory articular facet is present between the sacrum and the super-numerary L6 vertebra of Inh. 74 (♂). In Inh. 104 (a) (♂) the same condition exists but in this case it is bilateral. Inh. X (♀) has an L5 which is sacralized on the right and, in addition, the right sacro-iliac joint extends upwards to articulate with the vertebra, whereas the left sacro-iliac joint is limited to only the S1/2 segments. In Inh. 18 (♂) there is partial lumbarization of the S1 segment and in Inh. 46 (♀) the right sacral ala has an accessory articulation with the iliac bone in addition to its normal sacro-iliac joint.

In accordance with the tendency for vertebral anomalies to be multiple and of different kinds in a single column, it should be noted that at least five of these persons had more than one spinal anomaly — exclusive of such pathological conditions as osteoarthrosis, osteophytosis and Schmorl's nodes, etc.

A few other congenital anomalies or variations remain to be noted. Inhs. 117 (♀), 127 (♀) and 246 (♂) have a cervical rib attached to the C7 vertebra. Inh. 249 (♂) has the same condition bilaterally. All these are small, the largest being those of Inh. 249 which measure 48 mm (L.) and 53 mm (R.) in length. None of them articulated with the normal first thoracic rib but they may have had a fibrous cord extending from their free end to the adjacent bone. Inh. T (♂) has another costal anomaly: a left middle rib is bifid at its sternal end.

A few cranial variations have been recorded in the section on non-metrical variants, including inca bones. These are bones which are separated from the superior part of the occipital squama, usually by an anomalous suture extending from one half of the lambdoid suture to the other. Nine males and one female have this condition but there is much variation in its appearance. Most of these inca bones are isolated structures separated from the rest of the occiput by a single suture but it is quite common to find the supernumerary bone itself subdivided by one or more additional sutures to give bipartite or tripartite inca bones. A few typical examples, with their diameters, are given in Table 56.

Table 56: Type and size of inca bones

Inh.	Sex	Type	Maximum diameters (mm)	
			Sagittal	Transverse
81	♂	Bipartite	45	60
139	♂	Bipartite (Symmetrical)	44	73
249	♂	Single	48	63
336	♂	Bipartite (Symmetrical)	56	75

In Inhs. 139 and 336 the second dividing suture cuts the inca bone into two virtually sym-metrical halves. In Inh. 249, the bone is wholly partitioned out of the right side of the occiput, its antero-lateral border being bounded by the right lambdoid suture. Inh. 50 (♂) shows a very complicated arrangement. The superior part of the occiput is separated from the parietals by at least ten intersutural bones in the lambdoid suture. The large central elements of these could be described as a quadripartite inca bone.

The sternum is a bone which often survives badly in early burials but in Inhs. Z (♀), 216 (♂) and 288 (♂) it is well enough preserved to show that it had a congenital perforation. Inh. 179 (♂) has ossification of the transverse scapular ligament to convert the scapular notch into a foramen but it is uncertain whether this can properly be regarded as congenital or whether it was a condition which developed during later life. A number of femoral third trochanters have been noted in this series. Most are small and it has sometimes been difficult to decide if they are third trochanters or if they are nothing more than very craggy proximal thickenings of the linea aspera. But Inh. 142 (♂) is distinguished by the very large size of this structure which rises 10.8 mm above the surrounding bone. Inh. 194 (♂) has a processus supracondylis medialis on the right femur. This is a structure somewhat similar to a Wilbrand's tubercle. Finally, we may note Inh. 286 (♂) which has a double or "hour-glass" right mandibular condyle.

TEETH

Although many of the Cirencester jaws are damaged and unsuitable for metric study many retain much of the alveolus, with or without teeth, and yield information about the dentitions of these people.

In the adults recovered from south of the Fosse, parts of 116 male maxillae and 127 male mandibles, and parts of 51 female maxillae and 50 female mandibles survive. If these jaws contained complete normal dentitions 5504 tooth positions should be identifiable but owing to post-mortem damage only 4853 (88.2%) are now available for study. One hundred and forty-three (2.9%) of these positions showed that the teeth had never erupted, of which 133 (93.0%) were third molars. Of the 4710 erupted positions 1060 (22.5%) had been lost post-mortem and 399 (8.5%) had been shed during life. This leaves only 3251 teeth which can now be examined. Tables 57 to 63 show the frequency of ante-mortem loss from each tooth position, and the total male and female. (E.P. = Erupted positions; A-m loss = Ante-mortem loss).

Table 57: Male maxillary ante-mortem tooth loss

Tooth	8	7	6	5	4	3	2	1	1	2	3	4	5	6	7	8	Total
E.P.	61	94	101	105	106	106	103	103	103	103	104	103	100	97	97	67	1553
A-m loss	6	9	20	6	4	3	7	3	1	3	3	4	4	17	17	8	114
%	9.8	9.6	20.0	5.7	3.8	2.8	6.8	2.9	1.0	2.9	1.9	3.9	4.0	17.5	17.5	11.9	7.3

Table 58: Male mandibular ante-mortem tooth loss

Tooth	8	7	6	5	4	3	2	1	1	2	3	4	5	6	7	8	Total
E.P.	93	116	114	112	112	111	112	110	113	116	120	119	121	122	121	84	1796
A-m loss	18	10	19	8	2	1	4	5	10	7	2	2	11	20	15	6	130
%	8.6	8.6	16.7	7.1	1.8	0.9	3.6	4.6	8.8	6.0	1.7	1.7	9.1	16.4	12.4	7.1	7.2

Table 59: Female maxillary ante-mortem tooth loss

Tooth	8	7	6	5	4	3	2	1	1	2	3	4	5	6	7	8	Total
E.P.	23	38	41	42	42	42	43	41	43	44	44	46	45	44	39	25	642
A-m loss	2	8	10	6	4	4	4	4	3	6	4	5	9	8	7	3	87
%	8.7	21.1	24.4	14.3	9.5	9.5	9.3	9.8	6.9	13.6	9.1	10.9	20.0	18.2	17.9	12.0	13.5

Table 60: Female mandibular anti-mortem tooth loss

Tooth	8	7	6	5	4	3	2	1	1	2	3	4	5	6	7	8	Total
E.P.	31	45	46	45	46	47	47	47	49	49	49	47	47	48	46	30	719
A-m loss	4	6	9	2	2	1	2	3	3	2	1	2	4	13	10	4	68
%	12.9	13.3	19.6	4.4	4.3	2.1	4.3	6.4	6.1	4.1	2.0	4.3	8.5	27.1	21.7	13.3	9.5

Table 61: Total male ante-mortem tooth loss

E.P.   3349
A-m loss   244
%   7.3

Table 62: Total female ante-mortem tooth loss

E.P.   1361
A-m loss   155
%   11.4

Table 63: Total male plus female ante-mortem tooth loss

E.P.   4710
A-m loss   399
%   8.5

At 8.5 per cent the overall tooth loss is not especially high. (It was 11.1 and 15.9% respectively at the late Saxon sites of North Elmham and Thetford, Red Castle, both in Norfolk). But it would seem that the loss among women was about 56% more than among the men, in spite of the fact that the women died, on average, about three years younger than the men. This suggests a lower standard of oral hygiene among the females.

Tables 64 to 70 show the frequency of caries for each adult *in situ* tooth. (n = number of teeth).

Table 64: Adult male maxillary caries

Tooth	8	7	6	5	4	3	2	1	1	2	3	4	5	6	7	8	Total
n	41	76	72	83	87	78	55	45	52	52	80	84	75	72	71	44	1067
Carious	1	11	10	6	5	1	0	0	0	0	3	7	4	11	17	4	80
%	2.4	14.5	13.9	7.2	5.7	1.3	0.0	0.0	0.0	0.0	3.7	8.3	5.3	15.3	23.9	9.1	7.5

Table 65: Adult male mandibular caries

Tooth	8	7	6	5	4	3	2	1	1	2	3	4	5	6	7	8	Total
n	77	95	85	90	91	87	88	55	54	69	88	94	94	93	99	67	1315
Carious	4	6	3	3	0	0	0	0	0	0	1	1	1	9	8	4	40
%	5.2	6.3	3.5	3.3	0.0	0.0	0.0	0.0	0.0	0.0	1.1	1.1	1.1	9.7	8.1	5.9	3.0

Table 66: Adult female mandibular caries

Tooth	8	7	6	5	4	3	2	1	1	2	3	4	5	6	7	8	Total
n	20	31	31	35	37	34	27	23	24	27	38	37	35	32	29	21	481
Carious	2	2	2	2	1	0	0	0	0	0	0	2	2	3	2	1	19
%	10.0	6.4	6.4	5.7	2.7	0.0	0.0	0.0	0.0	0.0	0.0	5.4	5.7	9.4	6.9	4.8	3.9

Table 67: Adult female maxillary caries

Tooth	8	7	6	5	4	3	2	1	1	2	3	4	5	6	7	8	Total
n	12	25	27	29	30	28	22	13	15	26	28	31	28	29	24	16	388
Carious	0	1	4	2	1	0	0	0	0	0	0	2	4	11	2	1	28
%	0.0	4.0	14.8	6.9	3.3	0.0	0.0	0.0	0.0	0.0	0.0	6.5	14.3	37.9	8.3	6.2	7.2

Table 68: Total adult male caries rate

n	2382
Carious	120
%	5.0

Table 69: Total adult female caries rate

n	869
Carious	47
%	5.4

Table 70: Total adult male plus female caries rate

n	3251
Carious	167
%	5.1

The overall caries rate as shown from the tables is 5.1%, with negligible difference between the sexes. This is a moderately low figure though not exceptionally so. It may be compared with a few other early populations as shown in Table 71.

Table 71: Caries rates of adult teeth

Source	Date	% Carious		Author
Trentholme Drive, York	Romano-British	4.4		Cooke et al, 1968
Pooled	Romano-British	11.4		Emery, 1963
Pooled	Early Saxon	8.1		Hardwick, 1960
North Elmham, Norfolk	Late Saxon	6.4		Wells, 1977
Danubians	Merovingian	5.2		Gröschel, 1937
Ciply, Belgium	Frankish	12.5		Brabant, 1963
Iona, Scotland	7th–11th century	0.4		Wells, 1981
Pooled English	18th century	19.7	(♂)	Krogman, 1938
Pooled English	18th century	31.3	(♀)	Krogman, 1938

At Cirencester the combined male plus female maxillary caries rate is 7.4% compared with only 3.3% for the mandibular teeth. An additional 310 permanent teeth were present in the jaws of juveniles less than eighteen years of age. None of these was carious, so the total caries rate of the second dentition is reduced to 4.7%. Some of the caries in these teeth was probably due to severe attrition which has opened the pulp cavity. It is difficult to estimate how much was caused in this way but it is unlikely that primary pulp exposure accounted for more than 2–3% of dental decay.

In all populations caries is closely related to diet and the relatively low decay rate at Cirencester probably implies that moderately abundant supplies of meat were available to these people and that their reliance on carbohydrates was not excessive. It almost certainly indicates that fine milled flour and sugars, such as honey and raisins, were a negligible part of their food. The 167 caries cavities in sexed adult jaws were distributed as shown in Table 72.

Table 72: Distribution of caries in crania

Sex	No. of crania with teeth	No. of crania with caries	%
♂	140	55	39.3
♀	56	24	42.9
♂ + ♀	196	79	41.6

The deciduous dentition also has a fairly low caries rate. One hundred and fifty milk teeth survive of which four (2.7%) are carious. These four decayed teeth occur in three (13.6%) of twenty-two children.

Six of the 167 adult carious teeth have two separate caries cavities, giving a total of 173 foci of decay. In forty-five of these it is impossible to determine the site of origin because of the advanced destruction of the tooth. Table 73 shows the location of the remaining 128 cavities.

Table 73: Location of caries cavities

Location of caries	n	%
Occlusal	27	21.1
Cervical	10	7.8
Interstitial	91	71.1

All the cervical foci were on the buccal surface of the teeth. Of the interstitial foci two (2.2%) are in canines, twenty-eight (30.8%) in premolars and sixty-one (67.0%) in molars. The interstitial cavities were approximately twice as frequent at contact areas than at the cemento-enamel junction. In deciduous teeth one cavity was occlusal, three were interstial.

Periodontal disease was not extensive at Cirencester. In the 4710 erupted tooth positions there are fifty-nine (1.2%) alveolar abscess cavities. These cavities are distributed among thirty-seven persons: twenty-five males with forty-two cavities and twelve females with seventeen. From 177 mandibles fourteen (7.9%) had them. The commonest position for periodontal disease was adjacent to the first or second molars, with 71.2% of all abcess cavities occurring there. Table 74 shows the distribution of these lesions.

Table 74: Distribution of periodontal abscess cavities

Tooth Position	8	7	6	5	4	3	2	1	1	2	3	4	5	6	7	8		
♂ maxillae	0	4	4	2	2	0	0	0	1	0	0	1	0	7	5	1	=	27
♂ mandibles	1	1	6	0	0	2	0	0	0	0	0	0	1	4	0	0	=	15
♀ maxillae	0	0	1	0	2	0	0	0	0	0	1	1	1	5	1	1	=	13
♀ mandibles	0	0	0	0	0	0	0	0	0	0	0	0	0	3	1	0	=	4
Total	1	5	11	2	4	2	0	0	1	0	1	2	2	19	7	2	=	59

(Abscess cavities)

A common cause of periodontal abscess is extreme attrition of the teeth, with opening of the pulp cavity. This seems to have been infrequent at Cirencester and the cause of these persons' abscesses might have been the result of spicules of bone, husks of grain, etc. becoming wedged between tooth and gum or, more probably, due to alveolar extension from gingivitis, sometimes aggravated by deposits of tartar. The improbability of bony spicules becoming lodged in their tooth sockets may suggest that fish was a relatively uncommon item of their diet.

Apart from abscess cavities, which when present usually drained through the buccal surface of the jaw, generalized alveolar infection or osteitis is seldom found here and is never severe.

This low overall incidence of periodontal disease should not be taken to imply that tooth-picks, tooth-brushes or other devices of oral hygiene were used. It is more likely that satisfactory diet was responsible and that they were well enough fed to have no need to gnaw the coarsest or most damaging foods.

As noted above 143 teeth had never erupted, 133 of them being third molars out of 547 identifiable M3 positions — an incidence of 24.3%. There are 396 M3 positions in male jaws, with 91 (22.9%) unerupted, and 151 in the females, with 42 (27.8%) unerupted. The higher incidence of this condition in the women has been observed in other populations, e.g. a medieval group from Clopton, Cambridgeshire (Tattersall, 1968) and the North Elmham Anglo-Saxons (Wells, 1980). The combined male and female rate of maxillary M3 suppression is 23.5%; the mandibular is 23.5%.

Apart from third molars ten teeth remain unerupted, of which two (both canines) are in the maxilla of Inh. 43 (♀) and four are in the mandible of Inh. 224 (♂).

In most jaws the teeth were well spaced and showed good occlusion but at least twenty-four had some overcrowding, always of the anterior teeth, and in a few cases this was severe. In general the teeth were well formed except that at least forty-four persons had some degree, usually very slight, of enamel hypoplasia. This is a condition due to some morbid process which affects the development of the tooth in infancy and it is characterized by pits or ridges deforming the enamel of one or, more commonly, several teeth. The frequency with which the different teeth are affected gives some indication of the age of the child when it suffered the morbid process. Today the commonest teeth to be attacked are I1, I2, M1 and C in that descending order. At Cirencester a higher incidence of canines and second molars was found and this suggests that, whatever the causes may have been (infections, dietary deficiency, weaning troubles etc.) they attacked these children between the ages of two and four years old, rather than during the first eighteen months of life as is now usual.

Abnormally shaped teeth are rare in this series although several peg shaped third molars were found (for example, Inhs. 232 and 330) and a few maxillary incisors are slightly shovel shaped (for example the medials of Inhs. 145 and 232 and the laterals of Inh. 138).

Occlusion was mostly good and indicated strong functional use of teeth throughout the period of jaw development. The normal pattern here was edge-to-edge or slight overbite. But there are a few exceptions. Inh. 334 (♀) has gross overbite and bevelling of what remains of her anterior teeth. A few cases of impacted teeth, mostly third molars were found.

Calculus (i.e. tartar) was widespread among these people, with at least 105 persons affected. In fifty-eight it consisted of quite small (though often widespread) deposits; in fifteen it was of medium severity; and in thirty-two it was heavy. In contrast to what is found in modern jaws, at Cirencester the tartar tends to affect many or most teeth in a jaw rather than being concentrated on surfaces opposite the salivary ducts, and it is often of mixed labial, buccal and lingual distribution. Compared with some early populations the incidence of tartar here is fairly low and this is further evidence that a moderate amount of meat and coarse bread supplied much of their diet, and that little was eaten in the form of soft paps or porridges. The relatively mild extent of tartar here was also probably partly responsible for the lowish rate of periodontal infections in these jaws.

No evidence of dental filling, ornamentation or the use of prostheses was found at Cirencester. Dentistry, if practised at all, was presumably limited to the occasional extraction of decayed and painful teeth.

Toothwear was heavy in this population when compared with modern dentitions, but only moderate by the standard of many early groups. In view of the small sample available no attempt has been made to assess the attrition on each separate tooth position. Instead, a simple categorization has been made into five degrees: 0 = absence of attrition; 1 = in which the enamel and cusps are worn down with no more than one or two tiny uncoalesced exposures of dentine; 2 = in which separate areas of exposed dentine have coalesced, most of the occlusal enamel is worn away but with no more than an occasional small concavity of the tooth surface; 3 = in which extensive concavity of the tooth surfaces is present, with considerable reduction in crown height but with these changes often somewhat compensated by proliferation of secondary dentine; 4 = extensive destruction of the crowns of the teeth, opening the pulp cavity and often with the roots separately exposed.

Virtually no difference was found between the sexes. In males 129 jaws totalled 290 degrees of attrition i.e. an average of 2.24; in females 54 jaws totalled 122 degrees for an average of 2.26. Figure 84 shows that tooth wear was present in all adult jaws. The women had a slightly higher rate of first degree attrition than the men but lacked the gross fourth degree that had eroded the crowns in 3% of the men.

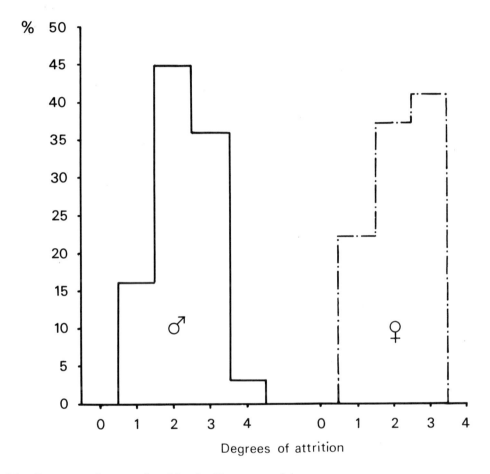

Fig. 84.   Percentage degrees of attrition in Cirencester adults

TORUS

Thirteen persons (10♂, 3♀) have torus mandibularis. It is difficult to make a precise estimate of the occurrence of this condition at Cirencester owing to damage to some of the jaws but these thirteen cases have been identified in 193 mandibles or substantial fragments thereof. This is a frequency of 6.7%.

In contrast to the large masses of bone which characterised the mandibles in a remarkable 8th–11th century group from Iona (Wells, 1974a) most of these Cirencester cases were very small, consisting of nothing more than a slight localized thickening of the alveolus. Only in three males, Inhs. 121, 185 and 307, was the condition slightly more developed. When present torus mandibularis was always bilateral except in Inh. 336 (♂) who had three very small tori on the right side only. The presence of these three nodules is not remarkable: in at least six persons the condition was multiple on one or both sides. In every case the anomaly is on the lingual surface of the alveolus, usually in the region of the lateral incisor or the premolars.

Inh. 229 (♀) was the only clear case of maxillary tori. They were small, bilateral, and on the labio-buccal surface of the bone.

No example of torus palatinus was found here but Inh. 311 (♀) has a small lump blocking about half the left external auditory meatus. It is uncertain whether this should be considered as a torus auditivus or as an osteoma.

OSTEOARTHROSIS

As with most other ancient burial grounds, the commonest identifiable disease at Cirencester is osteoarthrosis. South of the Fosse at least 134 (44.8%) of the 299 adults have this condition. But the total incidence must have been much higher than this. No skeleton in the whole series is complete. Most are very deficient and either lack many of the bones which are likely to be affected by arthrosis or, in the case of the larger limb bones, have their articular surfaces damaged to a degree which prevents recognition of the disease. Of the 299 adults probably at least ninety-seven have less than fifteen per cent of their articular surfaces surviving for inspection. This leaves only 202 persons with moderately extensive articulations, which raises the incidence of arthrosis to 66.3% and would undoubtedly have been higher still if more of those skeletons had been nearly complete. It seems likely that, in life, not less than 80% of the Cirencester adults would have had osteoarthrosis.

Before looking more closely at its distribution in these persons it is perhaps worth commenting on the general significance of arthrosis (or osteoarthritis, as it is often called). It is a very different disease from rheumatoid arthritis, which seems to be hardly identifiable in early skeletons. In contrast to fractures, which are usually due to a single violent injury, osteoarthrosis is the result of a succession of traumata — often of a very minor kind but continued over many months or years. It reflects, above all, what may be called the "wear and tear" of joints as a result of the minor strains and stresses inseparable from a normally vigorous and physically active life. It is the most useful of all diseases for reconstructing the life style of early populations. Its anatomical localization reflects very closely their occupations and activities, and its high frequency enables it to be treated statistically when comparing different groups.

In many cases of arthrotic joints, e.g. the shoulder, one of its component bones may be more severely affected than the other and often only one bone will be involved. For example, in the case of osteoarthrotic shoulders the scapula tends to be more commonly affected than the humerus; in the knee the femur is affected more often than the tibia. From a functional point of view it is better to think in terms of the joints which are affected rather than the individual bones which comprise the articulation. But affected bones as well as joints should always be recorded.

A common result of arthrosis is that a flange of newly formed bone — an osteophyte — develops around the margin of the affected joint. In the spinal column two different kinds of articulations occur: the posterior, intervertebral or "true" joints, and the articulations between successive vertebral bodies. These latter junction areas have certain features which distinguish them from other joint surfaces but, nevertheless, they are very commonly affected by an outgrowth of osteophytes which, when severe, may lead to fusion of some or even all of the vertebrae. Although they often occur in the same spine and commonly on the same vertebra it is useful to distinguish excrescences of the vertebral bodies (osteophytosis) from those of the posterior joints (osteoarthrosis). And in discussing the Cirencester spines these two terms will be consistently used in this distinguishing way.

Arthrosis can affect any joint in the body except the synarthroses but its incidence varies greatly in different populations. In the group of burials recovered from south of the Fosse its site of election was the vertebral column. Parts of 190 adult spinal columns were found, 127 male and 63 female. If all these columns had been complete, with their sacra, 4750 bones should be present. For assessing the presence of these lesions it is useful to consider each vertebra as consisting of a superior and an inferior part — or hemivertebra — thus giving a potential forty-nine hemivertebrae for each column (only the superior part of the sacrum being relevant). Unfortunately damaged or missing vertebrae greatly reduce the number of observations which can be made. Table 75 shows the number of observable hemivertebrae and the frequency of arthrosis and osteophytosis.

Table 75: Vertebral pathology (affected hemivertebrae)

Number of hemivertebrae observable for:

Sex	Arthrosis			Osteophytosis			Schmorl's Nodes		
	n	+	%	n	+	%	n	+	%
♂	4237	287	6.8	3857	1034	26.8	4126	318	7.7
♀	1889	132	6.9	1720	262	15.2	1804	101	5.6
♂ + ♀	6126	419	6.8	5577	1296	23.2	5930	419	7.1

It will be seen that the women's spines were arthrotic as often as those of the men, but the male rate of osteophytotic lipping was significantly higher than the female. There is nothing remarkable about the frequency of these lesions in the men: at Kingsworthy and North Elmham the male rates for arthrosis were 6.1% and 7.3% respectively; for osteophytosis they were 27.9% and 27.5%. However, it is unusual to find that the women have almost as much arthrosis as the men, though this does happen occasionally. At Kingsworthy and North Elmham their respective rates were only 2.0% and 4.4%, although their rates for osteophytosis were marginally higher than at Cirencester. It seems certain that the Cirencester women must have used their spinal columns vigorously and it is likely that much of their vertebral pathology was due to humping heavy burdens, yoked buckets of water perhaps, aggravated by torsional stresses, probably from digging, hoeing and other agricultural tasks.

That the male and female rates for these lesions were not dependent on large differences in severity affecting only a very few members of one sex is shown by Table 76 which records the percentage of men and women who were affected by these diseases.

Table 76: Distribution of arthrosis, osteophytosis and Schmorl's Nodes

Sex	Parts of spinal columns n	Lesion					
		Arthrosis		Osteophytosis		Schmorl's Nodes	
		+	%	+	%	+	%
♂	127	58	45.7	89	70.1	59	46.5
♀	63	22	34.9	36	57.1	24	38.1
♂ + ♀	190	80	42.1	125	65.8	83	43.7

It will be seen that in each case the female frequency of the lesions is roughly three quarters of the male rate and, although the difference between the sexes is significant, it is clear that the vertebral pathology was spread over a substantial number of women, not concentrated in a few persons.

Osteophytosis varies greatly in severity, ranging from a tiny, barely detectable, lip of a bone projecting from the border of a vertebral body to great excrescences springing from adjacent vertebrae and fusing into a single block of bone. These different severities can be expressed in various ways, some of which are very elaborate. The Cirencester lesions have been assessed on a simple five point scale: O = absence of osteophytosis; 1 = the lipping projects less than 3 mm; 2 = the lipping projects 3–6 mm; 3 = the lipping projects more than 6 mm but without synostosis of adjacent bones; 4 = adjacent bones are fused by large osteophytes. Tables 77 and 78, mf. 3/4, show the distribution by hemivertebrae of the five degrees of lipping.

An Index of lipping has been devised and is expressed as D x 100/V, where D is the total number of degrees of osteophytosis scored by the entire column, and V is the number of hemivertebrae available for inspection. At Cirencester, for the whole column, the Index is 168 in the males, 150 for the females. But the results can be shown separately for each major region and Table 79 does this for both sexes.

Table 79: Vertebral index of lipping severity

Region	Index ♂	♀
Cervical	141	163
Thoracic	155	142
Lumbar	195	161
Sacrum	186	150
Total	168	150

The Index for the whole vertebral column is not greatly higher for males than for females (at Kingsworthy the women scored only 140 to the men's 200) but there are interesting differences in the four regions. The fact that the women have slightly more severe lesions in the neck may be partly the result of a relatively weaker neck and shoulder musculature which afforded less protection to the column in that region. But it also raises the possibility that these women were in the habit of carrying loads on their heads, as is still the custom in many societies. The higher lumbo-sacral scores of the males reflect the fact that the really heavy work such as heaving logs, lifting building materials, etc., was performed by men because it is the lower spinal region which normally takes most of these heavy stresses. A further indication that, on average, the men were straining their columns more than women is that simple osteophytotic synostosis of adjacent vertebrae (degree 4 on our scale) is nowhere present in the females' spines but occurs between a minimum of twenty-one vertebrae, including two sacra, in at least eight males.

Whilst these spinal lesions are being discussed it is appropriate to refer to another form of pathology which is commonly found: a Schmorl's node. In childhood and adolescence the intervertebral discs consist of a gelatinous or semi-fluid nucleus contained in a tough fibrous capsule which, in turn, is surrounded by a thick elastic membrane. If the disc is subjected to too severe a strain, especially by compression forces from carrying heavy weights, the fibrous layer of the capsule may rupture and allow its gelatinous contents to escape. But the outer elastic layer stretches without tearing and a globule or bubble of jelly is then formed which presses against the body of the adjacent vertebra above or below the ruptured disc — often against both vertebrae. When this happens the bone, plastic as always, yields to the pressure and gradually a small pit or cavity is formed in its body. This is a Schmorl's node. The process usually takes place during or close to the adolescent period when heavy tasks may be undertaken but before the central nucleus of the intervertebral disc has become a solid rather than a gelatinous structure. The lesion in the vertebra probably first develops where vestigial remnants of the notochord have left a focus of weakness.

Table 80 shows the frequency of Schmorl's nodes. Although they were common in both sexes, the 5.6% affected vertebrae in the women is an unusually high rate. At Kingsworthy the male and female incidence was 3.1% and 1.1%; at North Elmham it was 6.5% and 1.6% respectively. Table 80 shows the distribution of Schmorl's nodes and the frequency of affected hemi-vertebrae for all levels where they occurred in males and females.

Table 80: Distribution of Schmorl's Nodes

Segment	Females			Males			Segment
		n	%	%	n		
T4		0 of 39	0.0	1.2	1 of 85		T4
T4		1 of 40	2.5	2.5	2 of 83		T4
T5	6/244	1 of 39	2.6	3.5	3 of 85	24/523	T5
T5	= 2.5%	0 of 38	0.0	7.1	6 of 85	= 4.6%	T5
T6		1 of 40	2.5	3.3	3 of 90		T6
T6		3 of 40	7.5	10.2	9 of 88		T6
T7		3 of 40	7.5	7.7	7 of 91		T7
T7		5 of 43	11.6	22.7	20 of 89		T7
T8	33/268	5 of 46	10.9	9.3	8 of 86	75/555	T8
T8	=12.3%	6 of 45	13.3	7.7	7 of 91	=13.5%	T8
T9		6 of 42	14.3	12.1	11 of 91		T9
T9		8 of 43	18.6	22.7	22 of 97		T9
T10		6 of 41	14.6	15.2	14 of 92		T10
T10	42/251	9 of 41	21.6	27.8	27 of 97	135/587	T10
T11	=16.7%	8 of 43	18.6	16.5	17 of 97	=22.9%	T11
T11		10 of 42	23.8	33.3	33 of 99		T11
T12		6 of 39	15.4	28.1	25 of 89		T12
T12		3 of 38	7.9	18.8	19 of 101		T12
L1		4 of 37	10.8	19.4	18 of 93		L1
L1		3 of 37	8.1	12.8	12 of 94		L1
L2	18/221	4 of 34	11.8	14.0	14 of 100	70/585	L2
L2	= 8.1%	2 of 36	5.6	12.0	12 of 100	=11.9%	L2
L3		3 of 35	8.6	9.5	9 of 95		L3
L3		2 of 35	5.7	5.4	5 of 93		L3
L4		1 of 36	2.8	7.7	7 of 91		L4
L4	2/179	0 of 37	0.0	3.3	3 of 90	14/451	L4
L5	= 1.1%	0 of 35	0.0	1.1	1 of 89	= 3.1%	L5
L5		0 of 36	0.0	2.2	2 of 90		L5
S1		1 of 32	3.1	1.2	1 of 86		S1

No node was found above the T4 vertebra in either sex and this is a common finding. The greatest incidence occurred on the inferior surface of T11, where a third of all male vertebrae and nearly a quarter of all female vertebrae had some degree of cavitation. It is interesting to see that down to that segment the inferior surface of vertebral bodies were more often affected than their superior surfaces, whereas from T12 to L5 this was reversed. Table 81 sums up these differences.

Table 81: Frequencies of Schmorl's Nodes on superior and inferior surfaces

Sex	Segments	Affected superior surfaces			Affected inferior surfaces		
		n	+	%	n	+	%
♀	T4–T11	330	30	9.1	332	42	12.7
	T12–L5	186	18	9.7	219	10	4.6
♂	T3–T11	717	64	8.9	728	126	17.3
	T12–L5	557	74	13.3	568	53	9.3

The evidence of Schmorl's nodes at Cirencester reinforces what was inferred from the vertebral arthrotic and osteophytotic lesions. It shows that these people used their spines to carry out numerous heavy tasks and that, compared with many other populations, the women undertook a disproportionately large share of the total work. It also shows that this workload was fairly severe for teenagers and was probably already imposed on young persons even in their late childhood. The arthrotic and osteophytotic lesions no doubt resulted from a mixture of stresses such as torsional strains, humping burdens, sudden jerks and excessive flexions. The Schmorl's nodes argue rather more specifically for the carrying of heavy weights and other compressional forces.

But stresses on the spinal column are not only shown by changes in the intervertebral joints and body borders. Some of the pathology is carried over to the ribs and these may have osteo-arthrotic changes on their heads and, or, their lateral articular facets. These sites articulate, respectively, with the bodies and transverse processes of thoracic vertebrae, and arthrosis may affect either bone of these joints. The condition is very common although precise details of its frequency are virtually unrecorded.

At Cirencester 68 persons (52♂, 16♀) had one or other of their costal joints affected. Table 82 summarizes the frequency of these lesions.

Table 82: Frequency of arthrotic ribs

	Rib articulation							
	Head				Lateral			
Sex	n	+	%	N	n	+	%	N
♀	576	18	3.1	6	560	41	7.3	16
♂	1294	63	4.9	29	1315	109	7.5	45
♀+♂	1870	81	4.3	35	1875	150	8.0	61

(n = number of observable rib facets; + = number of arthrotic facets; N = number of affected persons).

The male rate of arthrotic heads of ribs is nearly 60% higher than that of the females and presumably reflects a more vigorous and traumatic use of muscles, such as the pectoralis major, which have their origins attached to the rib cage. Whether, at Cirencester, the overall rates for arthrosis of these rib joints are high, average or low is uncertain in view of the paucity of comparative data. But lesions in these positions should not be lightly dismissed. They are important indicators of the use or abuse of certain specific trunk muscles and must derive from a precise range of muscular and articular stresses.

In the absence of records from other sites no attempt will be made here to analyse the significance of these pathologies in further detail. It is to be hoped that the data given in Table 82 will stimulate further interest in costal arthrosis.

The frequencies given above for osteoarthrosis include those for the posterior lumbo-sacral articulation. But it is convenient here to consider also another part of the axial skeleton: the sacroiliac joint. This shows arthrotic lesions in at least sixteen persons (10 ♂,6 ♀), either on the sacrum, the innominate or both. Owing to the defective state of many of the component bones of these joints it is often difficult to make an assured diagnosis and, especially, to determine the frequency of these lesions. It seems likely that the male rate was ten (4.5%) of 223 joints and the female rate six (7.7%) of 78 joints. It is uncertain why the women should have had a higher frequency than the men. If this can be relied on, as seems probable, it may be related not only to the burdens they had to carry but also to the increased vulnerability of these joints during and after pregnancy, at which time some loosening of the articulation occurs, with an increased potential for slipping under heavy strains. Unfortunately, in only one woman with arthrotic sacroiliac joints (Inh. 56) is it also possible to estimate the number of children she had produced but she emerges as one of the most fertile members of the group. We can be fairly confident that she had had at least six to eight children and possibly ten or twelve.

As noted above 134 (44.8%) of the 299 adults have osteoarthrosis. Omitting the few which have not been sexed we find that 104 (51.5%) of the 202 adult males are affected and 30 (32.9%) of the 91 females. An overall sexual difference of this order is not exceptional.

The costo-vertebral lesions have been discussed above. Leaving these aside we find that, of the 134 affected persons, 104 (79 ♂, 25 ♀) have arthrotic joints elsewhere than in the vertebrae, sacrum or ribs (although often coincident with those lesions). These non-vertebral arthroses have a strong tendency to be multiple. In the seventy-nine affected males they occur in two or more joints fifty-two times, i.e. 65.8% of the men have multiple non-vertebral lesions. In the twenty-five women sixteen (64.0%) have more than one joint affected. In many of these inhumations, e.g. 59 (♀), 205 (♂), 213 (♂), 272 (♂) and 311 (♀) the disease is widespread and occurs in several joints bilaterally. It is not easy to determine the total number of bones which are affected but in the 104 persons with arthroses, other than costo-vertebral lesions, at least 570 bones are involved. The commonest single joint to be affected is the hip. Twenty-eight men have between them a total of 47 arthrotic hip joints (24L., 23R.), 10 women have 17 (8L., 9R.). In 19 of the men and seven of the women the disease is bilateral. It is interesting that, when both bones of the joint are present, the lesions are rather more common on the acetabulum than on the femur (45:27 ♂; 14:12 ♀). The severity of the disease varies a great deal. In some cases, e.g. Inh. 182 (♀) gross collars of osteophytotic lipping spring from the acetabular border to encircle the femoral head. But it should also be noted that in several of these persons the condition is present in a very mild form, sometimes to a degree that can be described as hardly more than incipient. In a few of these cases opinions might differ as to whether the condition should properly be diagnosed as pathologically arthrotic.

These sixty-four arthrotic hips no doubt reflect the stresses and trauma consequent to performing heavy agricultural tasks, lumberjacking, stone quarrying, humping heavy loads, and being subjected to the jerks and torsions inevitable in such occupations. But hip joints do not, of course, function in isolation and many tasks, indeed most tasks, which impose heavy stresses on hips also throw great strain on the knees. It would be expected, therefore, that these people would have a number of arthrotic knee joints. This is borne out on examination of their skeletons.

Eighteen men have 27 arthrotic knees between them (11L., 16R.) and five women have ten such joints. In nine of the men and all the women the disease was bilateral. It is also significant that nine men and three women had lesions in their hips and in their knees concurrently. As was the case with the hip lesions, there are differences in the frequency with which the bones of the knee joint are involved. Lipping or other remodelling is present on twenty-seven patellae, twenty-four femora but on only twelve tibiae.

Osteoarthrosis of the knee, as well as being a common result of minor concussional injuries such as kicking spades into hard soil, is especially likely to result from torsional strains of the joint, as in pivoting the trunk on the leg, and from violently abducting the leg from the thigh — a common cause of "footballer's knee". Both these movements are likely to loosen or split the medial meniscus of the tibia, i.e. they produce what is commonly known as a "torn cartilage". It is possible that some of these arthrotic knees began in this way. In modern clinical experience osteochondritis, especially when it occurs in the knee, is very likely to lead to arthrosis if left untreated. In early populations this tendency seems to be less pronounced but it may be noted that two of the Cirencester persons who had osteochondritis of the knee, probably beginning during their teenage years, went on to develop osteoarthrosis of the same joint. These were Inhs. 199 (♂) and 312 (♀). However, in nine other cases of osteochondritic knees no arthrotic changes were found.

Occupations which impose heavy strains on hips and knees usually involve the ankle and foot joints in extensive trauma as well. At Cirencester thirty-three men and eight women have osteoarthrosis of ankle and, or, foot joints. These lesions tend to be bilateral but in four men the disease was limited to one ankle joint only. Any bone of the foot can be affected but the talus, calcaneus, navicular and the first metatarsal are especially prominent as sites of election. A few of these lesions are very mild and it is occasionally difficult to be sure that they are truly pathological and not merely rugosities around the surface of the joint. But it seems likely that 98 male and 21 female foot bones have some degree of arthrotic change.

These lesions would, in general, have been due to the same sort of long continued, repeated minor injuries which cumulatively produced the hip and knee arthroses. But they probably also reflect a number of sudden, isolated episodes of trauma in which tears and wrenches occurred from twisting their feet on tussocky, pitted or root-entangled ground. That this sometimes happened is, indeed, suggested by the presence of several tarsal exostoses which hint at torn ligaments and the avulsion of joint capsules.

At modern orthopaedic clinics osteoarthrosis of the shoulder is not an especially common disease. At Cirencester it occurred almost as often as arthrosis of the hip. Omitting Inhs 9 (♀) and 53 (♂) p. 175 — the two chronic dislocations — thirty men have forty-six arthrotic shoulders between them (19L., 27R.) and six women have nine (3L., 6R.). In sixteen males and three females the disease affected both shoulders. In twenty-nine men and five women only one bone of the joint was affected and in several cases the lesion was so mild as to make the diagnosis difficult. In most cases the disease was less severe in the women than the men. Lesions on the scapula tended to be rather more extensive than those on the humeral head but, in this series, there was little difference in their frequency.

Osteoarthrosis of the elbow joint was less common than in the shoulder. Twenty males had twenty-six affected elbows between them (8L., 18R.); six females had seven (3L., 4R.). In six men and one woman the condition was bilateral. The higher frequency of lesions in the elbow probably reflects the normal right handedness of the average man and his use of this arm for the most demanding work. In contrast to what was found in the shoulder there was a marked difference in the frequency with which the three component bones were involved. In the total of thirty-three arthrotic elbow joints the ulna was affected twenty-six times, the humerus twenty but the head of the radius only four.

In all active, hardworking peoples arthrosis of the wrist and hand is common. This was the case at Cirencester. At least twenty men and ten women had the disease. In most instances where it was present it was bilateral and affected more than one joint on each side. It is difficult to be precise but it seems likely that the radius and, or, ulna was the only bone affected in eleven male and five female wrists; and that about fifty carpals and metacarpals are arthrotic in men, twenty-five in women. Many of these lesions must have been due to such strained and traumatic occupations as ploughing, axing timber, smithing, and in the case of women perhaps, to hoeing or basket weaving. But some of these lesions may have been the result of single episodes of violence — a misdirected hammer blow, a hand crushed between two building blocks or a finger suddenly wrenched backwards when trying to restrain a restive horse.

Table 83 summarizes the distribution of osteoarthrosis in men and women for the shoulder, elbow, hip and knee joints.

Table 83: Distribution of osteoarthrosis

Shoulder:

46 shoulders	(19L., 27R.)	in 30 men	(16 bilateral)	30 scapulae 26 humeri 16 clavicles	} 72 bones
9 shoulders	(3L., 6R.)	in 6 women	(3 bilateral)	7 scapulae 7 humeri 1 clavicle	} 15 bones

Elbow:

26 elbows	(8L., 18R.)	in 20 men	(6 bilateral)	17 humeri 20 ulnae 2 radii	} 39 bones

| 7 elbows | (3L., 4R.) | in 6 women | (1 bilateral) | 3 humeri
6 ulnae
2 radii | } 11 bones |

Hip:

| 47 hips | (24L., 23R.) | in 28 men | (19 bilateral) | 45 acetabula
27 femora | } 72 bones |
| 17 hips | (8L., 9R.) | in 10 women | (7 bilateral) | 14 acetabula
12 femora | } 26 bones |

Knee:

| 27 knees | (11L., 16R.) | in 18 men | (9 bilateral) | 18 femora
17 patellae
6 tibiae | } 41 bones |
| 10 knees | (5L., 5R.) | in 5 women | (5 bilateral) | 6 femora
9 patallae
6 tibiae | } 21 bones |

It is interesting not only to see the distribution of these pathological conditions but also to record the frequency with which they occur among the total number of surviving bones. Table 84 shows this.

Table 84: Percentage of bones with osteoarthrosis

Location	% Osteoarthrosis	
	Male	Female
Ribs (Head)	4.9	3.1
Ribs (Lateral)	8.1	7.5
Clavicle (Medial)	5.1	3.9
Clavicle (Lateral)	14.7	2.6
Humerus (Proximal)	14.1	12.3
Humerus (Distal)	8.0	2.2
Femur (Proximal)	12.6	7.2
Femur (Distal)	7.6	8.3
Patella	10.7	11.7
Tibia (Proximal)	3.3	4.1
Tibia (Distal)	4.9	0.0

One unusual feature here is the high female arthrosis rate, compared with that of the males, on each of the three component bones of the knee joint. The reasons for this are uncertain and probably complex. No attempt will be made to analyse them here because, being largely anatomical and physiological, they are unlikely to contribute greatly to the interpretation of the way of life of these persons. But the difference in the frequency of arthrosis between the men and women is relatively slight at several other locations and the overall evidence of the limb bones in Table 84 appears to reinforce what was inferred above on the basis of the vertebral lesions: that, compared with the sexual differences in many other populations, the Cirencester women probably performed a disproportionately high amount of the total heavy work load of the group.

Some distinction can be made between the various actions and injuries which lead to arthrotic changes at the proximal, in contrast to the distal, articulations of the long bones. It is less easy to do this for the two rib facets so it may be noted that the frequency of arthrosis for the head and lateral rib facets combined is 172 (6.6%) of 2609 male joints and 59 (5.1%) of 1136 female joints, these lesions being distributed over fifty-three men and sixteen women.

Arthrosis of the sterno-clavicular joint is represented by a probable nine male and three female examples. In seven of these the lateral end of the same clavicle is also affected.

Finally, seven cases (3♂, 4♀) of osteoarthrosis of the jaw — the temporo-mandibular joint — must be noted. The condition is unilateral in Inhs. L (♀), 97 (♂), 270 (♀), and 311 (♀); bilateral in 130 (♂), 278 (♂) and 341 (♀). These arthrotic jaws imply their use on tough, resistant diets. In each of these persons the arthrosis reinforces the evidence given by the extent of dental attrition, which is moderately heavy in Inh. 270 and very severe in the six other persons.

The overall evidence of the osteoarthrotic lesions in these Cirencester people leaves no doubt that they led physically strenuous lives in which they were often exposed to much strain over long periods. But it must again be stressed that few early populations fail to show such a picture and that, by the average standard of such groups, the Cirencester people were not more severely affected than many or most others.

Table 85 summarizes the distribution and probable number of arthrotic bones, other than costo-vertebral elements.

Table 85: Number of arthrotic bones (costo-vertebral lesions excluded)

Jaw	7
Clavicle (Medial end)	9
Shoulder (including lateral clavicle)	95
Elbow	50
Wrist and hand	91
Sacro-iliac	39
Hip	98
Knee	62
Ankle and foot	119
Total	570

A word may be said about eburnation, a condition which sometimes results from severe osteoarthrosis. It shows itself as a smooth, highly polished area on the joint surface of a bone. It is due to destruction of the articular cartilage so that the two opposing articular surfaces come into direct contact and eventually develop a dense, ivory-like texture on the face of one or both bones. Although it usually implies a severe degree of arthrosis eburnation is merely a part, albeit an extreme part, of the total arthrotic process: it is not a separate disease entity.

In the 570 non-costo-vertebral arthrotic bones thirty (5.3%) have well marked patches of eburnation. They cover a wide anatomical range which includes the humeral head (Inh. 53 ♂); the capitulum of the distal end of the humerus (Inh. M, ♂); the distal end of the ulna (Inh. 73, ♂); the acetabulum and femoral head (Inh. 64, ♂); the carpal scaphoid and lunate (Inh. 174, ♂); and the heads of metatarsals (Inhs. 205 (♂) and 312 (♀)). But a common site of election is the metacarpus, especially the first metacarpal (on its base and head). In the present group eburnation is thus located in Inhs. 174 (♂), 182 (♀), 198 (♂), 270 (♀) and 308 (♂). The lesion sometimes affects equivalent joints bilaterally as in the femoral heads of Inh. 251 (b) (♂) and the distal ulnar articulations of Inh. 341 (♀).

In addition to these sites eburnation also occurs in various costo-vertebral joints. At Cirencester it is found on the posterior intervertebral articulations of C3 and C4 in Inh. 93 (♀); on the left inferior facet of C2 in Inh. 297 (♂); and on the mutually articulating facets of L4 and L5 in Inh. 110 (♂). In Inh. 175 (♀) there is an eburnated area on the lateral facet of a right middle rib.

These few examples, which are not exhaustive, are an additional indication of the distribution and severity of some of these osteoarthrotic lesions.

FRACTURES

South of the Fosse Way at least sixty persons (53 ♂, 6 ♀, 1 unsexed) have a minimum of 144 fractures (127 ♂, 16♀, 1 unsexed). In a few other instances there is a possible or probable fracture but owing to post-inhumation damage or some other cause there remains a modicum of doubt. When these uncertain cases are included the figures rise to at least 155 fractures (137 ♂, 17 ♀, 1 unsexed) in sixty-five persons (57 ♂, 7 ♀, 1 unsexed). These figures do not include injuries which are almost certainly due to sword cuts or other weapon wounds.

By far the commonest fractures are those of ribs: 25 males have a minimum of 77 broken ribs; two, probably three, females have 8 or 9 broken ribs. Among the men Inh. 261 has five fractures in four ribs; Inh. 307 has seven fractures; Inh. 124 has certainly seven and perhaps eight; whilst Inh. 212 has at least fifteen and probably seventeen. In all these cases the fractures have healed well with only trivial deformity. In the women Inh. 223 has not less than seven soundly repaired ribs. In antero-posterior crushing injuries or in accidental falls forward on to the chest there is a tendency for the ribs to snap at the angle or in their posterior third. With direct blows to the chest wall the fracture is rather more likely to occur in the middle or anterior part of the rib (the body of the rib). At Cirencester about three-quarters of all these fractures occur in the body of the ribs, only a quarter at the angle. This suggests that at least some of the injuries were due to deliberate aggression. No evidence of non-union or pseudar-throsis was found in any of these lesions. Many of the injuries are detectable from only small scraps of rib which show the fracture clearly but are too short, and sometimes too deformed, for its side to be determined. In the thirty-eight fractures where the laterality is unambiguous thirteen were on the right, twenty-five on the left. Ribs are, of course, often broken accid-entally in falls upon a hard object or in similar mishaps but direct, deliberate voilence is also a common cause. When this happens as a result of striking a man with a cudgel, or even perhaps with the fist, the injury is more likely to occur on the left than the right. That fractured ribs were almost twice as common on the left as the right at Cirencester is yet another hint that at least some of these injuries were the result of aggression rather than accident. Multiple bilateral rib fractures such as those of Inh. 212 strongly suggest severe antero-posterior crushing of the thorax under falling masonry, heavy wagon wheels etc.

After ribs, the next most common fracture at Cirencester was of the fibula. Ten men and two women had broken this bone, always unilaterally except for Inh. 272 (♂) in which both fibulae are fractured. Eight of these breaks are on the left, five on the right. Tripping over un-noticed objects or stumbling on rough ground, causing a violent eversion of the foot or the leg, is the usual prelude to a Pott's fracture of the fibula. Broken tibiae may be similarly caused but are also common as a result of falling from a height. Eight persons (7 ♂, 1 ♀) have a fractured tibia, six of these being on the left. In every case the fibula of the same leg was found to be broken also, except in the case of Inh. 335 (♂) which, although well preserved, showed no evidence of injury. Although deliberate blows on the leg can cause fractures of either bone, this is not a frequent occurrence. It is much more likely that all these lesions were the result of accidental falls, twisted ankles or jumping from heights.

Fractures of the forearm, which are often seen, commonly occur in two ways: (a) as a result of accidentally tripping and falling forward on to an outstretched hand; (b) as a result of raising the forearm to ward off a blow, aimed at the head, by club or cudgel. The first typically produces the well known Colles' fracture of the radius, about 20–30 mm proximal to the wrist joint. The second results in a mid-shaft break of the ulna i.e. what is commonly called a "parry" fracture. Both these lesions are found. In one case, Inh. 54 (♂), only the L. ulna survives and it has a fracture of its styloid process - the most distal tip of the bone. This often occurs in conjunction with a Colles' fracture so probably this man broke his wrist in falling forward on to his left hand. But fractures of the styloid process are occasionally caused by a direct blow. Inh. 142 (♂) also has this lesion but in his case the radius has survived and is unbroken so perhaps he incurred his injury by being hit on his R. wrist. This could then be a very distal and rather unusual form of parry fracture. Inhs. 163 (♂), 210 (a) (♂), 215 (♂), 248 (♂) and 20 (unsexed all have fractures of the ulnar shaft typical of a parry fracture — especially so as in each case it is the left forearm which is broken. If this is how they were incurred, the blow must have been a savage one in the case of Inhs. 163 and 210(a) because the radius also was broken. Inh. V (♀) also had a fracture of the ulnar and radial shafts, in her case of the right forearm. Inh. 304 (♂) is more of a problem. He had an exostosis of the L. ulna and radius in the distal third of the interosseous membrane but there is some irregularity of the bones which suggests that these lesions were due to incomplete fractures which caused negligible deformity of the shafts. A "greenstick" fracture might account for what is found. In this case also it is the left forearm which was injured and it, too, could have been a parry fracture.

When considering the probable cause of a fracture those of the metacarpals are especially ambiguous. They are commonly due to direct aggression, a blow from a stick for example, but they also occur as a result of innumerable occupational injuries such as having a hand crushed by masonry or even as a consequence of an ill-directed hammer blow. A further, and far from rare, cause is due to an aggressor violently punching someone's head and fracturing one of his own metacarpals on impact. In the group six persons (5 ♂, 1 ♀) have fractured metacarpals. It does not seem firmly possible to decide the cause of any of these lesions but it is worth noting that in four of the six it is the fifth metacarpal which is broken. This is the metacarpal of the little finger, the most exposed part of the hand when it is raised to ward off a threatened blow. It may be relevant to note that three of the men with broken metacarpals also have other injuries. Inh. 61 has two fractured ribs, as well as a broken right tibia and fibula; Inh. 212 is the person with fifteen or seventeen broken ribs; Inh. 215 has a fractured left rib, a parry fracture of the left ulna, and a fracture of his right talus and calcaneus. Several of these broken bones might have been due to deliberate attacks. Alternatively, they may indicate that these men led physically severe lives in occupations especially conducive to trauma. In either case we have a hint that these persons were of inferior social status, perhaps numbered among the ill-treated slaves of the community.

To a great extent fractures of the phalanges of hands, especially of the proximal phalanges, are caused in the same way and have the same significance as broken metacarpals. At Cirencester Inh. 320 (♂) has a fractured proximal finger phalange. It is almost certain that Inh. 307, the man with seven rib fractures, also has a broken phalange. Unfortunately there is a trace of ambiguity about this bone: a small exostosis is present on it which seems likely to have been associated with a well-healed break.

Fractures of the foot bones are seldom due to deliberate violence. In Inh. 206 (♂) the R. talus and calcaneus are much deformed by arthrosis and here again there is some evidence that this was the result of a compression fracture involving the head of the talus and the sustentaculum of the calcaneus. Inh. 215 (♂) has a well-marked crush fracture of his R. talus and calcaneus. In each of these men the injury might have been due to landing heavily on their heels after falling from a height, when house building or lumber-jacking, for example. Inh. 215 has already been noted above as a possible serf or low class labourer. Inhs. Y (♂) and 285 (♂) are the only ones to have fractured metatarsals — a soundly healed break with negligible deformity, of the fifth right. These are usually caused by such injuries as dropping a heavy weight on the foot or being trampled by a restive horse or ox.

A more difficult lesion to interpret is the deformed left elbow joint of Inh. M (♂). All three bones, the humerus, ulna and radius, are grossly arthrotic and their articular surfaces have undergone extensive remodelling. The humerus, especially, is much affected and there is some evidence that these changes were due to a fracture which involved the distal articular surface of this bone. A lesion of this kind is not uncommon as a result of falling on the elbow. In the present instance considerable limitation of movement would have followed this injury.

The fractured L. scapula of Inh. D (♂), pl. 32 has been fully described, mf. 3/5. The scapula is an extremely mobile bone which, until the modern age of high speed vehicle accidents and similar injuries, was rarely fractured other than by deliberate aggression or the occasional severe crushing catastrophe. Inh. D was surely the victim of some such attack but there remains uncertainty about its precise nature. It appears likely that he may have been hit by a club but it is probable that a cutting weapon also played a part. Perhaps this was the result of a peasant's brawl in which a sharp-edged mattock was used with undue vigour.

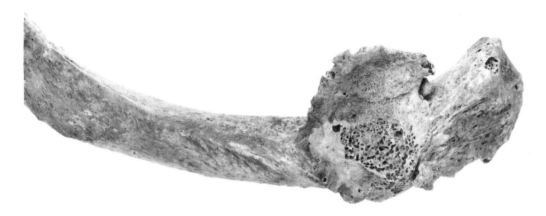

31. Inhumation 107, arthrotic rib

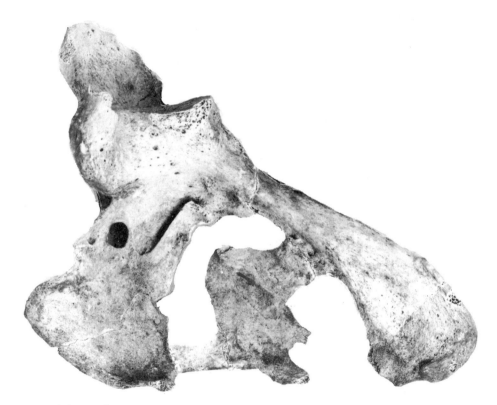

32. Inhumation D, left scapula

Broken noses may be due to many accidents. In this group two persons had sustained this injury: Inhs. 97 (♂) and 185 (♂) each had both their nasal bones fractured with slight displacement. But this lesion is also one of the most typical results of violent bickering and it is possible that these men were the recipients of a well directed punch on the nose. No way of distinguishing between accident and aggression is available here.

A number of head injuries at Cirencester were clearly due to sharp weapons such as swords or lance thrusts and are described in the section devoted to wounds. There are others, however, which are of less certain cause. Four cases are worth noting here. A round or elliptical depressed fracture is present on the frontal bone of Inh. 39 (♂), pl. 33, the R. parietal of Inhs. 108 (♂) and 165 (♂), and the L. parietal of Inh. 118 (♂). All these injuries could have been caused by an accidental blow on the head from a hammer or other blunt tool wielded by a clumsy workmate or by a drunken fall against a corner of a table. But each could equally well be a battle wound

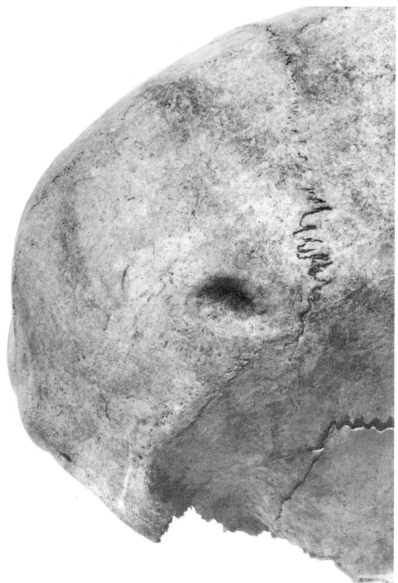

33.   Inhumation 39, slingstone wound

caused by an accurately directed slingshot. No final decision is possible but it should be noted that Inh. 118 has a second, quite distinct, fracture on the same parietal and that this other lesion closely resembles an injury caused by deliberately striking the skull with some such weapon as a light poker or garden hoe — even a blunt sword. There is no way to decide whether the two wounds were caused on the same or different occasions.

One of the commonest of accidental injuries is a fractured clavicle due to falling on the point of the shoulder. Three persons have this lesion: Inh. 4 (♂), on the right, and Inhs. 244 (♂) and 337 (♂), both on the left. All are firmly healed and, despite some deformity, they should have given rise to negligible disability. But another cause of clavicular fractures is a direct blow from a club or other weapon. It not uncommonly happens that when an aggressor seeks to bludgeon an opponent's skull the intended victim evades the blow by side-stepping. If, however, he dodges too little or too late the blow may indeed miss the skull only to fall instead on one or other shoulder, smashing the collar bone as it does so. Any or all of these Cirencester clavicular lesions could have been produced in this way.

The only other fractures to be noted here are the collapsed T4 and T5 vertebrae of Inh. 58 (♀), pl. 34, and the fractured T3 laminae of Inh. 288 (♂). For the former some such cause as a

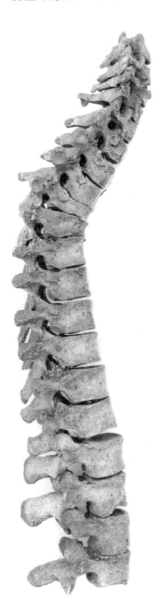

34.   Inhumation 58, fractured vertebrae

severe crushing injury or a heavy fall from horse back or house top must be sought. It is likely that the event was accidental although a deliberate attack of extreme violence cannot be excluded.

Table 86 summarizes the distribution of the fractures which have been discussed here.

Table 86: Distribution of fractures

A. Males
Inhumation   Fracture

Inhumation	Fracture
A	L. middle rib
D	L. middle rib; L scapula
M	?L. humerus — distal articulation
Y	R. 5th metatarsal
4	R. clavicle

A. Males (*contd.*)

Inhumation	Fracture
5(a)	Two ribs
31	L. tibia; L. fibula
39	L. frontal
48	R. 6th or 7th rib
53	Three ribs
54	L. ulna — styloid process
61	L. 6th & 7th ribs; R. 3rd metacarpal; R. tibia: R. fibula
77	L. fibula
97	L. & R. nasals
108	R. parietal
110	L. middle rib
113	R. middle rib
118	L. parietal
124	Two L. & two R. ribs; ?four other ribs
134	L. 3rd or 4th rib
140	R. middle rib
142	R. ulna — styloid process
163	L. ulna; L. radius
165	R. parietal
183	L. (?6th) rib; L. fibula
185	L. & R. nasals
198	L. fibula
199	L. (?5th, & 6th) ribs
203	L (?5th, 6th & 7th) ribs
205	Three ribs; R. tibia; R. fibula
206	?R. talus; ?R. calcaneus
208	R. radius
210(a)	Four ribs; L. ulna; L. radius
212	Fifteen (or ?17) ribs; L. 5th metacarpal.
215	L. 3rd or 4th rib; L. ulna; R. 2nd metacarpal; R. talus; R. calcaneus
225	L. 5th metacarpal
244	L. clavicle
248	L. ulna
249	L. middle rib; 2 R. ribs
261	Four ribs (one with two separate fractures)
272	L. tibia; L. & R. fibulae
276	Two L. and 3 R. middle ribs
285	R. 5th metatarsal
287	Three L. ribs: ?R. rib
288	Laminae of T3 vertebra
302	L. tibia; L. fibula
304	?L. ulna; ? L. radius
307	Seven ribs; ?proximal phalange of a finger
313	R. 5th metacarpal
320	Proximal phalange of a finger
324	L. 1st metacarpal
335	L. tibia
337	L. clavicle
344	Two middle ribs
346	L. middle rib

A. Males (contd.)
Inhumation   Fracture

347	L. tibia; L. fibula
352	R. fibula

B. Females
Inhumation   Fracture

V	R. ulna; R. radius; L. tibia; L. fibula
46(a)	L. middle rib
58	4th & 5th thoracic vertebrae
223	Seven ribs
341	R. 5th metacarpal
349	?L. middle rib
357	R. fibula

C. Unsexed
Inhumation   Fracture

20	L. ulna

A few details in the above table are worth noting. Firstly, the fracture rate among these people was fairly high, especially among males. At least 55 (26.7%) of 206 adult men had a fracture. The female rate was much lower: only 6 (6.6%) of 91 women had fractures. No doubt the rate would have been higher still for both sexes if the skeletons had been in better condition. In the Late Saxon population of North Elmham, Norfolk, the combined fracture rate for both sexes was about 9.0% of 206 skeletons.

In Table 86 a number of lesions have been recorded as "?" fractures, rather than as definitely so. It should, perhaps, be said that this is in spite of all doubtful bones having been radio-graphed. Contrary to popular belief X-rays often prove to be useless in diagnosing these injuries. Fractures associated with little callus and negligible initial deformity may repair so well that, even in known clinical cases, later investigation may reveal no trace of them.

None of the persons shown in Table 86 are juveniles. In most early populations, as in modern ones, fractures (other than those caused by car accidents) are relatively uncommon in children. Moreover, when they do occur, later repair of the bone may obliterate all evidence of the event.

Among the North Elmham Late Saxons the overall impression given by their fractures was that few were likely to have been due to deliberate violence. At Cirencester a very different picture is presented. Clearly these people led vigorous, energetic lives and sustained many accidents but we know from the evidence of their skull lesions that they also received wounds in battles, in gladiatorial combat or in private affrays. Many of their fractures could also have been due to violent attacks. The ulnar shaft "parry" fractures are likely candidates for this distinction and so are the broken noses. A substantial number of the ribs probably fall into this category. The scapula undoubtedly does. At least one radius, perhaps some of the metacarpals, one or more of the clavicles and some or all of the head injuries could also make a strong claim for inclusion. Proof almost always eludes us but it need impose no strain on credulity to suggest that at least forty of these broken bones might have been due to deliberate acts of aggression.

The absence of certain fractures may be noted. No broken jaws were detected, although the occasional isolated loss of incisor teeth, as in Inh. 43 (♀), invites speculation whether this was due to a punch in the mouth and was, therefore, yet another fracture of aggression. No fracture of the femur was found. The absence of femoral neck fractures is no doubt partly a reflection of the relatively short life-span of these people. Femoral shaft fractures, like those of the pelvis which are also absent here, usually suggest falls from a great height and are rare before Late Saxon and medieval times when lofty churches or castles were being built. No fractured patellae were detected.

The distribution and numbers of fractures shown in Table 86 needs to be put in perspective. Table 87 goes some way towards doing this. It shows the number of fractured limb bones in relation to the total number recovered.

Table 87: Frequency of fractured limb bones

Bone	Males			Females		
	n	#	%	n	#	%
Clavicle	201	3	1.5	90	0	0.0
Humerus	205	1	0.5	89	0	0.0
Ulna	201	7	3.5	71	1	1.4
Radius	213	4	1.9	87	1	1.1
Femur	242	0	0.0	93	0	0.0
Tibia	239	7	2.9	95	1	1.1
Fibula	195	11	5.6	79	2	2.5
Patella	164	0	0.0	65	0	0.0
Metacarpal	856	6	0.7	297	1	0.3
Metatarsal	622	2	0.3	303	0	0.0
Phalange	1652	2	0.1	609	0	0.0
Total	4790	43	0.9	1878	6	0.3

A total of 6668 limb bones, exclusive of carpals and tarsals, were well enough preserved and complete to show whether they had ever been fractured. Of these, 49 (0.7%) had probably been broken; 45 indubitably so. Splitting for the sexes shows that the overall male fracture rate was three times that of the females for the bones recorded in Table 87.

Finally, something may be said about the treatment of these fractures since we can have little doubt that, for some or many of them, the victims would have sought help from medicus or quack. Fractures vary greatly in the amount of deformity, overlap, shortening, angulation, comminution, callus formation, etc. which they show and today it is well recognized that to achieve the best possible repair of a fracture demands a high level of surgical skill. All the Cirencester fractures are strongly healed: no case of non-union was detected. But some have healed in bad positions which would have led to functional impairment and limitation of use. And it must be said that in no case does the repair of any of these fractures seem to own anything to surgical expertise and endeavour. In all cases the final appearance is no better than would have been expected if they have been left to heal by the powers of unaided nature. Only those fractures in which the original deformity was trivial have repaired in good position. This is the usual finding in early populations (Wells, 1974b).

WEAPON WOUNDS

Weapon wounds can be divided, very broadly, into two main categories, (a) those caused by sharp weapons which incise the bone and (b) those caused by blunt instruments which dent, crack or splinter it. Usually the former are easier to recognize than the latter. In early communities a cleanly cut skull is unlikely to be caused by anything other than a sword, battle axe or similar weapon. A depressed fracture may have been due to some blunt weapon such as a club or hammer but it could also result from falling on to the head, from being accidentally hit by collapsing masonry or a broken tree branch, from being kicked by a horse, and many other mishaps. In the group under discussion both kinds of injury are found.

35. Inhumation 24, skull wound

At least eight, perhaps eleven persons, appear to have received incised wounds. Inh. 24 (♂), pl. 35, has a narrow wound across his frontal bone, surrounded by a rough area of periostitis which was no doubt due to an infection which accompanied the process of healing. We may note here, parenthetically, that it is rarely possible, in the absence of healing, to know whether a sharp incision was inflicted during life or soon after death. From their severity it is obvious that some wounds would be rapidly fatal (Wells, 1964, plate 20) but there is always the possibility that they were mutilations inflicted on a corpse. Inh. 81 (♂) has a more perplexing lesion. It is in the midline of the frontal bone and looks as though it may have been caused by an arrowhead or lance which lightly cut the bone in tangential flight. It is well healed with negligible evidence of adjacent infection. A similar uncertainty is found in Inh. 58 (♀) who had a wound, again well-healed, of her R. parietal. It does not greatly resemble a sword wound unless the weapon was most gently — almost caressingly! — wielded. It suggests, rather, the kind of injury which might have been inflicted by a garden trowel, a light kitchen chopping knife or even the sharp edge of a hurled platter. Inh. S (♂) has a triangular depressed area on the frontal bone which might, perhaps, be due to septic erosion and necrosis of the outer table from an infected scalp lesion such as a carbuncle. It is, however, more likely to be the result of some sharp sword or dagger thrust which removed a sliver of bone but which was eventually followed by healing with only slight deformity. With Inh. 101 (♂) we are on firmer ground.

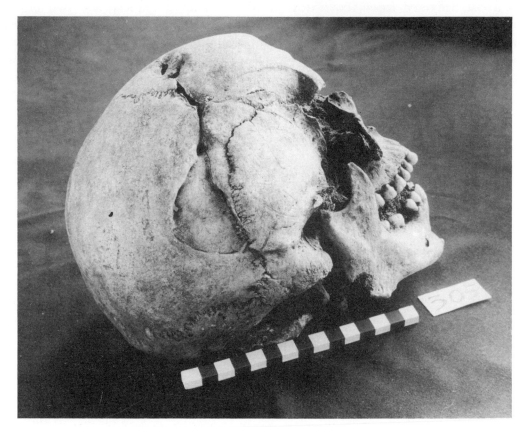

36. Inhumation 305, skull wound

37. Inhumation 305, skull wound

He has a cut delivered from above downward on to his L. parietal and two other, well separated, cuts delivered from his left on to his R. parietal. All three injuries are soundly healed and must have been inflicted months, probably years, before his death. Unfortunately it is impossible to know in what order they were incurred. Nor can one tell whether they were inflicted with long intervals between them or in quick succession during a single affray.

The most interesting of the cranial wounds is that of Inh. 305 (♂) pls. 36 and 37. This man had received a severe gash into his R. parietal which, as well as incising the bone, had fractured it so that a triangular area had become separated from the rest of the parietal and was depressed inwards towards the meninges. Despite the severity of the injury it eventually healed firmly but is likely to have caused various neurological after-effects. There is also an elliptical opening, with smoothly bevelled sides, in the superior part of his frontal bone. This appears to be a trephination. It was probably performed therapeutically in an attempt to relieve symptoms which had been caused by pressure on the brain from the depressed triangle of parietal. This case has been described in detail elsewhere (Wells, 1977).

In addition to these persons with cranial wounds four others have incised lesions of the limbs. Inh. 14 (♂) has a wound on the shaft of the R. humerus which was probably inflicted by a sword cut. A flake of cortex was lifted from the bone but it consolidated on to the shaft again and the lesion is now firmly healed. Inh. 288 (♂) has a closely similar wound just distal to the head of the L. tibia on the medial surface of the bone. In Inh. 21 (♂) a R. humerus has two cuts on its medial surface in mid-shaft. This is an exceedingly dangerous place in which to be wounded. Any incision which cut into the bone in this region would almost certainly sever the brachial artery — the main blood supply to the upper limb — with catastrophic haemorrhage. This seems to have happened in the present case because neither cut shows any trace of healing and it is likely that death ensued within a few minutes. It is worth noting that in hand to hand sword fights this is a very typical site in which to be injured. A man raising his right arm in order to strike a blow exposes the inner side of his humerus to a quick slash from a right-handed opponent.

An unusual lesion is seen in Inh. 163 (♂). A slice has been cleanly cut from the outer border of the lateral condyle of its L. femur. No trace of healing is present and death must have followed rapidly though it is likely that this was not, by itself, the lethal wound. Parts of this skeleton are missing or in poor condition and no evidence of other wounds can be detected.

Finally, Inh. D (♂) has already been mentioned in the section on Fractures, p. 162. The L. scapula has been smashed, probably as a result of a beating, but there is doubt about what weapon was used. At least part of this multiple injury seems to have been due to a moderately sharp implement.

Apart from the incised wounds which have been noted in this material there are several skeletons with injuries that were probably caused by blunt implements. Some of these (e.g. the cranial lesions of Inhs. 39(♂), 108(♂), 118(♂) and 165(♂) have already been described, p. 163). They are all ambiguous, however, and each could be the result either of accident or aggression. A few other more or less problematical lesions are present. Inh. 5(a) (♂) has a shallow depression, with evidence of mild infection, in the L. parietal; Inh. 23 (♀) has a dent on the L. side of her frontal bone. On balance it seems likely that both these injuries were more likely to be due to assault than to accident. A difficult case is that of Inh. 30 (♂) with linear lesions on both parietals, in each case with an irregular defect on the interior aspect of the skull. Unfortunately, here again some of the details are masked by post-inhumation damage. Finally Inh. 278 (♂) has two healed lesions on the left side of his frontal bone. No certainty is possible but in these cases, also, the weight of evidence suggests aggression rather than misadventure.

We have, then, a number of wounds which prove beyond all reasonable doubt that fighting — in battle, arena or "pub" — was a commonplace event with these people. In view of this we may be inclined to surmise that some of their more ambiguous lesions were also the legacies of assault rather than accident. Although many occupational or domestic mishaps can produce dents or cuts in the skull they are not, in fact, very frequent in such early communities as these Cirencester people. The cumulative effect of so many traumatic lesions which must or might have been due to aggression (there are at least twenty-five such injuries) suggests, rather com-

pellingly perhaps, that where ambiguity exists the cause is most likely to have been a deliberately inflicted wound — a view which is reinforced by the evidence that many of the simple
fractures here were also the result of aggression.

Finally, three more cases must be mentioned. Inh. 28 (♂) has a lesion of the R. tibia which
closely resembles what is seen when a varicose ulcer penetrates to the bone. But this man was
probably not much more than twenty-five years old, which is an unusually young age for
severe varicose ulceration, so it may be that his tibial lesion was the result of some kind of shin
wound, whether accidental or deliberate cannot be known. In Inh. 44 (♂) an exostosis is present
on the L. humerus. It was probably due to ossification of a blood clot after tearing a few muscle
fibres but the possibility of its having resulted from a wound cannot be entirely excluded.
Similarly, a penetrating wound of the joint giving rise to septic arthritis is a possible, though
somewhat unlikely, cause for the ankylosed left knee of Inh. 174 (♂).

38.   Inhumation 199, right tibia with up-turned spike

EXOSTOSES

Disregarding the osteophytes which are associated with joints, various kinds of exostoses are present. A probable thirty-one persons (27♂, 4♀) have about thirty-seven of these lesions (32 ♂, 5♀). In a few instances the cause of the exostosis is obvious, in some it cannot be determined, in most a plausible conjecture can be made.

Inhs. 61 (♂) and 276 (♂) each have an exostosis on two adjacent left middle ribs. In Inh. 61 they have grown towards each other to form a pseudarthrosis; in Inh. 276 they are sharp needle-like processes rising from the superior border of the ribs. Inh. 349 (♀) also has an exostosis on a left middle rib. In each of these five ribs the lesion has developed at the site of a fracture which was no doubt the cause of the exostosis. Inh. 183 (♂) has an exostosis arising from the medial surface of the left fibula in its distal third and another on the lateral surface of the left tibia. They have grown towards each other and form a pseudarthrosis articulating through a large flat surface about 35 x 26 mm across. They presumably result from a severe tear of the interosseous membrane which appears to have been due to a well-healed (?greenstick) fracture of the fibula. In Inh. 304 an exostosis has grown from the interosseous border of the left ulna and radius in the distal third of the bones but in this case pseudarthrosis has not developed between them. The cause here is probably another greenstick fracture involving both bones.

In all these cases it might be thought that the exostoses are merely surplus masses of callus from an over-exuberant repair of the bone. This is probably true of the rib exostoses but is unlikely in the case of the long bones where the original lesion could hardly have been much more than a fine crack in the cortex.

The commonest site for exostoses at Cirencester is the leg with six tibiae (5 ♂, 1 ♀) and three fibulae (♂) affected. But these lesions are not homogeneous and they probably represent slight differences in aetiology. Inh. 183 has been noted above. In Inhs. 14 (♂) and 256 (♂) the lesion is at the distal end of a tibia, in Inh. 62 (♂) it is distally on the left fibula. All these were probably due to tearing part of a ligament or the capsule of the joint. Two exostoses involve the proximal end of the leg — Inh. 145 (♂), left fibula, and Inh. 325 (♂) which has a small knob like an exostosis on the lateral condyle of the left tibia. Inh. 199 (♂) has two exostoses: one of which is on the infero-lateral border of the right patella. The other is an interesting lesion which arises from the anterior border of the right tibia about 85 mm proximal to the ankle, pl. 38. It is a stout up-curved spike, 10 mm broad, which curves proximally for 23 mm. It has the appearance of a miniature meat-hook and in this extremely vulnerable subcutaneous position it must have been an annoying disability for this man. He could hardly hope to perform much active work without repeatedly knocking it and breaking the overlying skin. A well marked periostitis is present on this bone and this probably represents a reaction to frequent episodes of minor infection consequent on damage to this bizarre lesion. That this happened and led to him to adopt some preventive measures is suggested by the fact that, adjacent to the exostosis, the bone is bronze stained. This was a rare finding at Cirencester and in this burial it is likely to be the result of wearing some sort of shin guard or protective covering in an attempt to prevent injury to the lesion. It is probable that, although they were caused in different ways, all these leg exostoses were in some way due to trauma.

An uncertain lesion is the exostosis of Inh. 146 (♀). This is on the left tibia in a mid-shaft position. This, too, might have been due to injury but the shaft of the bone is thickened and dilated by osteitis or a low grade osteomyelitis and it is possible that the exostosis was in some way an associated result of the infection and not precedent to it. The general impression given by these exostoses is of legs vigorously used and exposed to much stress. This is reinforced by a number of exostoses in the feet. Inh. 143 (♂) has one on the right calcaneus, Inh. 288 (♂) on the left navicular, Inh. 324/334 on the left first cuneiform. Inh. 273 (♀) has two lesions: one at the postero-medial angle of the right talus and one on the sustentaculum tali of the right calcaneus. All these foot exostoses are likely to be the result of torn ligaments after having wrenched the foot in some way. A small haemorrhage would occur at the site of the tear and after the blood had clotted "organization" of the clot would take place, i.e. it would be invaded by osteoblasts and converted into bone.

The only other exostosis of the lower limb is one on the left femur of Inh. 179 (δ). It is situated at the proximal end of the great trochanter and was probably due to a tear of the insertion of the Obturator internus, Gemelli and, or, the Piriformis muscles.

The only exostoses of the forearm are those noted above for Inh. 304. But three such lesions are present in the arm. Inh. 48 (δ) has one on the lesser tubercle of the right humerus which was probably due to a tear of the insertion of the subscapularis muscle during a violent attempt to draw the arm towards the trunk or to resist its abduction. Inh. 214 ($\circ$) has one at the distal part of the insertion of the left Deltoid which was probably due to tearing some of its fibres. A much more ambiguous lesion is present on the left humeral shaft of Inh. 44 (δ). This might have been due to tearing a muscle or, as mentioned on p. 172, it could perhaps have been the consequence of a penetrating wound of the bone.

In contrast to the scarcity of exostoses in the forearm they are relatively common in the hand. Six, perhaps seven, persons — all male — have them. In Inh. 3 the site is on the head of the right first metacarpal; and in Inh. 346 on the volar surface of the left third metacarpal. In Inhs. 10, 171 and 307 the exostoses are on proximal phalanges. All these lesions were probably due to various kinds of trauma and, cumulatively, they show the vulnerability of hands and fingers among these, as among most, people. Inh. 277 has a lesion on the head of the left first metacarpal but some doubt exists whether this is an exostosis or a simple osteoma.

Of the remaining four exostoses one (Inh. 113, δ) is on the medial end of the left clavicle and is likely to have been due to a tear of the capsule of the sterno-clavicular joint or its associated ligaments. The rest are pelvic lesions. Inh. 53 (δ) has an exostosis above the left acetabulum and Inh. 187 (δ) a craggy one on the left pubic ramus. The first probably developed from tearing a few fibres of the reflected tendon of the Rectus femoris muscle, the second from a tear of the origin of the Adductor longus. In Inh. 165 (δ) there is an exostosis of the left ilium which appears to have synostosed with the left ala of the sacrum. It is of uncertain aetiology but probably traumatic. Table 88 summarizes the distribution of these lesions.

Table 88: Distribution of exostoses

Inh.	Site of exostosis (Male)
3	R. 4th metacarpal
10	Proximal phalange, 3rd finger
14	L. tibia: distal end
44	L. humerus: shaft
48	R. humerus: lesser tubercle
53	L. acetabulum: superior border
61	L. 6th and 7th ribs
62	L. fibula: distal end
113	L. clavicle: medial end
143	R. calcaneus
145	L. fibula: 30 mm distal to head
165	L. ilium
171	R. 3rd finger: proximal phalange
179	L. femur: great trochanter
183	(a) L. tibia; (b) L. fibula
187	L. pubic ramus
199	(a) R. patella: inferior border; (b) R. tibia: anterior border
227	L. 1st metacarpal
256	R. tibia: distal malleolus
276	L. middle ribs (two)
288	L. navicular: supero-proximal border

(*contd.*) Inh.	Site of exostosis (Male) (CONTD.)
304	(a) L. radius; (b) L. ulna. Interosseous borders
307	Finger: proximal phalange
324/334	L. 1st cuneiform: distally
325	L. tibia: lateral condyle
331	R. 1st metacarpal: head
346	L. 3rd metacarpal: volar surface

Inh.	Site of exostosis (Female)
146	L. tibia: mid-shaft
214	L. humerus: deltoid insertion
273	(a) R. talus; (b) R. calcaneus: sustentaculum tali
349	L. middle rib

The overall evidence of these exostoses once again shows clearly that these people were exposed to many and varied stresses and injuries. Many of these lesions must have been due to violent muscle strains or to excessive demands made on the peri-articular ligaments. In view of this it is especially noteworthy that the men were much more liable to develop exostoses than the women. The evidence of osteoarthrosis leaves no doubt that the women were subject to much articular "wear and tear" but this is likely to have been due to relatively mild stresses distributed over many months or years. The evidence from exostoses reinforces that from fractures: that sudden violence and shock injuries were usually sustained by the men.

DISLOCATIONS

Clear evidence of dislocation has been identified in only two of the Cirencester skeletons: Inhs. 9 (♀) and 53 (♂). In Inh. 9 the glenoid fossa of the right scapula and the right humeral head have been almost destroyed by severe arthrosis and remodelling of the bone. A false joint has developed between the two bones on the antero-inferior surface of the neck of the scapula and there is little doubt that this was due to a chronic unreduced dislocation of the shoulder pls. 39–40. In Inh. 53 the left shoulder joint is severely arthrotic. The glenoid fossa is rough, ringed with osteophytes, and there is a craggy platform of bone, 37 x 35 mm, on the anterior surface of the scapula just medial to the articular surface. The left humeral head has suffered post-inhumation damage but it, too, is arthrotic and deformed. A make-shift joint was present between the two bones and it is certain that this was due to an unreduced chronic dislocation of the shoulder joint.

Both these cases must have had very severe limitation of movement at the affected joint and this is perhaps reflected in the extensive arthrosis that was present in their undislocated shoulders. This was presumably due to the additional stresses sustained by the unaffected joints. In Inh. 53, pl. 41, the left clavicle is smaller and lighter than the right, probably an atrophy due to disuse of the whole forequarter after dislocating his shoulder.

Dislocated shoulders are, of course, common mishaps which may result from various kinds of accidental falls or torsion of the arm. But they may also be due to deliberate acts of aggression in which the arm is violently twisted, usually behind the victim's back. There is no evidence in either of these cases to favour one or other of these possibilities.

A more puzzling lesion is present in Inh. 297 (♂). There is, again, well marked osteoarthrosis of the left shoulder joint but in this case the glenoid fossa does not face laterally, as is normal. It

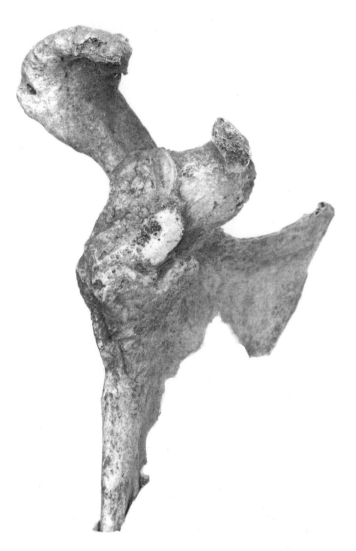

39.   Inhumation 9, lesion and dislocation of shoulder

is displaced and rotated backwards to face about forty degrees posteriorly. The remodelling of the bone does not appear to have been due to a fracture and it is uncertain whether a minor dislocation or subluxation was present.

Three adult males have a lesion which is not uncommon in early skeletons but which has received little attention from palaeopathologists. It consists of a defect in the rim of the acetabulum, usually in the supero-posterior quadrant. This defect, which may extend for 10–40 mm along the bone, takes the form of a flattened flange, usually 3–4 mm below the level of the unaffected part of the rim. It is sometimes referred to as "acetabular flange lesion". The cause of this defect is not fully understood but it seems likely that it is produced by a transient, incomplete, upward dislocation of the femoral head. The femur is usually unaffected in these cases but the acetabulum is damaged severely enough to leave permanent evidence of the event. At Cirencester Inh. 174 has a very mild lesion of this kind on the right acetabulum. Inh. 276 also has it on the right, with the flange extending for about 10 mm along the rim. In Inh. 336 it is the left side which is affected cind in this case both the acetabulum and the femoral head are mildly arthrotic. The lesion has been discussed and illustrated by Wells (1976).

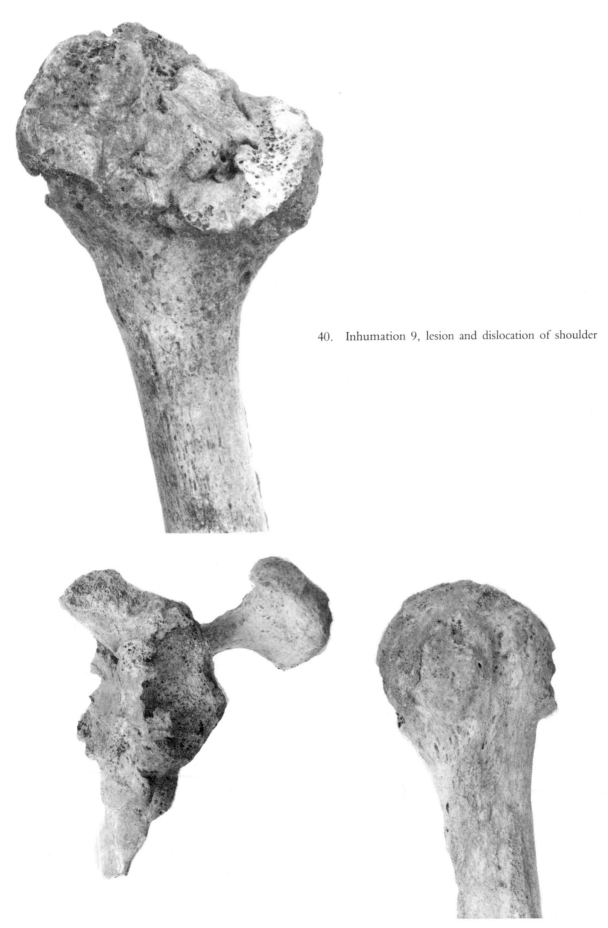

40. Inhumation 9, lesion and dislocation of shoulder

41. Inhumation 53, dislocated shoulder

OSTEOCHONDRITIS DISSECANS

Osteochondritis dissecans is a lesion of uncertian aetiology although it seems probable that trauma plays at least a contributory role in its onset. It consists of an aseptic necrosis of a small area of the articular cartilage of a joint, together with necrotic loss of the underlying bone. The condition is usually revealed by a pit in the bone but healing sometimes occurs and the cavity may be obscured by an infill of new osseous tissue. Occasionally this is too exhuberant and rises proud of the normal surface of the bone. The lesions vary in size from two or three millimetres in diameter to about twenty or twenty-five in the largest examples. It is seldom more than about eight millimetres deep. Osteochondritis is extremely common in modern clinical practice. It almost always starts between the ages of twelve and eighteen years, and about 85 per cent of all lesions occur in the femoral condyles, usually the medial one, where it is the commonest cause of a foreign body in the knee joint — a "joint mouse". Apart from the femoral condyles it is found in the talus and less frequently in the elbow or other joints.

A few sporadic cases of osteochondritis have been recorded in the literature of palaeopathology, e.g. by Perrot (1976) but the only general review of the disease is a brief article by Wells (1974c).

In early populations its femoral site of election is much less obtrusive than in modern orthopaedic practice and a wide scatter of other joints is commonly affected. This is well shown in this series of skeletons. Thirty-nine persons (25♂, 11♀, 3 juv.) had one or more osteochondritic lesions. It is a condition which tends to be bilaterally symmetrical and it was so here in at least seven persons (3♂, 3♀, 1 juv.). (Others may have had symmetrical lesions which are not now detectable owing to loss or damage of one of the pair of bones). Of the men, Inh. 222 had it bilaterally in the tibial condyles, Inh. 313 in the sustentacula tali of his calcanei, and Inh. 322 in the glenoid fossae of his scapulae. Of the women, Inh. 257 had a lesion in the distal articular surface of each tibia and Inh. 312 had one in the base of her hallucial proximal phalanges. The juvenile Inh. 57 had it in the femoral condyles.

But apart from their frequent bilateral symmetry osteochondritic lesions are often multiple without being symmetrical. Inh. 167 (♂) has a distal tibial and also a calcaneal lesion; Inh. 216 (♂) has a lesion of the axis and of the base of the L. 1st metatarsal; and Inh. 222 (♂) has a lesion of the head of the L. 1st metatarsal in addition to his bilateral tibial pitting. Inh. 127 (♀) has a lesion of the R. talus and R. calcaneus; Inh. 332 (♀) has lesions of the R. 1st metatarsal base and of the R. hallucial proximal phalange; whilst Inh. 312 (♀), in addition to her symmetrical phalangeal lesions, has an osteochondritic pit in her L. scapula, L. femoral medial condyle, L. patella and L. tibial head.

It is impossible to determine to which side two damaged phalanges belong. Of the remaining fifty-six lesions, twenty-eight occur on the left and twenty-eight on the right. The most commonly affected bone is the femur with one lesion proximally and ten distally. The distal lesions occur on the medial condyle (5), the lateral condyle (2) and the intercondylar patellar surface (3). Six scapular lesions occur, of which five are on the left. When osteochondritis affects the intervertebral articular facets this is almost always in the cervical region of the column. Cirencester is no exception to this rule. In both Inh. 71 (♂) and 216 (♂) the lesion is on the axis, in Inh. 322 (♂) it is on the C4.

The commonest single joint to be affected in this series is the knee, of which twelve (6♂, 4♀, 2 juv.) have a total of fourteen bones involved. But considered as a unit the foot is decidedly more vulnerable. Twenty-one persons (14♂, 7♀) have osteochondritic lesions of their feet, with a total of twenty-six joint surfaces affected (16♂, 10♀). This shows that 44.8% of all lesions occurred in the foot, compared with only 24.1% in the knee. These figures exclude the six persons (4♂, 1♀, 1 juv.) with osteochondritis of the ankle, of whom Inh. 257 (♀) had it bilaterally. In Inh. 354, a juvenile aged 15–16 years, the osteochondritic pit occurred in the unfused distal epiphysis of the R. tibia.

Five (8.6%) of the lesions had healed and what was originally a pit became filled with new bone which was raised about ½–1 mm above the normal articular surface. These four cases are the L. scapula of Inh. 261 (♂), the medial femoral condyles of Inhs. 262 (♀) and 312 (♀), and the L. femoral head of Inh. 331 (♂). This 8.6% repair rate is not an unusual frequency for early populations.

The uncertain aetiology of osteochondritis dissecans makes it impossible to interpret these lesions with assurance. It is likely, however, that they reflect, to some extent, stress conditions occurring especially in adolescence. If so we must infer that for some reason or other young persons of both sexes were required to use their feet and knees for vigorous and sometimes traumatic occupations. Also that their shoulder joints were often subjected to strains from which their musculature was not yet strong enough to protect them. The numbers are few but in this connection it may be relevant that of the six affected shoulders five (88.3%) were on the left side.

Table 89 summarizes the distribution of osteochondritis.

Table 89: Distribution of osteochondritis dissecans

A. Males

Inh.	Site of lesions
71	Axis: R. superior facet
112	R. Femur: lateral condyle
140	L. Scapula
167	(a) R. tibia: distal; (b) R. calcaneus: posterior articular surface
179	R. talus: posterior inferior articulation
184	L. calcaneus: posterior articular surface
186	R. calcaneus: sustentaculum
199	R. femur: medial condyle
207	L. scapula
208	R. talus: trochlear surface
210(a)	L. femur: mid-condylar
216	(a) axis: L. superior facet; (b) L. 1st metatarsal: base
222	(a) L. tibia: lateral condyle; (b) R. tibia: lateral condyle; (c) L. 1st metatarsal: head
227	L. tibia: distal
261	L. scapula
263	R. 1st metatarsal: base
280	R. femur: medial condyle
287	R. 1st metatarsal: base
302	L. talus: trochlear surface
305	L. navicular: proximal surface
309	R. hallucial proximal phalange: base
313	L. & R. calcanei: sustentacula
322	(a) L. scapula; (b) R. scapula; (c) C4 vertebra: L. superior facet; (d) C4 vertebra: R. superior facet; (e) R. hallucial proximal phalange: base
331	L. femur: head
333	Hallucial proximal phalange: base

B. Females

Inh.	Site of lesions
46	L. femur: lateral condyle
56	L. 1st metatarsal: head
103	L. talus: posterior inferior articulation

B. Females (*contd.*)

Inh.	Site of lesions
127	(a) R. talus: posterior inferior articulation; (b) R. calcaneus: sustentaculum
255	R. talus: posterior inferior articulation
257	(a) L. tibia: distal; (b) R. tibia: distal
262	(a) L. femur: medial condyle; (b) R. femur: medial condyle
269	L. acetabulum
312	(a) L. femur: medial condyle; (b) L. patella; (c) L. tibia: lateral condyle; (d) L. hallucial proximal phalange: base; (e) R. hallucial proximal phalange: base; (f) L. scapula
332	(a) R. 1st metatarsal: base; (b) R. hallucial proximal phalange: base
334	Hallucial proximal phalange: base

C. Juveniles

Inh.	Age	Site of lesions
57	16	(a) L. femur: mid-condylar; (b) R. femur: mid-condylar
138	12–13	Mandible: R. condyle
354	15–16	R. tibia: distal

Table 90 sums up the distribution of these lesions.

Table 90: Osteochondritis: affected joints and bones

Location	n
Knee joint	14
Hallucial proximal phalange	7
Talus: trochlear and inferior surface	6
Shoulder joint	6
Ankle joint	5
1st metatarsal	6
Vertebrae	4
Calcaneus	6
Hip joint	2
Mandible	1
Navicular	1

It will be seen that 47 (81.0%) of these lesions are in the lower limb. This is a normal finding. The lesions vary in size from small pits only 3–4 mm in diameter to cavities 8–10 mm across. In seven instances paired lesions occurring on the left and right were present. In a few cases partial or complete healing has occurred — i.e. the osteochondritic cavity has been filled with regenerated bone. In modern clinical practice untreated osteochondritis dissecans often progresses to give arthrotic changes in the joint. At Cirencester there was little evidence of this.

INFECTIONS

There is often much ambiguity in the diagnosis of infections in early skeletons. Some are easy and self-evident, such as paradontal abscesses or flamboyant cases of leprosy and osteomyelitis. But the latter two diseases tend to be somewhat limited in the areas and especially the periods of their most obtrusive occurrence. A major difficulty with ancient material is to know whether a bone which shows strong evidence of periostitis or osteitis was, in fact, infected or whether the abnormal response was due to some other cause such as trauma. Apart from paradontal disease, which is dealt with in the section on teeth, there is very little unequivocal evidence of infection in the Cirencester skeletons.

Of the specific infections it can be said at once that there is no evidence to suggest that any of these persons had leprosy or syphilis. A few lesions, e.g. the synostosed phalanges of Inhs. 333 (♂) and 338 (♂) are common in leprosy but the overall evidence of these skeletons is quite insufficient to sustain the diagnosis and it seems probable that neither this disease nor syphilis was present in the Cirencester population.

The problem of tuberculosis is less easily resolved. Most untreated cases of leprosy and syphilis eventually affect bones and thus become skeletally recognizable. Most cases of tuberculosis do not and therefore remain elusive. The lungs, lymph glands, kidneys, meninges, skin, peritoneum and other soft tissues may be affected without osseous involvement. (Different strains of organism are concerned). The most likely case of tubercular infection here is Inh. S (♂), a man aged about twenty to twenty-one, whose first lumbar vertebra showed a type of cavitation and collapse similar to that which is often found in Pott's disease (tuberculosis of the spine). However, staphylococcal, mycotic and other infecting organisms might produce an identical appearance and, on the basis of this specimen, it would not be justifiable to assert that tuberculosis was present among these people. A few other cases could perhaps have been caused by this disease, e.g. the anklyosed knee joint of Inh. 174 (♂) or the disorganised ankle of Inh. 17 (♂), but both these are extremely unlikely diagnoses and the possibility of tuberculosis at Cirencester must rest on the insecure evidence of Inh. S.

A no less difficult problem arises with poliomyelitis. At least four persons, Inh. 23 (♀), 101 (♂), 305 (♂) and 312 (♀), had unilateral atrophy of a limb which could typically have been caused by this disease. In Inh. 23 the R. humerus and ulna are smaller than those of the left side. In Inhs. 305 and 312 the L. humerus, ulna and clavicle are smaller than those on the right. The differences are well marked in both skeletons but in neither of them can the full extent of the lesions be assessed owing to post-inhumation damage. A number of other possible explanations for these deformities might be proposed, e.g. that their arms were damaged during a difficult delivery when these persons were born. This would be especially likely to happen if they had been breech births. But no other evidence is available to support this and an attack of anterior poliomyelitis in middle childhood remains, perhaps, the most likely diagnosis. The same element of doubt applies to Inh. 101 whose left humerus, ulna and radius are similarly smaller than the bones of his right arm. In his case, however, still another possibility must be considered. He had several head wounds which seem to have been inflicted long before death and his diminished left arm (including its musculature) may have been a neurological consequence of severe intracranial injury. Nevertheless the cumulative impression of four cases of unilateral limb atrophy goes some way to suggest that poliomyelitis was indeed present among these persons.

With sinusitis we are on firmer ground. A maxillary antrum which is rough and pitted by osteitis, sometimes with a fistula draining from it into the roof of the mouth, is clear evidence of an infected sinus.

No doubt most cases of sinusitis begin by extension of a nasal infection. In many early communities the ordinary living quarters consisted of a small hut with central, open hearth and poor ventilation. Under such conditions irritant smoke from the fire would have provoked much coughing and sneezing. Inevitably droplet infections of viruses and streptococci would have passed from one occupant to another, with sinusitis as a common result. This would especially happen in regions where for much of the year the climate was cold and damp. The sinusitis, in turn, must sometimes have led to chronic respiratory infections, such as bronchitis, which would undoubtedly have been a not infrequent cause of premature death.

At Cirencester at least seven persons (4♂, 3♀) showed evidence of antral infections. As far as one can tell the disease usually began in the maxillary sinuses and remained localized there. But in Inh. 327 (♀) an alternative mode of onset can be seen. A large periodontal abscess was present in the alveolus around the maxillary left first molar and instead of discharging adequately into the mouth it formed a fistula going upward to discharge into the antrum, which subsequently became chronically infected. A similar fistula is present in Inh. 333 (♂) but in this case an extensive bony reaction occurred round its orifice in the sinus, with the formation of a large collar of bone about 27 mm high inside the cavity and surrounding the fistula.

Osteomyelitis is uncommon in most early burial grounds. This is in marked contrast to what is found in post-medieval cemeteries where the rapid rise in the frequency of this disease is exceeded only by that of rickets. At Cirencester only one case, Inh. 146 (♀), can be identified and even this is open to some slight doubt. When it is not the result of an open wound of the bone, perhaps even penetrating to the marrow cavity, osteomyelitis is usually due to a blood borne staphylococcal infection. It is a disease of bad hygiene and poor living conditions such as were typical of urban slums under the first impact of the industrial revolution. Although exceptions to this are often found its absence from the Cirencester group indicates a moderately good standard of living, including nutrition and general hygiene.

A few cases of periostitis, probably the result of infection after an open wound, have been noted in the section on wounds and no further comment on these is needed here.

A curious lesion is that of the R. ischial tuberosity of Inh. 213 (♂). The bone, which is rough and craggy, appears to have been the site of a chronic bursitis of the kind commonly known as "weaver's bottom" on account of its being an occupational hazard of this trade. In the present case it is difficult to decide whether the reaction was associated with an infection or whether the lesion is wholly traumatic in origin.

Perhaps the most perplexing, certainly the most interesting, lesions of this kind are the cases of periostitis or osteitis of the tibiae and fibulae. This is a well known lesion in early skeletons where it is characterized by a "grained" or "fluted" appearance of the leg bones. Slight cortical thickening is the rule but this is not invariably present though sometimes it may be extensive and must be called an osteitis rather than a simple periostitis. No rigid distinction can be drawn in practice: the one condition merges imperceptibly into the other. The lesion usually involves the medial (i.e. subcutaneous) and lateral (i.e. interosseous) surfaces of the tibia but is mostly absent or extremely slight on the posterior surface. When present the lesion commonly involves the middle three-fifths of the bone, sometimes more. Occasionally less than a quarter of the shaft is affected. The fibula is concurrently involved in about half the cases. When present the lesion has a strong tendency to be bilateral. Although sometimes found in juveniles it is rare in young children. At least 95 per cent of cases occur in full adults. In some early groups these periosteitic or osteitic legs are found in 10–20 per cent of the skeletons: sometimes more. One of the difficulties in interpreting this pathology is that it seems to be a disease unknown in modern clinical practice. There is certainly nothing like it which occurs with similar frequency.

In the group south of the Fosse twenty-six persons (18♂, 7♀, 1 unsexed) have these leg lesions which involve fifty-three bones (36 tibiae, 17 fibulae). All are adult except the unsexed person Inh. 63, an adolescent aged 12–13, and Inh. 57 (♂), a youth aged sixteen years. However, in both these juveniles the lesion is slightly atypical and they should probably be excluded from the rest of the group. In Inh. 63 strong evidence of trauma is present; in Inh. 57 Osgood-Schlatter's disease may account for the pathology. The woman Inh. 197 ought also to be removed from this group. A localised area of periostitis on her left tibia, which is small (40 x 15 mm) and narrowly circumscribed, strongly suggests that it was due to an infected ulcer penetrating to the bone through the overlying tissues. If so, this could have been a chronic varicose ulcer or the result of simple trauma. Inh. 28 (♂) has an even more convincing varicose ulcer lesion of the right tibia.

Discarding these four cases leaves forty-eight leg bones with periostitis (or a low grade osteitis). Only tibiae and fibulae are affected: the disease seems never to involve the upper limbs or feet. Owing to the poor state of the Cirencester material, with many of the leg bones fragmentary and eroded, it is impossible to estimate the frequency of this lesion with any confidence but it seems likely that it occurs in about 10–12 per cent of the adult tibiae, with little difference between the sexes. A clinician must inevitably wonder what symptoms were present during life and what limitation of activity these lesions imposed on the sufferers. No guidance can be found in the extensive early medical texts but it should be said that in the limited number of modern diseases which produce periostitis of the shin the bone is usually exquisitely painful to touch, leg movement much limited and general malaise often obtrusive. The aetiology of these lesions is so uncertain that we cannot even be sure whether they were due to some infection such as a relatively non-virulent staphylococcus or whether they are inflammatory reactions of a non-infective type. They are also found, with widely different frequencies, in various Iron Age, Gallo-Roman, Anglo-Saxon, Merovingian, Ancient Egyptian, American Indian and other populations, so it is probable that they reflect a pathology of multiple causation. Even so it is also likely that most of the Cirencester examples are the result of a single causal agent.

Three persons have well marked periosteitic lesions in the hand. Inh. 322 (♂) has an affected R. 5th metacarpal; whilst Inh. 188 (♂) has three proximal phalanges and Inh. 140 (♂) has two middle phalanges affected — one of the latter having had its head partly destroyed by the lesion. All three cases reflect the vulnerability of the hand and its susceptibility to infection. Inh. 140 has a lesion which may sometimes be produced by a severe and long continued whitlow.

NEOPLASMS

Not more than six persons (4♂, 2♀) have neoplastic lesions and in four or five of these the tumour is nothing more than a simple ivory or "button" osteoma — if these can properly be called neoplasms.

Inh. 163 (♂) has an ivory osteoma, 9 mm in diameter, on the left side of the frontal bone; Inh. 311 (♀) has a similar but smaller one on the right parietal. Both Inhs. 198 (♂) and 304 (♂) have an osteoma in the floor of an acetabulum. That of 304 is 8 mm in diameter. It is of interest that in Inh. 198, a man aged 40–50, very slight osteoarthrosis was present in the affected left hip joint (on both bones), whereas in Inh. 304, a younger man aged about 27–35, no arthrotic changes were found in his right hip in spite of the size of the osteoma. Inh. 227 (♂) had a small, 7 x 5 mm, tumour on the head of the left first metacarpal. It is uncertain whether this is a true osteoma or an exostosis. If the latter, it was probably traumatic in origin from a torn ligament or a misdirected hammer blow. Whatever its status may be there can be little doubt from its size and position that it would have substantially limited the functioning of the metacarpo-phalangeal joint. In addition to her parietal osteoma Inh. 311 has a small mass of bone which blocks about half the orifice of her left external auditory meatus. It is perhaps a matter of indifference whether this should be called an osteoma or a torus auditivus. Finally, Inh. 314 (♀) has an unusual lesion in the left maxilla, just below the orbital border. It consists of a small cavity in the bone, about 6 mm diameter. Some post-inhumation roughening obliterates the finer details but it has a slightly raised margin. Whether this is due to osteoblastic activity or to passive expansion of the bone from whatever growth or cyst made the cavity is uncertain. The lesion bears some resemblance to a secondary malignant deposit of low virulence but a firm diagnosis does not seem to be possible.

SYNOSTOSES

In several inhumations synostosis (ankylosis) of two or more bones is present. The commonest location for this is the spinal column, which is affected by different synostosing pathologies in not less than seven persons. Osteoarthrosis of the posterior intervertebral joints has fused C2/3 in Inh. 73 (♂); C3/4 in Inhs. 184 (♂) and 210(a) (♂); and T3/4 in Inh. 274 (♀). The C2/3 vertebrae of Inh. 73 are also fused by osteophytosis of their bodies. And Inh. 210(a) has a second pair of fused segments, L5/S1, also due to osteophytosis of their bodies. In Inh. 288 (♂)

the T3/4 are ankylosed but in this case the synostosis is the result of a fracture of the laminae of T3. The vertebrae are fused by their spinous processes and by their bodies at the left costal facets, with the T3 tilted slightly downwards to the left on the T4. In Inh. 190 (♀) the C2/3 are fused by their posterior intervertebral joints and also by their arches but in this case there is no evidence of fracture or other pathology. The synostosis appears to be congenital, as a result of incomplete segmentation of the spinal column at this level. Finally, Inh. 191 (♀) has lumbo-sacral fusion. This, too, appears to be a congenital abnormality. The woman had six lumbar vertebrae and the L6 is fused to the right ala of the sacrum. This vertebra is wedge-shaped, narrow to the left, and also has a supernumerary articulation (which is not ankylosed) with the left sacral ala.

42.   Inhumation 174, ankylosed knee

As well as his two pairs of fused vertebrae Inh. 210(a) has synostosis of the left and right sacroiliac joints. Apart from the synostosis there is no visible pathology to indicate its cause. But in Inh. 208 (♂) there is severe osteoarthrosis of the iliac surface of the right sacro–iliac joint. The sacrum is missing but the damaged iliac osteophytes show that the two bones had become ankylosed during life. The sacrum of Inh. 165 (♂), though present, is considerably damaged but it seems to have been fused to the left ilium. In this case the cause was an exostosis of the ilium which articulated with the left sacral ala and had seemingly became synostosed with it.

Apart from these vertebral and sacroiliac lesions few other examples of ankylosis are recognizable. Inh. 320 (♂) has fusion of the left fourth and fifth ribs along 45 mm lateral to their necks. There is no clear evidence of fracture or other pathology and the condition is apparently congenital. Inh. 272 (♂) has the left tibia and fibula united by an excess of callus after a simple Pott's fracture of the fibula. The fusion of the two bones extends for 42 mm in the distal quarter of the leg. A more ambiguous lesion is present in Inh. 174 (♂), pls. 42, 43. Here the left femur, patella and tibia are firmly ankylosed with the leg forming an angle of about 80°–85° on the thigh. There is, again, no clear evidence of fracture here but extensive periostitis of the left femoral shaft is present with mild inflammatory changes in the tibia. Apart from the ankylosis there is no great deformity of the joint and its cause must remain uncertain. It was probably infective in origin but the causal organism can only be surmised. Tuberculosis is an unlikely possibility. A more probable origin would be a penetrating wound of the joint. There is some evidence that this lesion was present several years before death. It would have been impossible for this man to have walked and unless he hopped on his sound limb he would have been committed to the use of some kind of crutch or peg-leg.

Inh. 278 (♂) has extensive pathological changes in both feet. These largely consist of destruction of the bases of heads of metatarsals from gout but both tarsalia and metatarsalia are extensively affected by osteoarthrosis and there is synostosis of the left cuboid with the fifth metatarsal, and of the third cuneiform with the fourth metatarsal. Severe limitation of function must have resulted from these lesions and it is likely that walking would have been almost impossible at times.

Finally, two men, Inhs. 333 and 338 had ankylosis of a middle to a distal toe phalange. In neither is it possible to determine the cause though trauma, perhaps with a hair-line fracture involving the joint, is a likely possibility.

Excluding congenital fusion, these synostoses are mostly the expression of different kinds of stress and trauma. In this they reinforce the overall evidence of the Cirencester skeletons that these persons led an active and vigorous life, with a wide range of physical occupations which would impose much strain on their joint surfaces and the surrounding ligamentous capsule.

43. Inhumation 174, ankylosed knee

CRIBRA ORBITALIA

Cribra orbitalia is a common lesion in many early populations. It was first extensively studied by Welcker (1888) since when much debate and numerous articles have been devoted to it. This was largely because its aetiology and significance were unknown and it therefore became the focus of conflicting theories. Even today there are different views about it, and it undoubtedly presents a variety of problems. However, a wide concensus of opinion now believes that cribra orbitalia (like cribra cranii or porotic hyperostosis) is an expression of an iron-deficiency anaemia. In its early stages it takes the form of a fine sieve-like pitting in the roof of the orbit, usually towards the lateral side. At a later stage the pitting becomes coarser, with a reticulum of new bone between the holes, whilst the affected area of the orbit becomes thickened. The lesion is usually bilateral and is more common in children than adults. It often accompanies the cribra parietalis, cribra frontalis, etc. of porotic hyperostosis which, in various early populations, are manifestations of iron-deficiency anaemias such as those induced by thalassaemia (Cooley's syndrome), sickle-cell disease, and sphaerocytosis. In its earliest stages cribra orbitalia may be difficult to distinguish from the fine punctate pitting or 'pseudopathology" produced by post-inhumation erosion of the orbital roof. Cirencester has several cases in which this uncertainty exists.

It seems likely that cribra orbitalia is present in thirty-five persons (20 ♂, 7♀, 8 juveniles), who between them have fifty-three affected orbits. Of these fifty-three lesions forty-seven (88.7%) are very mild. A few are so slight that it is difficult to be sure that they are true cases of cribra. Six (11.3%) are slightly more advanced and can be classified as of second degree on a six degree scale. In adult skulls 226 orbits are well enough preserved to reveal the presence or absence of cribra and in these skulls forty (17.7%) orbits have the disease. In the thirty-five persons who are affected by the condition both sides are available for inspection in twenty-three cases. In twelve cases only one orbit is present. When both orbits are present the lesion is bilateral in eighteen (78.3%), unilateral in five (21.7%). All cases in which it was unilateral were very early lesions. In any skull where the disease was clearly established the lesions were always bilateral and all juvenile cases were bilateral. It is interesting to see that, at Cirencester, cribra orbitalia was about fifty per cent more common among the men than the women. Males have thirty (19.9%) affected orbits out of 151 available for inspection; females have ten (13.3%) out of seventy-five. The thirteen lesions among juveniles were noted from thirty-seven orbits, a frequency of 35.1%.

These findings need to be interpreted with caution. If the current view of the aetiology of cribra orbitalia is correct its occurrence at Cirencester must indicate that iron-deficiency anaemia was widespread in these people, even if not severe. The reason for the anaemia is obscure. No hint of such causal agents as Cooley's syndrome is present here and genetic anomalies of this kind need hardly be considered. The cause is more likely to be found in a dietary deficiency. But the nature of this is problematical. It is likely that their water was somewhat lacking in iron salts: much of it was probably derived from shallow surface supplies which were intermittently rain-fed. To envisage a deficiency of iron severe enough to produce anaemia we must postulate that the diet of these persons contained inadequate amounts of green vegetables and of meat. This may have been the case. On the other hand the overall physical development of these men and women suggests that they enjoyed a moderately abundant and well-balanced diet. A further difficulty is to understand why the men have a higher frequency of cribra than the women. Does this imply that, by reason of being mistresses of the kitchen, the women and girls were free to filch choice morsels from the stewpot and to maintain a level of flesh and protein intake which gave them some protection against anaemia — a protection denied to the men whose daily work and relaxation took them away from the home?

The much higher incidence of cribra in the orbits of the children is an almost universal finding in early communities. But this, too, poses difficulties. Apart from any problems about its cause, what were its effects? Does the higher juvenile rate imply that this was often a lethal condition from which they died young, or was it a self-limiting syndrome from which most of them recovered, leaving fewer traces of its existence in the adults?

Parenthetically here, it may be of interest to note evidence from the temple of Nodens, at Lydney, Gloucestershire, which is not far from Cirencester. At this site the *ex voto* of a hand has been found which shows the condition of koilonychia — dorsally concave or spoon-shaped finger nails. This syndrome is a well known result of iron-deficiency anaemia and it is possible that the votive was presented to the temple by someone — perhaps from Cirencester! — who suffered from anaemia. The shrine was situated beside a deposit of ferruginous gravel which was mined for iron ore in Roman times and from which iron impregnated water still drips. Drinking this in small quantities would undoubtedly have had excellent therapeutic effects on anyone with a low haemoglobin level or a diminished red cell count — and presumably on any sufferer from cribra orbitalia.

MISCELLANEOUS LESIONS

Several of the Cirencester skeletons show a variety of lesions which do not fit comfortably into any of the previous sections. There is a wide range of this unclassified pathology and whilst some of the abnormalities are well known, others are of uncertain aetiology and not properly understood.

Inh. 3 (♂) has an irregular area for the insertion of the Biceps brachii muscle on the right radius. It was probably due to tearing some fibres of the tendon when, contrary to his custom, he was called upon to lift a very heavy weight, perhaps, or trying to restrain a violently cantankerous horse. A closely similar condition is present on the right radius of Inh. 208 (♂). It is possible, however, that this craggy bicipital tuberosity was partly due to an extremely powerful development of this man's Brachialis and Biceps muscles and that his occupation had been one involving the habitual carrying of extremely heavy burdens.

A number of vertebral anomalies are present. Inh. 103 (♀) has an L5 which, viewed from the front, is wedge-shaped with its narrow side to the right. The sacrum is scoliotic in this skeleton and the L5 defect appears to be partly compensatory for this. Several large Schmorl's nodes are present higher up the column but no other significant abnormality. Inh. 168 (♀) also has a wedge-shaped L5, narrow to the left. In this case it has a large lateral mass articulating with a facet, 29 x 21 mm, on the right ala of the sacrum. This was presumably a developmental defect. In Inh. 191 (♀) a somewhat similar condition exists, but here it is an extra, or L6, vertebra which is wedge-shaped with the narrowing to the left. It articulates through a supernumerary facet with the left sacral ala and is fused with the sacrum on the right. Inh. 224 (♂) has slight anterior wedging of the T8 and T9 which gave a slight forward bowing of the spine. In Inh. 307 (♂) the atlas is asymmetrical, with two occipital facets on the right, one on the left. This was no doubt a congenital anomaly. Inh. 349 (♀) has severe scoliosis (lateral curvature) of the spinal column, concave to the left, with advanced wedging of the T7 to T10 vertebrae and accompanying osteophytosis. This could have been a developmental orthopaedic defect which became slowly progressive during childhood and early adult life. Two sacra are of especial interest. In Inh. 55 a lip of bone protrudes from the right side of the sacral promontory. And in Inh. 324/334 there is a six-piece sacrum which has a slight collapse or non-development of the S3 segment. This is an unusual lesion which is probably due to a developmental anomaly in childhood. In this skeleton there is also a partial collapse of the T9 vertebra.

Three persons had unusual anomalies of ribs. Inh. 9 (♀) has a right middle rib with a deformity of the body. The bone is depressed and bowed inwards towards the pleura, the pleural surface of the rib being longitudinally ridged. In Inh. 206 (♂) at least eight ribs have borders which are very slightly sinuous. It is just possible that this could be due to the serious congenital defect of coarctation of the aorta — probably in a mild form. In Inh. 288 (♂) at least nine ribs (5L., 4R.) have a slightly sigmoid torsion between the head and the body. In each of these three cases the interpretation of the lesion is extremely ambiguous.

Both Inhs. 3 (♂) and 213 (♂) have a cavity immediately above the left acetabulum. The larger of the two (Inh. 213) measures about 22 x 22 mm. These lesions are not uncommon in early skeletons although they have attracted little interest from palaeopathologists. Their aetiology is uncertain but is probably traumatic. They have been discussed and illustrated by Wells (1976). Inh. 213 also has the ischial irregularity which, because of its frequent occupational origin, is commonly known as "weaver's bottom". It is a form of bursitis which can be caused in various ways. The present case is slightly ambiguous and is briefly noted in the section on infections.

44.   Inhumation 134, hole in scapula

Various exostoses, osteophytoses and other examples of remodelled bone have already been recorded above. A few more remain to be noted here. Inh. 48 (♂) has an elongated broad process of bone which projects medially and posteriorly from the spine of each ilium. It probably represents an ossification of the anterior part of the sacrospinous ligament, though it is uncertain why this should have occurred. In Inh. 64 (♂) there is a small elevated irregularity on the head of the right femur. It does not greatly resemble a healed osteochondritis and is perhaps due to an intra-articular inflammatory lesion of the synovial membrane — a synovitis of the joint. An unusual appearance is shown by the right calcaneus of Inh. 75 (♂). It has a large vault or overhang which projects laterally over the groove for the tendon of the Peroneus longus muscle. It is about 25 mm long and projects 12 mm beyond the normal surface of the bone. Inh. 142 (♂), a skeleton with a large left third femoral trochanter, also has a slight irregularity of the lateral epicondylar ridge of the right humerus. This may have been due to tearing some of the fibres of the muscles of the forearm when performing some violent movement involving the wrist and hand. In Inh. 307 (♂) there is a small remodelled area at the distal extremity of the sustentaculum tali of the R. calcaneus and also of the proximal border of the R. navicular. This is more likely to be the result of a torn ligament than of anything else. Inh. 335 (♂) has an area of low roughness involving the superior non-articular surface of the left talus but this is almost certainly due to trauma and tearing some of the ligamentous fibres of the ankle joint, consequent on the fracture of the fibula which this man sustained and its associated joint damage.

    A different form of anomaly is seen in Inh. 247 (♂). Here the right navicular has a strongly developed supernumerary facet on its tuberosity for the insertion of an extension of the tendon of the Tibialis posterior muscle. This foot also has well marked bowing, concave medially, of the fifth metatarsal which is likely to be the result of habitually wearing a sandal with a very tight thong, or some equivalently constricting footwear.

45. Inhumation 182

Inh. 312 (♀) has been noted above as a possible case of poliomyelitis. She also had severe osteoarthrosis, with eburnation of the head of her right second metatarsal and the base of its proximal phalange. The deformity of these bones makes it almost certain that she suffered from a cocked up "hammer toe". Another person with lesions of the phalanges is Inh. 252 (♀). This woman had a cupped deformity at the base of at least three distal finger phalanges. They are typical of the changes produced by Heberden's nodes.

A perplexing and unusual lesion is seen in Inh. 134. (♂), pl. 44. A small pit, 9 x 12 mm, with a low raised rim is present in the superior surface of the right scapular spine. It lies across the whole breadth of the spine and extends slightly above it to intrude for about 2 mm into the supraspinous fossa. This lesion may perhaps have been caused by tearing part of the origin of the Deltoid muscle or the tendon of insertion of the Trapezius.

A striking pathological change is found in Inh. 182 (♀), pl. 45. This woman has very severe osteoarthrosis of both hip joints. The right acetabulum surrounds the femoral head with a tight collar of lipping so that the two bones cannot be disarticulated. The femur can be moved in the socket only between about 85°–120° of flexion. The left hip must have been very similar but post-inhumation damage now allows the two bones to be separated. These hips also show the condition known as Otto's disease, in which the floor of the acetabulum bulges medially into the pelvic cavity — in this case to a depth of 13 mm. If the permanent flexion and extremely

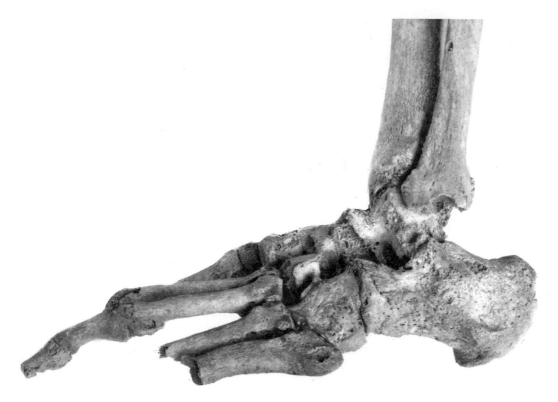

46. Inhumation 42, right foot with extensive cavitation around the ankle joint due to gout

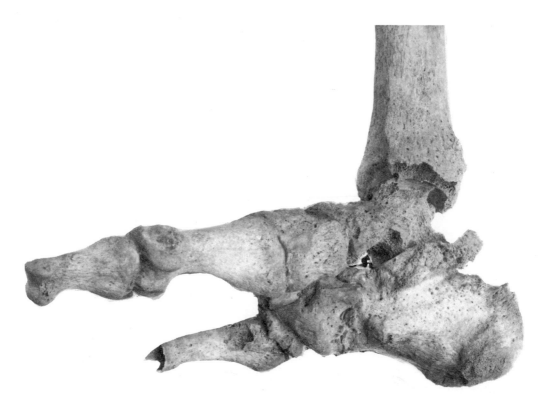

47. Inhumation 42, evidence for gout in the left foot

48.   Inhumation 42, right hand showing cupping of metacarpals and phalanges

limited movement possible in these two joints had not made it quite impossible for this woman to walk it is likely that one or both femoral heads would have perforated the acetabular floor and gone right through into the pelvic cavity.

Inh. 57 (♂) has a lesion at the proximal end of each tibia which may be due to Osgood-Schlatter's disease. This is one of a group of ill-understood syndromes which includes Kienbock's disease of the semilunar bone, Kohler's disease of the navicular, and similar lesions affecting the calcaneus (Haglund), and second metatarsal (Freiburg). Osgood-Schlatter's lesion, in common with the others, tends to develop in childhood and eventually be self-limiting. A typical case, in an Anglo-Saxon skeleton from Norfolk has been described by Wells (1968).

One of the most interesting discoveries at Cirencester is shown by Inhs. 42 (♂), 278 (♂) and 331 (♂). These three men have, in various degrees, evidence of gout. Until the first of these cases was described (Wells, 1973) the only indisputable case of gout in the literature of palaeopathology was that of an Egyptian mummy of an elderly man, of Coptic date, which was described by Elliot Smith and Warren Dawson in 1924. The characteristic lesions in these Cirencester skeletons consist of destruction of joint surfaces, mostly in the hands and feet, and small para articular pits in different bones. Inh. 42 is the most severely affected, with widespread lesions affecting most bones in both feet, with others in the hands, ulnae, radii, patallae and tibiae, pls. 45–48. In Inh. 278 (♂) most of the tarsals and metatarsals are affected. Much remodelling of these bones has occurred and there is synostosis of some of the foot elements. Gouty lesions are also present elsewhere, e.g. the patellae. Inh. 331 is the least affected but this is probably partly due to its being the least well preserved of the three skeletons. Nevertheless it has typical gouty destruction of the bases and, or, heads of several metatarsals and of phalanges of fingers.

Finally it is worth mentioning the double Inh. 243. This burial contained the remains of two very small infants, newborn or only a few days old. One is fractionally larger than the other but no more than is often found in newborn babies of different lengths and weights. There is no osteological evidence that these two babies were related but it can be emphatically said that if, by chance, they do happen to be siblings they must without any question be twins. If so, it would be likely that their early death was due to one of the obstetric complications which are a common hazard of twin pregnancies.

PARITY

A recent development of great interest and importance to palaeodemographers is the estimation of parity, i.e. the number of children a woman has borne. This is based on changes which pregnancy and childbirth produce in the pelvis — specifically in the area of the preauricular grooves and around the pubic symphysis. The method is still in need of much refinement but already it can offer information which is unobtainable in any other way.

Unfortunately the pelvis, especially the middle part of the pubes, is often badly damaged in early burials. This was the case at Cirencester and as a result it was possible to estimate in only thirteen women how many children they had borne. The results are shown in Table 91.

Table 91: Number of births per woman

Inh.	Age	Number of births Min.	Max.	Mean
R	45 ± 5	3	5	4
X	50 ± 5	2	3	2.5
1	42 ± 7	1	2	1.5
9	45 ± 10	8	10	9
56	50 ± 10	6	8	7
103	35 ± 5	1	3	2
104(b)	45 ± 15	5	7	6
175	55 ± 5	5	7	6
182	60 ± 5	6	8	7
262	55 ± 5	5	7	6
270	39 ± 3	2	4	3
295	45 ± 5	1	2	1.5
312	51 ± 3	4	6	5
n = 13		49	72	60.5
$\bar{x}$ =	47.5	3.8	5.5	4.7

In view of the uncertainties still inherent in the method it would be pretentious to make closer estimate than those shown. Taking the mean of the suggested numbers indicates that these thirteen women would have produced about sixty children between them — an average of 4.7. This seems to be slightly higher than the figure for the North Elmham Anglo-Saxons. It has often been supposed that in the absence of contraceptive techniques women in early populations passed rapidly from one pregnancy to another, producing ten or even twenty children during their reproductive lives. Very strong evidence exists to refute this hypothesis and the matter has been extensively discussed by Wells (1975). The onset of menstruation does not usually imply that a girl is immediately able to conceive and it it likely that, with menarche occurring somewhat later for Romano-British girls than for modern western Europeans, many or most young women would have been unlikely to conceive before eighteen years. It is also probable that the menopause occurred earlier then than now and that their reproductive life was correspondingly shorter. Indeed, it may have been little more than about fifteen years on average, since many women must have died well before attaining the menopause. An average of between four and five children, such as these Cirencester women appear to have had, would then represent one pregnancy about every four or three years. This is a very probable figure. In western Europe today the tendency is for mothers to wean their babies early and rear them on the safe substitutes of tinned or pasteurized milk. In former times lactation was much more

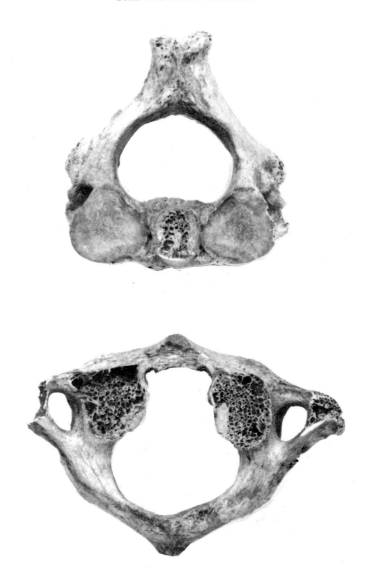

49.   Inhumation R, decapitation cutting through the atlas vertebra

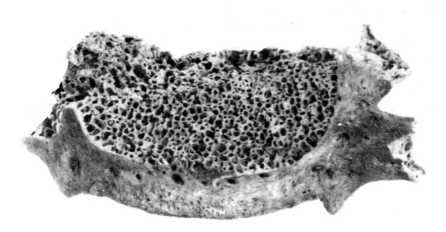

50.   Inhumation 215, decapitation through the C4 vertebra

prolonged — often for two or three years. This was because a baby who was not breast fed often had almost no chance of survival when the only alternative was cow's milk which was heavily contaminated with the organisms of dysentery and enteritis. (Wet nurses were probably the rare prerogative of a few socially elite women). The extended period of lactation would not, as is sometimes believed, have prevented further pregnancies but it would undoubtedly have reduced their frequency. Moreover it is extremely probable that these people, in common with almost all others, practised some kind of contraception or abortion which would have further diminished the number of live births. And even if this was not the case there is always a spontaneous miscarriage rate which tends to be about 20% of all pregnancies. This implies that the thirteen women we are considering here would have had about seventy-five conceptions spontaneously reduced to the sixty births.

A somewhat unusual situation is found here. It happens that most of these thirteen persons were fairly long-lived by the standards of their time and it is likely that at least eleven of them had survived for what would have been their full child-bearing potential. Two may have died with a few potentially fertile years left to them. It is likely that between them they had lived for about 160 reproductive years. They would thus have averaged one conception perhaps every 3.5 years and a full-time birth about once every 4.3 years.

DECAPITATION

At least six persons had been decapitated.

Inh. R (♀) had been beheaded through her atlas vertebra — a most unusual and exceptionally high level, pl. 49. Its inferior articular facets have been cleanly cut off by a blow that was inflicted from back to front. The odontoid process of her axis has also been severed just above its base. Inh. 123 (♂) was decapitated, again from back to front, through the C3 vertebra. The axis is now missing but was probably wounded by the blow which had also truncated the R. mastoid process and incised the R. ramus of the mandible. Inh. 215 (♂) had been beheaded through the C4 vertebra but in this case the stroke was inflicted from front to back, pl. 50. In Inh. 216 (♂) the decapitation was through the C4 vertebra, with a tiny slice of bone removed from the C3 as well. Here the blow traversed the neck from back to front. In Inh. 304 (♂) it is again the C4 vertebra which was sectioned. The bone has been damaged post-mortem but it is virtually certain that this stroke was also delivered from behind. Finally, the dramatic Inh. 305 (♂) shows a clean cut through the C3, with a tiny sliver removed from the axis, the blow sweeping on to leave a clean shallow incision in the posterior border of both mandibular rami.

It is interesting that one of these persons was a woman. Five of the six were decapitated from behind forwards. In every case the bone had been cut very cleanly and there is no doubt that the weapons must have been razor sharp. Apart from Inh. R, all the transections were through the C3 or C4 segments. It may also be noted that the head was not necessarily removed from its normal position for burial. It was the examination of the bones, not the excavation of the graves, which revealed what had happened. This suggests the possibility that after the cervical spine and the spinal cord had been severed the heads may still have remained attached to the trunk by the anterior tissues of the neck. If so, these heads cannot have been removed as trophies to venerate or as spoils of war to gloat over and we may be inclined to think that penal decapitation is a more likely reason for these injuries.

GNAWED BONES

At Cirencester it is common to find bones which have been gnawed by various kinds of animals. Accurate estimation is impossible but it seems likely that at least five per cent of skeletons have been attacked in this way. Usually it is the long bones of the limbs which are affected, especially those of the leg. But this is probably due to the fact that much of the tibia, being thinly covered by soft tissues, is easily reached and nibbled by small rodents — in contrast to the femur which is mostly protected by thick thigh muscles. A few typical cases will serve to show what is found.

51. Gnawing on the left humerus of Inhumation 55, and the right tibia of Inhumation S

In Inh. 208 (♂) the right tibia is gnawed along about 50 mm. This seems to have been caused by a small rodent. Inh. 170 (♂) also shows gnawing of the right tibia for 55 mm along the anterior border in the middle of its shaft. The fibula is similarly affected and the marks on both bones suggest that they were made by a small, mouse-size rodent. Much larger toothmarks extend for 140 mm along the R. femoral shaft of Inh. 203 (♂). These were probably made by a fox or a moderately large dog. Inh. 141 (♂) has gnawing of 110 mm of the interosseous borders of the right ulna and radius. In this case a smaller dog or fox seems to have been responsible. Inh. 22 (♂) has rodent gnawing both of the forearms and of the legs. In Inh. 55 (♀) the left humerus is extensively chewed pl. 51; in Inh. P (♂) the right clavicle is nibbled; and in Inh. 168 (♀) it is the left scapula which is mostly affected. The right radius if Inh. 176 (♂) and the left tibia of the nine year old Inh. 133 have both been gnawed by more than one sort of animal. These bones show evidence of fox or dog teeth as well as those of some small rodent about the size of a mouse. Other examples could be quoted.

The sum of this evidence suggests that many of the Cirencester corpses were interred in shallow graves which were not firmly compacted. They were thus easily reached by burrowing predators as large as dogs. It must also indicate that the graves were neglected soon after the burial. What "soon" means in this context is difficult to say: less than five years is likely, though up to fifty is possible. No evidence of post-inhumation erosion of bones by coleoptera was found here, although it must be conceded that this is often difficult to identify. It is also interesting that no skeleton was found with gnawing of the skull though, in some cemeteries, the borders of the orbits, of the zygomata and of the mandibular rami and body are common sites of rodent activity.

In view of the uncertainty about the date of introduction of black rats into the Brisish Isles it is worth noting that in a few cases, such as Inhs. F (Juv., 12 years), S (♂) pl. 51, 16 (♂) and 133 (Juv. *c.* 9 years) some of the toothmarks look extremely like those which are known to have been produced by rats on modern bones.

NORTH OF THE FOSSE WAY

THE MATERIAL AND ITS CONDITION

On average the state of this group can be described as considerably more defective than that to the south of the Fosse, poor though that is.

SEX AND AGE

The 45 burials in this group may be taken to represent the remains of no more than 45 persons. They are all single inhumations and the only duplication found was the occasional isolated fragment of bone in two or three of these graves. These are so insignificant that they may be disregarded.

The 45 burials comprise 34 males, 4 probable males, 3 females, and 4 probable females. All were adult, except Inh 709. This was an adolescent, aged about 13 years, who is almost certainly a male. A juvenile burial rate of only 2.2%, such as this, is an extremely unusual occurrence although a similar situation was found in a series of at least eighty skeletons of the 7th-12th century from Martyrs' Bay, Iona. At that site the only juvenile, aged about 16 years, was represented by one solitary bone — a radius with an unfused distal but newly fused proximal epiphysis (Wells, 1981).

The mean age at death of the 20 adult males whose ages could be assessed with some assurance was 40.2 years; of the 5 females it was 35.5 years.

The other outstanding difference between the two groups is the sex ratio. Only three (6.7%) of the 45 inhumations can be assessed as female with any assurance, although four others might possibly have been women which would give a percentage of 15.5% females. By contrast the 300 sexed burials to the south of the Fosse included 93 (31.0%) females.

PHYSICAL TYPE

The universal deficiency of crania makes it impossible to say anything of significance about the physical affinities of these people. However a few brief observations may be made.

STATURE

In stature the skeletons do not differ greatly from those of the main group south of the Fosse. The mean height of 24 adult males was 1707 mm (5ft 7in), with a range of 1620 (5ft 3¾in)-1778 (5ft 10in). These estimations are probably slightly less reliable than those of the main group because, owing to the small number available, seven have had to be calculated from bones of the upper limb. Table 92 mf. 3/5 gives the measurements of male long bones.

The only females whose height could be reliably estimated were Inh. 718 at 1680 mm (5ft 6in) and Inh. 739 at 1538 mm (5ft 0¼in).

NON-METRICAL VARIANTS

The identification of non-metrical variants, especially those of the skull, was made extremely

197

difficult by the poor condition of this series. For many of the features listed in Table 51 only one or two, sometimes no, observations could be made. This being so it seems of little use to comment on, or even record, each character. Table 93 shows the frequency of all variants where three or more observations were possible.

Table 93: Non-metrical variants

Variant	n	+	%
Metopism	8	3	37.5
Bregma bone	4	0	0.0
Inca bone	4	0	0.0
Supra-orbital notch	5	3	60.0
Parietal foramina	6	4	66.7
Double supra-orbital foramen	6	0	0.0
Huschke's foramen	16	0	0.0
Double or hour-glass occiptal condyle	7	1	14.3
Post condylar canal	3	2	66.7
Double hypoglossal foramen	9	1	11.1
Pre-condylar tubercles	7	2	28.6
Sagittal sinus turns left	5	1	20.0
Blurred sub-nasal margin	12	5	41.6
Nasal fossiculae	8	2	25.0
Malar tuberosity	11	6	54.5
Marginal tubercle	10	2	20.0
Zygomaxillary tubercle	10	3	30.0
Multiple mental foramen	19	1	5.3
Gonial eversion	11	9	81.8
Infero-lateral mental tuberosity	14	4	28.6
Atlas bridge	12	2	16.7
Ossified dens	4	1	25.0
Septal aperture of humerus	26	2	7.7
Acetabular crease	11	2	18.2
Third trochanter	15	2	13.3
Vastus notch	5	0	0.0

MERIC AND CNEMIC INDICES

Only 18 meric and 15 cnemic indices were obtainable. Nothing of note was found. The mean Meric Index was 76.2, with a range of 61.9–89.7; the Cnemic Index averaged 70.7, with a range of 63.0–79.9.

SQUATTING FACETS

Fifteen tibiae (12 ♂, 3 ♀) can be examined for the presence or absence of squatting facets at the ankle. They are present in two (16.5%) of the males and one (33.3%) of the females. Both male facets are small (1st degree), the female facet is large (3rd degree). Differences of size and frequency such as these are normally found between the sexes in early populations.

TEETH

Very few teeth survive in this group. Only 394 dental places are recognizable and of these four (1.0%) were unerupted – all of them third molars.

Of the 390 erupted places nine (2.3%) had been shed ante-mortem. A further 50 have been lost post-mortem, leaving 331 teeth now present in the jaws. Of these 33 teeth 16 (4.8%) are carious but nine of them occur in one skull (Inh. 718 (♀)).

Only 17 inhumations have jaws or fragments on which the above data are based, the caries cavities being distributed among four (23.5%) of the specimens.

Sixteen skulls total 31 degrees of attrition, i.e. an average of 1.9. Tartar seems to have been uncommon but enamel hypoplasia was present on a few teeth.

OSTEOARTHROSIS

As is usual in early groups osteoarthrosis was the commonest lesion. In spite of the extremely defective state of most burials it was recognizable in at least 18 skeletons.

With relatively so few surviving here it must be unreliable to compare the severity and frequency of spinal lesions in this group with their occurrence in the main series, nevertheless a strong subjective impression is conveyed that they were less severe and the available figures show that they were less common. Eight men and two women had arthrosis and, or, osteo-phytosis of vertebrae. In addition to these, five men had one or more Schmorl's nodes, whilst Inh. 730 (♂) also had arthrosis of two ribs. Parts of the spinal column survived in 13 males.

Table 94 shows the total number of surviving superior and inferior hemi-vertebrae in the men, with the percentage which show these lesions.

Table 94: Frequency of male vertebral lesions

Number of hemi-vertebrae observable for:

Arthrosis			Osteophytosis			Schmorl's nodes		
n	+	%	n	+	%	n	+	%
349	7	2.0	348	26	7.4	346	15	4.3

Comparison with Table 75 will show that these lesions were significantly more common to the south of the Fosse.

Not included in the above figures are the female Inh. 718, who had arthrosis and osteo-phytosis of her vertebral column; so, too, had Inh. 713, a possible female, who also had well marked arthrosis on both bones of her L. hip joint.

Apart from these costo-vertebral lesions nine of the men have arthrosis, often affecting several joints and widely scattered throughout the skeleton. Inh. 704 has it on the L. scapula and humeral head; at the R. elbow and R. wrist on the radius; and in both hip joints on the ace-tabula. His L. knee is also severely affected and this is discussed below. His R. foot was arthrotic in the tarsus and metatarsus. This skeleton was also one of those with arthrosis, osteo-phytosis and Schmorl's nodes of the spinal column. Inh. 730 was another man with multiple arthrotic lesions. He had the most severely affected spine in this series with at least six Schmorl's nodes and seven of his 16 surviving vertebrae had osteophytosis. Arthrosis was also present on two of his seven ribs; at his elbows on the L. humerus and both ulnae; and at his hip joints on the heads of both femora. Clearly, this man had led a vigorous and physically demanding life.

Among the males, seven hip joints were affected in five persons; and six elbows in four. Other sites with arthrosis include both sacroiliac joints of Inhs. 714 (♂) and 768 (♂); and the L.

mandibular condyle of Inh. 768. An indication of the relative mildness of most of these arthrotic lesions is that none of them show evidence of eburnation.

FRACTURES

Nine fractures are identifiable. Inh. 703 (♂) has one and Inh. 712 (♂) has three well-healed fractures of left ribs. Inh. 715 (♂) has a soundly healed L. Colles' fracture together with its common accompaniment — a crack through the styloid process of the L. ulna. In Inh. 730 (♂) there is a well-healed oblique fracture through the mid-shaft of the L. tibia. There is no angulation of the bone but it is 14.2 mm shorter than its fellow. The L. fibula escaped being broken but there is slight arthrosis of its head which may be causally related to the tibial lesion. In Inh. 763 (♂) there is a gross fracture of the L. ulna and L. radius at the junction of their proximal and medial thirds. Both bones are solidly healed with much callus and two large callus exostoses extend between the bones. These exostoses apparently came into non-synostosed contact to make a kind of pseudarthrosis across the interosseous membrane.

Table 95 shows the overall frequency of fractures as far as it can be ascertained.

Table 95: Fracture frequency

Bone	n		%
Clavicle	19	0	0.0
Humerus	20	0	0.0
Ulna	19	2	10.5
Radius	22	2	9.1
Femur	24	0	0.0
Tibia	23	1	4.4
Fibula	17	0	0.0
Metacarpals	121	0	0.0
Metatarsals	101	0	0.0
Phalanges	249	0	0.0

EXOSTOSES

A few exostoses were found. Those associated with the forearm fractures of Inh. 763 have already been described. In Inh. 704 (♂) there is an exostosis 19 x 4 mm which rises about 4 mm above the surface of the bone adjacent to the lateral supracondylar ridge of the R. humerus. It does not resemble the supracondylar process which is associated with a normal foraminal arch of bone in the Felidae and which is occasionally seen in human material. Inh. 712 (♂) has an exostosis, 38 x 8 mm and 2 mm high, bordering the medial epicondylar ridge of the R. femur and another, 35 x 15 mm and 3 mm high, bordering its lateral epicondylar ridge. There is also some adjacent roughness of the lateral cortical surface of the bone. Inh. 729 (♂) also has two exostoses. One is 42 mm long, rising about 4.5 mm above the surface of the anterior border of the R. tibia. The other is a small excrescence from the lateral border of the L. first metatarsal. All these lesions were probably traumatic in origin and followed tearing of the ligaments or aponeuroses attached to the bones.

The only female with an exostosis was Inh. 718 who had a small out-growth from the L. pubic bone in the position of the pubic spine. Its cause must remain uncertain but it may have been produced by the trauma of pregnancy and childbirth.

MISCELLANEOUS LESIONS

Inh. 765 (♂) had a small wound about 10 mm above the L. orbit and lying parallel to its upper border. This lesion is 13 mm long and 5 mm wide. Its floor lies 2–3 mm below the normal surface of the bone and is well healed though slightly rough. It seems almost certain that it was caused, either accidentally or deliberately, by a penetrating wound of the scalp from some not very sharp instrument.

The only examples of osteochondritis were present in Inh. 703 (♂) who had a small irregularity about 3.5 mm in diameter on the capitulum of the L. humerus. This was presumably a lesion which had healed. In Inh. 729 (♂) there is a small pit in the head of the L. first metatarsal.

Cribra orbitalia was found only once, in Inh. 701 (♂). It was bilateral, but of first degree only.

In Inh. 729 (♂) there is a "flange" lesion, a defect about 24 mm long in the antero-superior quadrant of the rim of the L. acetabulum. These interesting lesions have been briefly noted above p. 176 and are more extensively referred to, and illustrated, in Wells (1976).

Inh. 704 (♂) has a perplexing condition. His L. femur is 18.8 mm shorter and much smaller in build than his R. one. The tibiae and fibulae are not precisely measurable but they, too, are much lighter and more slender than those of the R. side and were almost certainly somewhat shorter. There is gross destruction of the L. knee joint, which in life seems to have been flexed at about 80°, though without true synostosis between the femur and the tibia. The patella, however, is fused to the femur. The diagnosis of this condition is difficult. It could, perhaps, have resulted from poliomyelitis. But, on balance, it is more likely to have been due to an infection — either tuberculosis or a septic arthritis, perhaps from a penetrating wound of the joint. The bones have sinuses in them which presumably discharged pus during life. Functionally, this limb would have been almost useless and for locomotion he must have been dependent on his right leg. This probably explains the extensive arthrosis in it. Perhaps he was reduced to the use of crutches which may have partly accounted for the arthrosis of his L. shoulder, R. elbow and R. wrist.

Inh. 712 (♂) has a small tumour, 7 mm in diameter, in the lower part of the lingual surface of the mandible below the left second molar. It is probably nothing more than a cancellous osteoma but its exact status remains uncertain.

Developmental anomalies are uncommon in this series. In Inh. 703 (♂) the L5 vertebra has a detached neural arch. In Inh. 710 (♂) the L5 is sacralized and the inferior articular facets of L2 are very asymmetrical. Inh. 718 (♀) has a six piece sacrum.

Editorial Note

During excavation of CT 76 bone scatters were plotted and collected, p. 70. These were sent for analysis and following the method of small find recording Dr. Wells designated them the "Triangle" series.

CIRENCESTER "TRIANGLE" SERIES

The "Triangle" series is by far the most defective of all the Cirencester inhumations. It mostly comprises unarticulated fragments of bone, of doubtful association, which were probably derived from burials which had been cut by other burials. Thus, their main interest stems from the possibilities (a) that they may give some indication of the sequence of grave digging and (b) that they can give a minimum number of persons buried in the cemetery, additional to those

numbered burials which have been discussed above. Unfortunately the osteological examination of these remains throws no light on the sequence in which the graves were dug but a few
comments can be made on the persons represented.

The "Triangle" material was presented for examination in twelve separate small groups. It
was at once seen that probably half of these consisted of indescriminately pooled remains from
more than one individual.

At least twenty persons seem to be represented here of whom only one is definitely juvenile
— a child aged 10 to 12 years. Two others might be late adolescents about 17 years old or they
may already have been adults over 18 years. The remaining 17 individuals are fully adult. The
child is unsexable. Two other adults also consist of a few unsexable scraps but the remaining 17
can be diagnosed with considerable confidence as exclusively males. Although the amount of
surviving bone in each of these twelve groups is very small, and although in many of the lots
key diagnostic elements such as the pelvis or the skull are either absent or badly defective, this
determination of sex seems justified on the grounds of the sturdy build and strong muscularity
of most long bone fragments, the size of articular surfaces, the substantial development of ribs,
hand bones and other such features.

A detailed description of each group would be valueless but a few observations may be worth
making.

In the surviving scraps of jaws of the "Triangle" series 144 dental places are identifiable.
From these 20 (13.8%) teeth had been shed ante-mortem. None were unerupted but 42 have
been lost post-mortem, leaving 82 teeth for inspection. Of these, nine (11.0%) are carious
(from six different persons), a rate which is more than double that of the other burial groups
examined.

Stature can be estimated for only two persons: lot 228 (a) (♂) was about 1675 (5ft 6in) and lot
232 (♂) about 1786 mm (5ft 10¼in).

No non-metrical variants of any note were detected.

A few pathological conditions were found. In addition to the dental caries and ante-mortem
tooth loss in several of these groups, well marked radiculitis was present in lot 229 (b). Lot 228
(a) has periostitis of his only surviving (R.) tibia. In lot 232 an osteochondritic pit, 3 mm in
diameter, is present in the distal articular surface of a R. tibia. In the lot 299 complex, which
contains parts of at least three persons, the glenoid fossa of a R. temporal is arthrotic i.e. this
man had osteoarthrosis of his jaw. Unfortunately the corresponding mandibular condyle is
missing. A R. humerus of lot 329 has the congenital anomaly of a very small supra-condylar
process. Osteoarthrosis is not greatly in evidence in this series, presumably because of
the exceptional deficiency of its commonest anatomical sites of election here. But one of the
men in the 331 complex had well marked lesions on the costal facets of at least three vertebrae
and on the lateral articular facets of two out of five ribs. Another man in this lot had arthrosis of
the posterior intervertebral facets of the L4 and L5 vertebrae, osteophytosis on the superior and
inferior borders of the bodies of L1–L5, and a Schmorl's node on L2. This person, if the skeletal
association is reliable, also has two exostoses. One is a large lip of bone, 33 x 19 mm and rising
7 mm high, about 15 mm above the supero-posterior quadrant of the R. acetabulum. It is
possible that this lesion may have been due to trauma affecting the reflected tendon of the
Rectus femoris muscle. The second exostosis is 62 mm long, 12 mm wide, and rises 9 mm
above the surface of the bone on the lateral ridge of the linea aspera of the R. femur. This was
probably due to an extensive tear of the aponeurotic insertion of the Adductor magnus or
Vastus lateralis muscles.

HUMAN BONE LEAD CONCENTRATIONS
by
Tony Waldron

The uses to which the Romans put lead exposed them to a considerable risk of developing lead poisoning and there is a good deal of documentary evidence to suggest that the disease was common amongst them, and that on occasions, it assumed endemic proportions. There is not much in the way of scientific evidence to support this view, however, although it is a relatively simple matter to assess the degree to which ancient populations were exposed to lead by an analysis of the concentration of lead in bone. During life at least 90% of the lead which is absorbed into the body is fixed in the skeletal tissues where it tends to accumulate with age, at least until the fifth or sixth decades. A high bone lead concentration may thus be taken as an indication that the individual (or the population of individuals) was heavily exposed during his lifetime.

Some studies have already been undertaken to examine the lead content of bones from a variety of Romano-British sites, but the largest series so far has come from the excavations at Cirencester.

A total of 333 bones from this site, principally rib, vertebra or ulna, have been analysed from a total of 161 skeletons. Samples of different bone were taken from the same skeleton in order that the degree of variation in lead content from bone to bone could be determined. Each bone sample was cleaned, dried and weighed, and then wet ashed in a mixture of perchloric and nitric acids. The lead content was determined using atomic absorption spectrophotometry and all lead concentrations expressed as micrograms lead/gram (μg/g) dry weight of bone.

The reliability of the analytical method was tested by comparing the results obtained with those of a physical method employing neutron activation and with those of another laboratory using chemical analysis. In both cases, the results from the secondary analyses confirmed that the original method was sound. As a further check of the method, 27 duplicate samples from the same bone were sent for analysis without the prior knowledge of the analyst and the differences between the results were not statistically significant.

From the results of the analyses it seems clear that the inhabitants of the site — or at least those who came to be buried there — were heavily exposed to lead (see Table 96 and fig. 85 mf. 4/5). In the modern population, the mean concentration of lead in bone is variously quoted, but the maximum concentration seems to be between 40–50 μg/g. The concentrations in the Cirencester bones are markedly abnormal by present day standards and indeed, as can be seen from fig. 85, none is less than the contemporary maximum quoted above. The distribution of lead concentrations is very wide (fig. 85) and, especially in the rib and vertebra, noticeably skewed to the right. There is a substantial proportion of values (approximately 5% in all) in excess of 500 μg/g, indicating exposure on a massive scale even for this population.

There are no consistent sex differences (Table 96), nor is there any correlation between lead concentration and age (Table 97). In contemporary populations, bone lead concentrations are higher in men than in women and there is an increase in concentration with age, and the fact that this was not the case in the Cirencester bones was unexpected. It is possible that the similarity in lead concentration in the male and female bones is an indication that degree of exposure was the same, but since the differences noted in modern bones are thought to be due to an underlying difference in rates of absorption from the gut this seems, at first sight, unlikely. However, it is known that the absorption of lead from the gut is markedly affected by the constitution of the diet; it increases particularly if the levels of calcium and iron are low. Now if the people at Cirencester had a diet deficient in calcium and iron but at the same time were presented with a great deal of lead, this combination of factors might be sufficient to off-set the rather small differences in absorption seen in men and women on well balanced diets containing relatively small quantities of lead. Since we have no information on the composition of the diet of the Cirencester people, this has to remain a matter for speculation.

Failure to note an increase in lead concentration with increasing age may be due to a combination of circumstances, the most significant of which being the small numbers in some of the cells, the wide spread of the results within each cell, and the difficulties inherent in assigning a precise age to the bones. In most cases, especially with adult bones, the age can only be quoted as lying within a five, ten, or even fifteen year range. This necessarily makes the chances of demonstrating trends with age extremely difficult.

The variations in lead content in the different bones was expected, mean levels in rib and vertebra being higher than in the ulna by a factor of 1.6–1.7. The correlation between levels in rib and vertebra is highly significant (Table 98), but not between vertebra and ulna. There is a significant correlation between levels in rib and ulna in males but not in females; the reasons for this difference are obscure.

The practical consequences of the variation in lead levels are that in any other studies of this kind, the type of bone used should be specified in order to allow proper comparisons to be made with the results of other investigations.

The major source of lead to which the individuals on the site were exposed must have been the diet, but how the lead got into their food and drink remains unknown, and there are no clues from the excavation. This is an area in which there is an obvious need for further study both at this and other sites.

Contamination of the bones by lead in the soil has always to be borne in mind although in general this is not a serious problem since lead is firmly bound to organic materials in the soil and mobile only under conditions of high acidity, conditions which do not favour good bone preservation. Soil samples were analysed from several parts of one of the trenches on the site (see figs. 38 and 86 mf. 4/5) and the lead concentrations were in no way exceptional (Table 99).

The most important question which we have to consider is, did the high lead levels to which those folk living at Cirencester were exposed have any adverse effects on their health? Is it possible that any of them died of lead poisoning?

So far as the adults in the group are concerned, it is not possible to state categorically that any actually had lead poisoning since elevated bone lead concentrations may result if large (but sub-toxic) amounts of the metals are absorbed over a long period. Lead workers are an obvious example of those who may be subjected to prolonged heavy exposure and, as expected, their bones may contain several times the 'normal' concentration, and levels in excess of 200 μg/g have been reported. On the other hand, an enhanced intake of lead may also be due to environmental factors. In Glasgow, for example, where the water is extremely plumbosolvent, mean bone lead concentrations are almost twice as high as those in a hard water (non-plumbosolvent) area and in one study of autopsy material, 6.5% of the levels were in excess of 200 μg/g, the highest value being 540 μg/g; none of the patients had had symptoms of lead intoxication during life. Chronic, heavy exposure to lead may not be an immediate threat to life, but it may well be accompanied by an increased morbidity. For example, some of the Cirencester inhabitants with the highest exposure would very likely have been anaemic, and this would have rendered them less able to cope with infections and other relatively trivial illnesses.

If high bone levels in adults cannot be taken as necessarily implying a diagnosis of lead poisoning, then conversely, levels within the normal range do not exclude it. Most cases of severe clinical intoxication arise from the absorption of unusually large amounts of lead over a short period of time. This is expecially so in children. Now if previous exposure has been slight, bone lead concentrations before the onset of symptoms may be correspondingly low and although they will certainly rise following the intoxicating dose, the increase may not be sufficient to take the concentration outside the range of normal values.

These difficulties in the interpretation of bone lead concentrations apply equally to children as to adults, as noted above, although high concentrations in the bones of very young children are much more suggestive of clinical intoxication since infants are much less able to tolerate an increased burden of lead than older children or adults.

The results of the youngest children in the study are shown in Table 100 (mf. 4/5) and it seems highly likely that some of these children did actually die from lead poisoning.

THE ROMAN CEMETERIES OF CIRENCESTER

In order to enhance the examination of the Bath Gate cemetery a study of the known burial pattern around the town was undertaken. The full gazetteer, mf. 5/5, brings together all the recorded information of burials within the immediate environs of the Roman town, culled from journals, manuscripts, museum records, newspaper cuttings, and excavations. An open-ended numbering system was adopted to permit additions in the future, with blocks of numbers being assigned to the areas outside the west (A–1999 including those burials excavated in CS and CT 69–76), south (2000–2999), east (3000–3999), and north gates (4000–4999). Finds of human bones recovered from within the town defences are numbered 5000–5999; with unprovenanced finds 6000–6999. The divisions are geographical around the town, and in no sense chronological. Wherever possible each number represents a single burial. For the earlier very general descriptions of finds such as Leland's account of Grismunds Tower (Gazetteer 1000) where specific numbers of burials are not given the gazetteer number may represent more than one individual. Tombstones have been numbered individually. In those locations where either inhumations and/or cremations occur with tombstones, duplication of individuals by numbering the tombstone and the individual commemorated by the above ground marker may have occurred.

Fig. 87 serves to locate all those burials for which precise or more approximate find-spots are known.

To date the greatest number of recorded burials, have been recovered from the Roman cemetery to the west of the town. The earliest record of a burial was made by Stukeley in 1721 in describing Gazetteer burials 1063–1068, when 5 tombstones, and several urns were found "near the Querns, half a mile west of the town". The descriptions of the eminent antiquarians Leland and the Rev. Skinner are of great interest in themselves when discussing Grisminds Tower, gazetteer 1000, and the inhumations recovered during the digging of a pond to provide water for the cattle, gazetteer nos. 1107–1138.

Finds of burials to the south of the town are few. During the nineteenth century with the construction of the Midland and South Western Junction Railway and concomitant light industry and housing development, only three tombstones, gazetteer nos. 2003–2005, were recorded. Building development and service installations resulted in the recording of a spate of burials in the 1950's. Fuller observation in the nineteenth century for the more mundane and less obvious inhumations and cremations would no doubt have increased the total considerably and given a truer reflection of the size of the cemetery.

To the east of the town the construction of the eastern by-pass revealed 14 burials, gazetteer burials 3005–3018. The land immediately outside the east gate has been little developed and the eastern line of the second century defences has continued to contain the line of the town since the Roman period.

The line of Gloucester Street, northwards from the site of the north gate at the junction with Spitalgate Lane, is bordered by medieval and post-medieval houses and thus the scope for investigation of the Roman cemetery has been limited to the recovery of one skeleton, gazetteer no. 4000 in *c.* 1842. Burials 4001–4003 from Stratton, a mile from the town, are of interest, and possibly represent seventh to eighth century Saxon graves. The Anglo-Saxon burial dug through the floor of The Barton mosaic (Sewell and Powell, 1910, 67–8) and the finds of Anglo-Saxon burials in the gravel pits nearby (Whatley, 1894–5) point to Anglo-Saxon occupation in and use of this area.

The twenty-three sculpted and inscribed tombstones commemorate the names of ten individuals — Julia Casta (1063), Cast. Castrensis (1071), Publia Vicana (2000), Dannicus (2003), Genialis (2004), Philus (2005), Igennus (2021), Nemomnius Verecundus (2022), Petronius (2023) and Ingenuina (2036). As works of art the two military tombstones of Dannicus and Genialis are noteworthy, with the civilian Philus representing the third three-dimensional figure. The finely sculpted hand of gazetteer burial 2035 is arguably from a military tombstone also, with a provenance in the southern cemetery close to those of Dannicus and

Genialis. The only other military tombstone comes from the Bath Gate cemetery, where a fragment was found re-used in the footings for wall 2 of the roadside building, mf. 2/5. Re-use of tombstones, as for example the four civilian tombstones 2021-2024 in the base of the town rampart, would suggest that movement of tombstones from their original site and purpose was not an uncommon practice and the stray tombstone of military character in the Bath Gate cemetery may originally have stood outside the south gate, which appears to have been favoured by military personnel.

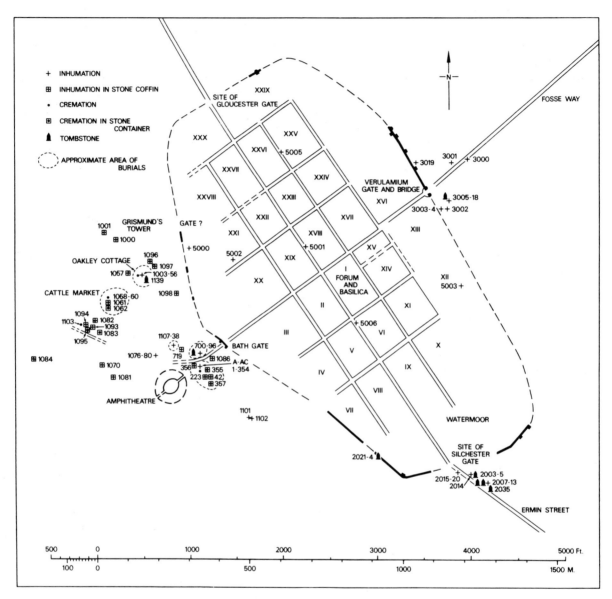

Fig. 87.   Plot of Gazetteer burials

Only seven tombstones give the age at death of the individuals commemorated, ranging from Igennus aged only six, to Nemomnius living to 75 years. Both Petronius and Genialis died at the age of 40, with Philus 45 years of age, Julia Casta 33, and Ingenuina 20. With the benefit of notes written by the Rev. Skinner of Camerton in 1824 (Brit. Mus. Ad. MSS 33679) it has been possible to substantiate the provenance of gazetteer 6010 as having been found in "Steep Stairs field", i.e. the area of the southern cemetery.

The transportation of large blocks of stone from the quarry source near the amphitheatre to the southern outskirts of the town would appear to have presented no difficulties, and makes it the more unusual that no stone coffins have been found anywhere else but in the Querns, where the total recovered is now twenty-five.

Similarly, cremation as a method of disposing of the dead appears more prevalent to the west of the town. The use of square blocks of limestone for 1002, 1062, 1073–5, 1083, 1088–1089, 1095, 2002 and 2006, with a hollow scooped to take either the ashes, or a pottery urn containing the ashes is in contrast to the less elaborate method of simple disposal in urns for cremations found in the grounds of Oakley Cottage, 1003–1056. An illustration in Buckman and Newmarch (1850, 111, fig. 44) illustrates clearly the form of these stone containers, on several occasions making use of column sections, and re-using blocks of limestone cut from the nearby quarries. From the cemetery outside the south gate an outstanding find of a cremation in a glass cinerary urn, 2002, was further wrapped in lead, according to several accounts, and placed within a cremation stone. Precise description of the stone is not given, but the form would presumably mirror closely one of those from the western cemetery. The second cremation stone from the southern cemetery, 2006, is doubtful, the receptacle possibly being a mortice and tenon fixing in a large slab of building stone.

All the pottery cinerary urns in the Corinium museum collection, reflect the general trend exhibited in other cemeteries in Roman Britain of cremation being a first-second century burial tradition, superceded by inhumation in the third and fourth centuries. The period of overlap of the two traditions is best illustrated in Cirencester in the grounds of Oakley Cottage 1003–1056 where the two forms are in close proximity to one another, but without physical overlap.

Lead as a medium for the encasing of cremated ashes has already been described in the context of burial 2002. In only two other instances has lead been recorded — in the case of burial 356 for an inhumation where the inner coffin of lead was placed inside one of stone, see p. 92, a simple St. Andrew's cross decorating the lid; and burial 6000 represented by a far more elaborate fragment, decorated with a St. Andrew's cross in cable pattern, ?paterae and a full-face female bust. By its nature, the fragment probably comes from one of the shorter sides of a coffin.

Perhaps one of the most interesting groups of burials are those catalogued 5000–5007, which by their very provenance, within the walls of the town, call for individual attention and discussion. Burial 5003, that of a small child, in an outside yard area of the Beeches Town House, is understandable in the context of Roman law and custom. The adult inhumations 5001 and 5006 lying in the ditch bordering Ermin Street have been used to argue for the decline of the towns population, disruption of civil administration (Wacher, 1974, 289–315) and retreat to the amphitheatre in times of unrest at the end of the fifth century. The tombstone fragment designating burial 5005 illustrates further the re-use of Roman material — in this case in the foundation trench of the Saxon Church, pre-dating the twelfth century Augustinian Abbey.

ABBREVIATIONS

A.E.	Année épigraphique
Am. J. Phys. Anthrop.	American Journal of Physical Anthropology
Antiq. J.	Antiquaries' Journal
Archaeol. Aeliana	Archaeologia Aeliana
Archaeol. Cambrensis	Archaeologia Cambrensis
Archaeol. Cantiana	Archaeologia Cantiana
Archaeol. J.	Archaeological Journal
Brit. Archaeol. Rep.	British Archaeological Reports
Brit. Dent. J.	British Dental Journal
Brit. Med. J.	British Medical Journal
Bull. Board Celtic Studies	Bulletin of the Board of Celtic Studies
Bull. Group. Int. Rech. Sc. Stomat.	Bulletin du Laboratoire de recherche de l'Institut de Stomatologie de l'Université, Bruxelles
Bull. N.Y. Acad. Med.	Bulletin of the New York Academy of Medicine
C.I.L.	Corpus Inscriptionum Latinarum
Dt. Zahn-Mund Kieferheilk	Deutsche Zahn-Mund und Kieferheilkunst
E.E.	Ephemeris Epigraphica
G.C.R.O.	Gloucester County Record Office
J. Archaeol. Sci	Journal of Archaeological Science
J. Brit. Archaeol. Ass.	Journal of the British Archaeological Association
J. Glass Studies	Journal of Glass Studies
J. Hist. Geography	Journal of Historical Geography
J. Hist. Med.	Journal of History of Medicine
J. Northampton Museum	Journal of the Northampton Museum & Art Gallery
Med. Biol. Illust.	Medical and Biological Illustration
Med. Hist.	Medical History
Norfolk & Norwich Archaeol. Soc.	Norfolk and Norwich Archaeological Society
Paleopath. Ass. Newsletter	Paleopathology Association Newsletter
Proc. Cotteswold Natur. Fld. Club	Proceedings of the Cotteswold Naturalist Field Club
Proc. Prehist. Soc.	Proceedings of the Prehistoric Society
Proc. Soc. Antiq. Scot.	Proceedings of the Society of Antiquaries of Scotland
Sussex Archaeol. Collect.	Sussex Archaeological Collections
Trans. Bristol Gloucestershire Archaeol. Soc.	Transactions of the Bristol and Gloucestershire Archaeological Society
Trans. London Middlesex Archaeol. Soc.	Transactions of the London and Middlesex Archaeological Society
Trav. Doc. Centre Paléoanthrop. Paleopath.	Travaux et documents du Centre Pierre Morel et Calvin Wells Centre de Paléoanthropologie et de Paléopathologie, Lyon
Wiltshire Archaeol. Natur. Hist. Mag.	Wiltshire Archaeological and Natural History Magazine
Z. Rassenk.	Zeitschrift für Rassenkunde

BIBLIOGRAPHY

Akerman, J.Y., 1857 — An account of researches in Anglo-Saxon cemeteries at Filkins, and at Broughton Poggs, in Oxfordshire, *Archaeologia*, 37, 140–6

Alarcao, J. de, 1975 — Bouteilles carrées à fond decoré..., *J. Glass Studies*, xvii, 49, 51

Almgren, O., 1923 — *Studien über Nordeuropäische Fibelformen der ersten nachchristlichen Jahrhunderte mit Berüchsichtigung der provinzialrömischen und südrussischen Formen*, Leipzig

Andrews, A.H. & Noddle, B.A., 1975 — Absence of premolar teeth from ruminant mandibles found at archaeological sites, *J. Archaeol. Sci.*, 2, 137–144

Annable, F.K., 1962 — A Romano-British Pottery in Savernake Forest, Kilns 1–2, *Wiltshire Archaeol. Natur. Hist. Mag.*, ccx, 142–155

Armitage, P.L. & Clutton-Brock, J., 1976 — A system for the classification and description of the cattle horncores from archaeological sites, *J. Archaeol. Sci.*, 3, 329–348

Atkinson, D., 1916 — *The Romano-British site on Lowbury Hill in Berkshire*, Reading

Atkyns, Sir Robert, 1712 — *The Ancient and Present State of Gloucestershire*

Baddeley, W. St. Clair, 1922 — The Excavation at Cirencester, *Trans. Bristol Gloucestershire Archaeol. Soc.*, XLIV, 100–15

Baddeley. W. St. Clair, 1924 — *A History of Cirencester*, Cirencester

Beck, H.C., 1928 — Classification and nomenclature of beads and pendants, *Archaeologia*, 77, 1–77

Beecham, K.J., 1886 — *History of Cirencester and the Roman City of Corinium*, Cirencester

Berry, B.Y., 1965 — *A Selection of Ancient Gems from the Collection of Burton Y. Berry*, Indiana

Böhme, A., 1970 — Englische Fibeln aus den Kastellan Saalburg und Zugmantel, *Saalburg Jahrbuch*, XXVII, 5–20

Böhme, A., 1972 — Die Fibeln der Kastelle Saalburg und Zugmantel, *Saalburg Jahrbuch*, XXIX, 5–112

Bonner, C., 1950 — *Studies in Magical Amulets, chiefly Graeco-Egyptian*, Ann Arbor, 6

Boon, G.C., 1966 — Roman Window Glass from Wales, *J. Glass Studies*, viii, 41–45

Boon, G.C., 1966 — Gilt glass beads from Caerleon and elsewhere, *Bull. Board Celtic Studies*, XXII, 104–9

Boon, G.C., 1977 — Gold-in-glass beads from the ancient world, *Britannia*, VIII, 193–208

Brabant, H., 1963 — Observations sur la denture humain en France et en Belgique a l'époque gallo-romaine et au moyen âge, *Bull. Group. Int. Rech. Sc. Stomat.*, 6, 169–296

Brailsford, J.W., 1962 — *Hod Hill, I: Antiquities from Hod Hill in the Durden Collection*, London

Breeze, D.J., 1974 — *The Roman Fort at Bearsden*, Edinburgh

Brodribb, A.C.C., et al., 1971 & 1973 — *Excavations at Shakenoak,* vols. II, IV, Oxford

Brothwell, D.R., 1972 — *Digging up Bones,* London

Brothwell, D., and Higgs, E., 1969 — *Science in Archaeology*

Brown, T.C., 1849 — Notes on discoveries..., *J. Brit. Archaeol. Ass.,* iv, 69–71

Brown, T.C., 1869 — Notes on discoveries..., *J. Brit. Archaeol. Ass.,* xxv, 102

Brown, P.D.C., & McWhirr, A.D., 1966 — Cirencester, 1965, *Antiq. J.,* 46, 240–53

Brown, P.D.C., & McWhirr, A.D., 1967 — Cirencester, 1966, *Antiq. J.,* 47, 185–197

Brown, P.D.C., & McWhirr, A.D., 1969 — Cirencester, 1967–8: Eighth Interim Report, *Antiq. J.,* 49, 222–243

Buckman, J. & Newmarch, C.H., 1850 — *Illustrations of the Remains of Roman Art in Cirencester,* Cirencester

Budge, E.A.W., 1903 — *An account of the Roman antiquities preserved in the museum at Chesters,* London

Bushe-Fox, J.P., 1914 — *Excavations on the site of the Roman town at Wroxeter, Shropshire,* Soc. Antiquaries of London, II, Oxford

Bushe-Fox, J.P., 1916 — *Third Report on the Excavations on the Site of the Roman Town at Wroxeter, Shropshire, 1914,* Soc. Antiquaries of London, IV, Oxford

Bushe-Fox, J.P., 1932 & 1949 — *Third and Fourth Reports on the Excavations of the Roman Fort at Richborough, Kent,* Soc. Antiquaries of London 10 and 16

Callender, M.H., 1965 — *Roman Amphorae,* London

Cardozo, M., 1962 — Pedras deanéis romanos en contradas em Portugal, *Revista de Guimaraes,* LXXII, 155, no. 28

Charlesworth, D., 1959 — Roman Glass in Northern Britain, *Archaeol. Aeliana,* 4 xxxvii 33–58

Charlesworth, D., 1966 — Roman Square Bottles, *J. Glass Studies,* VIII, 26–40

Chenet, G., 1941 — *La Céramique gallo-romaine d'Argonne du IVe siècle et la terre sigillée decorée à la roulette,* Macon

Chiesa, G. Sena, 1966 — *Gemme del Museo Nazionale di Aquileia,* Aquileia

Church, Sir Arthur — *Corinium Museum. A Guide to the museum of Roman remains at Cirencester,* editions printed in 1871, 1876, 1883, 1910 & 1922

Church, Sir Arthur, 1874 — Recent Roman finds at Cirencester, *Wiltshire Archaeol. Natur. Hist. Mag.,* XIV, 186–192

Clarke, G., 1979 — *The Roman Cemetery at Lankhills,* Winchester Studies 3, Pre-Roman and Roman Winchester, Part II, Oxford

Clifford, E., 1961 — *Bagendon: A Belgic Oppidum,* Cambridge

Cooke, C., & Rowbotham, T.C., 1968 — Dental report, in *The Romano-British cemetery at Trentholme Drive, York,* (ed. L.P. Wenham), 177–216

Corcoran, J.X.W.P., 1969 — The Cotswold-Severn Group, in *Megalithic Enquiries in the West of Britain,* (eds. T.G.E. Powell *et al*), 13–106

Coss, P.R., 1971 — *The Langley Cartulary,* unpubl. Ph.D. Thesis, Univ. of Birmingham

Coss, P.R., 1974 — The Langley Family and its Cartulary: a study in the late medieval 'Gentry', *Dugdale Society Occ. Papers* no. 22

Crawford, O.G.S., 1925 — *Long Barrows of the Cotswolds,* Gloucester

Cunliffe, B.W., 1968 — *Fifth Report on the Excavations of the Roman Fort at Richborough, Kent,* Soc. Antiquaries of London, 23

Cunliffe, B.W., 1971 — *Roman Bath Discovered,* London

Cunliffe, B.W., 1975 — *Excavations at Portchester Castle, Vol. I: Roman,* Soc. Antiquaries of London, XXXII

Darling, M.J., 1977 — Pottery from Early Military Sites in Western Britain, in *Roman Pottery Studies in Britain and Beyond,* (eds. J. Dore & K. Greene), 57–100

Deonna, W., 1953 — Mars tropaeophore, *Zeitschrift Fur Schweizerische Archaeologie und Kunstgeschichte,* XIV, 65–7

Detsicas, A., 1973 — *Current Research in Romano-British Coarse Pottery,* C.B.A Research Report, 10

Devine, M., 1977 — *The Cartulary of Cirencester Abbey, Gloucestershire*, vol. 3, Oxford

Dore, J. & Greene, K., 1977 — Roman Pottery Studies in Britain and Beyond, *Brit. Archaeol. Rep. (Supp. Series)*, 30, Oxford

Doppelfeld, O., 1966 — *Römisches und Frankisches Glas in Köln*, Köln

Down, A. and Rule, M., 1971 — *Chichester Excavations I*, Chichester

Driesch, A. von den, 1976 — *A Guide to the measurement of animal bones from archaeological sites*, Harvard

Dunning, G.C., 1936 — A Bastion of the Town Wall of London, and the Sepulchral Monument of the Procurator Julius Classicianus, *Antiq. J.*, xvi, 1–7

Dunning, G.C., 1968 — The Stone Mortars, in *Fifth Report on the Excavations of the Roman Fort at Richborough, Kent*, (ed. B.W. Cunliffe), 110–114

Dunning, G.C., & Jessup, R.F., 1936 — Roman Barrows, *Antiquity*, X, 37–53

Emery, G.T., 1963 — Dental pathology and archaeology, *Antiquity*, 37, (148): 274–81

Exner, K., 1939 — Die provinzialromischen Emailfibeln der Rheinlande, *Bericht des Romische-Germanische Kommission*, 29, 33–121

Farrar, R.A.H., 1973 — The Techniques and Sources of Romano-British Black-Burnished Ware, in *Current Research in Romano-British Coarse Pottery*, (ed. A. Detsicas), 67–103

Farrar, R.A.H., 1977 — A Romano-British Black-Burnished Ware Industry at Ower in the Isle of Purbeck, Dorset, in *Roman Pottery Studies in Britain and Beyond*, (eds. J. Dore and K. Greene), 199–227

Fossing, P., 1929 — *The Thorvalsen Museum, Catalogue of Antique Engraved Gems and Cameos*, Copenhagen

Fowler, E., 1960 — The Origins and Developments of the Penannular Brooch in Europe, *Proc. Prehist. Soc.*, XXVI, 149–77

Fowler, P.J., *et al.*, 1970 — *Cadbury-Congresbury, Somerset, 1968: An Introductory Report*, Bristol

Fox, A., 1940 — The Legionary Fortress at Caerleon, Mons.. Excavations in Myrtle Cottage Orchard, *Archaeol. Cambrensis*, 95, 101–153

Frere, S.S., 1972 — *Verulamium Excavations*, vol. I, Soc. Antiquaries of London, XXVIII, Oxford

Fremersdorf, F., 1958 — *Das Naturfarbene sogenannte Blaugrune Glas in Köln*, Köln

Friendship-Taylor, R.M., 1979 — The Excavation of the Belgic and Romano-British Settlement at Quinton, Northamptonshire, Site 'B', 1973–7, *J. Northampton Mus.*, 13, 2–176

Frisch, T.G., & Toll, N.P., 1949 — *The Excavations at Dura-Europos, Final Report*, IV.4.1, Yale

Fulford, M.G., 1975 — New Forest Roman Pottery, *Brit, Archaeol. Rep*, 17, Oxford

Fulford, M.G., 1977 — Pottery and Britain's Foreign Trade in the Later Roman Period, in *Pottery and Early Commerce*, (ed. D.P.S. Peacock), 35–84

Fuller, E.A., 1884–5 — Cirencester, the manor and the town, *Trans. Bristol Gloucestershire Archaeol. Soc., 9, 298–344*

Fuller, E.A., 1890–1 — Cirencester Castle, *Trans. Bristol Gloucestershire Archaeol. Soc.*, 15, 103–119

Furtwängler, A., 1896 — *Beschreibung der geschnittenen Steine im Antiquarium*, Berlin

Gechter, M., 1980 — Die Fibeln des Kastells Niederbieber, *Bonner Jahrbücher*, 180, 589–610

Gelling, M., 1978 — *Signposts to the Past*, London

Gerster, E.W., 1938 — *Mittelrheinische Bildhauerwerkstatlen im 1 Jahrhundert n.Chr.*, Bonn

Gillam, J.P., 1960 — The Coarse Pottery, in Steer (ed.), 113–129

Gillam, J.P., 1968 — *Types of Roman Coarse Pottery Vessels in Northern Britain*, 2nd ed., Newcastle-upon-Tyne

Gillam, J.P. & Mann, J.C., 1970 — The northern British frontier from Antoninus Pius to Caracalla, *Archaeol. Aeliana*[4], 48, 1–44

Goodchild, R.G., 1941 — Romano-British Disc-brooches derived from Hadrianic Coin-types, *Antiq. J.*, XXI, 1–8

Greene, K.T., 1973 — The pottery from Usk, in *Current Research in Romano-British Coarse Pottery*, (ed. A. Detsicas), 25–37

Grensted. L.W., 1959 — Contents of Brainpan of Skull, in Webster, G., 84–5

Griffith, A.F., & Salzmann, L.F., 1914 — An Anglo-Saxon Cemetery at Alfriston, Sussex, *Sussex Archaeol. Collect.*, 56, 16–53

Griffiths, N.A., 1978 — A fragment of a Roman cavalry tombstone from Cirencester, *Britannia*, IX, 396–7, fig. 5

Grigson, C., 1976 — The craniology and relationships of four species of *Bos*: 3, *J. Archaeol. Sci.*, 3, 115–136

Gröschel, W., 1937 — Pathologische Erscheinungen an den Zähnen und Kiefern der Alemannen aus den Begräbnisstäten der Merowingerzeit des Bezirkes Dillingen und der Donau *Dt. Zahn-Mund Kieferhlk*, 4, 370–386

Harcourt, R.A., 1974 — The dog in prehistoric and early historic Britain, *J. Archaeol. Sci.*, 1, 151–175

Harden, D.B., 1956 — Glass vessels in Britain and Ireland, 400–1000, in *Dark Age Britain:* Studies presented to E.T. Leeds, London

Harden, D.B., 1959 — New Light on Roman and Early Medieval Window Glass, *Glastechische Berichte*

Harden, D.B., 1960 — The Wint Hill hunting bowl, and other related glasses, *J. Glass Studies*, ii, 52

Harden, D.B., 1962 — *Eburacum: Roman York, Vol. 1,* The Glass, 136–140, Royal Commission on Historical Monuments, England

Hardwick, J.L., 1960 — The incidence and distribution of caries throughout the ages in relation to the Englishman's diet, *Brit. Dent. J.*, 108, 9–17

Hart, W.H., 1863–7 — *Historia et cartularium monasterii Sancti Petri Gloucestriae*, 3 vols.

Hassall, M.W.C., 1973 — Inscriptions 1969–1973, in McWhirr, 211–4

Hassall, M.W.C., 1982 — Epigraphic evidence for the auxilliary garrison at Cirencester, in *Early Roman Occupation at Cirencester*, (eds. J. S. Wacher & A.D. McWhirr), 67–71

Hassall, M.W.C., & Rhodes, J., 1974 — Excavations at the New Market Hall, Gloucester, *Trans. Bristol Gloucestershire Archaeol. Soc.*, XCIII, 15–100

Hassall, M.W.C., & Tomlin, R.S.O., 1977 — Roman Britain in 1976: Roman Inscriptions, *Britannia*, VIII, 439

Haverfield, F., 1893 — Romano-British Inscriptions, 1892–3, *Antiq. J.*, L, 285

Haverfield, F., 1917–18 — Roman Cirencester, *Archaeologia*, lxix, 161–200

Hawkes, C.F.C., & Hull, M.R., 1947 — *Camulodunum, First Report on the Excavations at Colchester, 1930–39,* Soc. Antiquaries of London, XIV, Oxford

Hawkes, S.C., 1977 — Orientation at Finglesham; sunrise dating of death and burial in an Anglo-Saxon cemetery in East Kent, *Archaeol. Cantiana*, 92, 33–51

Hearne, T., — *The Itinerary of John Leland the antiquary* published from the original manuscript in the Bodleian Library

Henkel, F., 1913 — *Die roemischen Fingerringe der Rheinlande*, Berlin

Henig, M., 1974 — A Corpus of Roman Engraved Gemstones from British sites, *Brit. Archaeol. Rep.*, 8, Oxford

Henig, M., 1976 — A silver finger-ring from Winchester Wharf, Southwark, *Trans. London Middlesex Archaeol. Soc.*, 256

Hermet, F., 1934 — *La Graufesenque (Condatomago)*, Paris

Hobley, B., & Schofield, J., 1977 — Excavations in the City of London, First Interim Report, 1974–5, *Antiq. J.*, LVII, 31–66

Hodder, I., 1974 — The Distribution of Savernake Ware, *Wiltshire Archaeol. Natur. Hist. Mag.*, 69, 67–84

Horsely, J., 1732 — *Britannia Romana*, or The Roman Antiquities of Britain, London

Household, H., 1969	*The Thames and Severn Canal*, Newton Abbot
Imhoof-Blumer, F., & Keller, O., 1889	*Trier und Pflanzenbilder auf Münzen und Gemmen des Klassischen Altertums*, Leipzig
Irvine, J.T., 1879	Antiquities at Cirencester and Berkeley, *Trans. Bristol Gloucestershire Archaeol. Soc.*, III, 256–257
Jackson, D.A. & Ambrose, T.M., 1978	Excavations at Wakerly, Northants., 1972–5, *Britannia*, IX, 115–242
Jewell, P.A., 1963	Cattle from British archaeological sites, in *Man and Cattle*, (eds. A.D. Mourant & F.E. Zeuner), 80–101
Keller, E., 1971	*Die spätrömischen Grabfunde in Südbayern*, Münchener Beitrage zur Vor- und Fruhgeschichte, 14
Kendrick, T.D., 1932	British Hanging Bowls, *Antiquity*, VI, 161–184
Kenyon, K.M., 1948	*Excavations at the Jewry Wall Site, Leicester*, Soc. Antiquaries of London XV, London
Kibaltchitch, T.W., 1910	*Gemmes de la Russie Méridionale*, Berlin
Kilbride-Jones, H.E., 1936–7	A bronze hanging bowl from Castle Tioram, Moidart: and a suggested Absolute Chronology for British Hanging Bowls, *Proc. Soc. Antiq. Scot.*, lxxi, 206–247
Knorr, R., 1910	Die verzierten Terra sigillata — Gefässe von i. Cannstatt und Kongen=Grinario, ii. Rottioeil, iii. Rottenburg-sumelocenna Stuttgart
Knorr, R., 1919	*Topfer und Fabriken verzierter Terra-sigillata ersten Jahrunderts*, Stuttgart
Krogman, W.M., 1938	The role of urbanization in the dentition of various population groups, *Z. Rassenk*, 7, 41–72
Leeds, E.T. & Shortt, H. de S., 1963	*An Anglo-Saxon Cemetery at Petersfinger, Salisbury*
Lehner, H., 1904	Die Einzelfunde von Novaesium, *Bonner Jahrbücher*, 111/112, 243–418
Lewis, Rev. S.S., 1876–80	On nine Roman signets lately found in the lead-mines at Charterhouse on Mendip, *Communications Cambridge Antiquarian Soc.*, IV, 277–284
London Museum Cat., 1930	*London in Roman Times*
Lukis, W.C.	*The family memoirs of the Rev. William Stukeley, M.D. and the antiquarian correspondence of William Stukeley, Roger and Samuel Gale, etc.* 3 vols. Surtees Society, lxxiii (1882), lxxvi (1883), lxxx (1887)
Lysons, S., 1792	Account of Roman Antiquities discovered in the County of Gloucester, *Archaeologia*, X, 131–6
Maclean, Sir John, 1886–7	Notes on a Roman inscribed stone at Weston Birt, *Trans. Bristol Gloucestershire Archaeol. Soc.*, XI, 336–339
Maiden, J., 1958	Three Gloucestershire Military Tombstones, *Trans. Bristol Gloucestershire Archaeol. Soc.*, LXXVII, 31–41
Manning, W.H., 1972	The Iron Objects, in *Verulamium Excavations*, (ed. S.S. Frere), 163–195
Manning, W.H., 1976	*Catalogue of Romano-British Ironwork in the Museum of Antiquities, Newcastle-upon-Tyne*, Dept. of Archaeology, Univ. of Newcastle-upon-Tyne
Marshall, F.H., 1907	*Catalogue of the Finger Rings, Greek, Etruscan and Roman in the Department of Antiquities, British Museum*, London
Maczunska M., 1974	A Glass Bead with Faces from Balice Mosciska District, *Bulletin Archaeologique Polonais*, XXXIX, 3, 297–300
McGrath, P., & Cannon J., 1976	*Essays in Bristol and Gloucestershire History*
McWhirr, A.D., 1973	Cirencester, 1969–1973: Ninth Interim Report, *Antiq. J.*, LIII, 191–218
McWhirr, A.D., 1976	Studies in Archaeology and History of Cirencester, *Brit. Archaeol Rep.*, 30
McWhirr, A.D., 1978	Cirencester, 1973–6: Tenth Interim Report, *Antiq. J.*, LVIII, 61–80

McWhirr, A.D., 1981   *Roman Gloucestershire*

Middleton, J.H., 1892   *The Lewis Collection of Gems and Rings in the Possession of Corpus Christi College, Cambridge*

Morant, G.M., 1922   A first study of the Tibetan skull, *Biometrika*, 14, 193–260

Mourant, A.D. & Zeuner, F.E., 1963   *Man and Cattle*, Royal Anthrop. Inst. occ. paper 18, London

Nash-Williams, V.E., 1932   The Roman Legionary Fortress at Caerleon, Mons. Report on the excavations carried out in the Prysg Field, 1927–9, *Archaeol. Cambrensis*, 87, 48–105

Neal, D.S., 1974   *The Excavation of the Roman Villa in Gadebridge Park, Hemel Hempstead, 1963–8*, Soc. Antiquaries of London, XXXI, Leeds

Niessen, C.A., 1911   *Beschreibung Römischer Altertümer Sammlung Neissen Coln*, Cologne

O'Neil, H.E., 1968   The Roman Settlement on the Fosse Way at Bourton Bridge, Bourton-on-the-Water, Glos., *Trans. Bristol Gloucestershire Archaeol. Soc.*, 87, 29–55

O'Neil, H., & Grinsell, L.V., 1960   Gloucestershire Barrows, *Trans. Bristol Gloucestershire Archaeol. Soc.*, lxxxix, 5–148

Partridge, C., 1981   *Skeleton Green, a Late Iron Age and Romano-British Site*, Britannia Monograph Series, 2

Peacock, D.P.S., 1967   The heavy mineral analysis of pottery; a preliminary report, *Archaeometry*, 10, 97–100

Peacock, D.P.S., 1977   *Pottery and Early Commerce: Characterisation and Trade in Roman and Later Ceramics*, London

Perrott, R., *et al.*, 1976   Anthropologie d'un abri-sous-roche préhistorique, Le Rond-du-hevrier (Haute Loire), *Trav. Doc. Centre Paléoanthrop. Paléopath.* 3, 1–261

Picard, G.C., 1957   *Les Trophees Romains*, Paris

Potter, K.R., 1955   *Gesta Stephani: the deeds of Stephen*, Oxford

Powell, T.G.E. *et al.*, 1969   *Megalithic Enquiries in the West of Britain*, Liverpool

Rahtz, P., 1978   Grave Orientation, *Archaeol. J.*, 135, 1–14

Rawes, B., and Gander, E.D., 1978   An Ancient Quarry at Manless Town in the parish of Brimpsfield, *Trans. Bristol Gloucestershire Archaeol. Soc.* XCVI, 79–82

RCHM Glos., 1976   *Iron Age and Romano-British Monuments in the Gloucestershire Cotswolds*, Royal Commission on Historical Monuments, England

Reece, R., 1962   The Oakley Cottage Romano-British Cemetery, *Trans. Bristol Gloucestershire Archaeol. Soc.*, LXXXI, 51–72

Reece, R., 1976   The Ashcroft Site, Cirencester, *Trans. Bristol Gloucestershire Archaeol. Soc.*, XCIV, 92–100

Reece, R., 1981   *Excavations in Iona, 1964–1974*, Institute of Archaeology, Occasional Publication, no. 5

Reece. R., 1982   Acta of the Berne International Numismatic Congress 1979, forthcoming

Reinach, S., 1895   *Pierres Gravées*, Paris

Rennie, D.M., 1971   Excavations in the Parsonage Field, Cirencester, *Trans. Bristol Gloucestershire Archaeol. Soc.*, XC, 64–94

Rhodes, J.F., 1964   *Catalogue of Sculptures in the Gloucester City Museum*, Gloucester

RIB   Collingwood, R.G., and Wright, R.P., *The Roman Inscriptions of Britain*, I, 1965

Richardson, K.M., 1960   A Roman Brooch from the Outer Hebrides, with Note on Others of its Type, *Antiq. J.*, XL, 200–13

Richardson, K.M., 1962   Excavations in Parsonage Field, Cirencester, 1959, *Antiq. J.*, XLII, 167

Richter, G.M.A., 1956   *Metropolitan Museum of Art, New York, Catalogue of Engraved Gems, Greek, Etruscan, and Roman*, Rome

Rigby, V., 1982 — The Coarse Pottery, In *Early Roman Occupation at Cirencester*, (eds. J.S. Wacher & A.D. McWhirr), 153–200

Riha, E., 1979 — *Die Romischen Fibeln aus Augst und Kaiseraugst*, Forschungen in Augst, Band 3, Augst

Rivet, A.L.F. & Smith, C., 1979 — *The Place-Names of Roman Britain*, Batsford

Rogers, G.B., 1974 — *Poteries sigillées de la Gaule Centrale, I: les motifs non figurés*, Gallia, Suppl. 28

Ross, C.D., 1964 — *The Cartulary of Cirencester Abbey, Gloucestershire*, vols. I & II, London

Rudder, S., 1779 — *A New History of Gloucestershire*, Cirencester

Rudder, S., 1800 — *A History of the Town of Cirencester*, Cirencester

Sewell, E.C. & Powell, A.H., 1910 — The Roman Pavement at the Barton, *Trans. Bristol Gloucestershire* Archaeol. Soc., XXXIII, 67–8

Silver, I.A., 1969 — Ageing in domestic animals, in *Science in Archaeology*, (eds. D. Brothwell & E. Higgs), 283–302

Skinner, Rev. J., 1824 — *Skinner Journals*, vol. XLVII, British Museum MS 33679

Slater, T.R., 1978 — Family, society and the ornamental villa on the fringes of English country towns, *J. Historical Geography*, 4, 129–144

Smith, A.H., 1964 — *The Place-Names of Gloucestershire*, Cambridge.

Smith, C.R., 1850 — *The Antiquities of Richborough, Reculver, and Lymne in Kent*

Smith, C.R., 1880 — Roman lead Coffins and ossuaria in *Collectanea Antiqua*, vii, London

Smith, G.E., & Dawson, W.R., 1924 — *Egyptian Mummies*, London

Stanfield, J.A., & Simpson, G., 1958 — *Central Gaulish Potters*, London

Stead, I.M., 1967 — A La Tene III burial at Welwyn Garden City, *Archaeologia*, CI, 1–62

Stead, I.M., 1980 — *Rudston Roman Villa*, The Yorkshire Archaeological Society, Leeds

Steer, K.A., 1960 — Excavations at Mumrills Roman Fort, 1958–60. *Proc. Soc. Antiq. Scot.*, 94, 113–129

Steiger, R., 1966 — Gemmen und Kameen im Romermuseum, Augst, *Antike Kunst*, 9, 29

Steiner, P., 1911 — *Sammlung des Neiderrheinischen Altertums Vereins*, Frankfurt

Stukeley, W., 1724, 1776 — *Itinerarium curiosum*, Centuria I, 1724; Centuriae I, II 1776, London

Swain, E.J., 1978 — *Excavations at the Chessells, Kingscote*, Kingscote Archaeological Association, Stroud

Swan, V.G., 1975 — Oare reconsidered and the origins of Savernake Ware in Wiltshire, *Britannia*, VI, 59–61

Sydenham, E.A., 1952 — *The Coinage of the Roman Republic*, London

Tattersall, I., 1968 — Dental paleopathology of medieval Britain, *J. Hist. Med.*, 23, 380–5

Taylor, C.S., 1889 — *An analysis of the Domesday Survey of Gloucestershire*, Bristol

Thawley, C.R., 1982 — The Animal Remains, in *Early Roman Occupation at Cirencester*, (eds. J.S. Wacher & A.D. McWhirr), 211–227

Thorpe, W.A., 1949 — *English Glass*, London

Toller, H., 1977 — Roman Lead Coffins and Ossuaria in Britain, *Brit. Archaeol. Rep.* 38, Oxford

Torrens, H.S. 1982 — The Geology of Cirencester and District, in *Early Roman Occupation at Cirencester*, (eds. J.S. Wacher & A.D. McWhirr), 72–78

Toulmin Smith, L., 1964 — *The Itinerary of John Leland in or about the years 1536–1539*, 5 vols., London Centaur Press

Toynbee, J.M.C., 1964 — *Art in Britain under the Romans*, Oxford

Toynbee, J.M.C., 1976 — Roman Sculpture in Gloucestershire, in *Essays in Bristol and Gloucestershire History*, (eds. P. McGrath & J. Cannon), 132

Trevor, J.C., 1950 — Anthropometry, *Chambers Encyclopaedia*, I, 458–62

Trotter, M., and Gleser, G.C., 1952 — Estimation of stature from long bones of American whites and negroes, *Am. J. Phys. Anthrop.*, 10, 463–514

Trotter, M., and Gleser, G.C., 1958 — A re-evaluation of estimation of stature based on measurements of stature taken during life and of long bones after death, *Am. J. Phys. Anthrop.*, 16, 79–123

Tudor, D., 1938–40 — Monumente inedite din Romula, *Buletinual Comisiuni Monumentelor Istorice*

Vanderhoeven, M., 1962 — *De Romeinse Glasverzameling in het Provincial Gallo-Romeins Museum*, Tongeren

Verey, D., 1970 — *The Buildings of England:* Gloucestershire, vol. I, The Cotswolds, Penguin

Vermeule, C., 1952 — Roman Imperial Gems, *Numismatic Circular*, Aug.–Sept. 1952

Wacher, J.S., 1961 — Cirencester 1960: First Interim Report, *Antiq. J.*, XLI, 63–71

Wacher, J.S., 1962 — Cirencester 1961: Second Interim Report, *Antiq. J.*, XLII, 1–14

Wacher, J.S., 1963 — Cirencester 1962: Third Interim Report, *Antiq. J.*, XLIII, 15–26

Wacher, J.S., 1964 — Cirencester 1963: Fourth Interim Report, *Antiq. J.*, XLIV, 9–19

Wacher, J.S., 1969 — *Excavations at Brough-on-Humber, 1958–61,* Soc. Antiquaries of London, XXV, London

Wacher, J.S., 1974 — *The Towns of Roman Britain*, Batsford

Wacher, J.S., 1976 — Late Roman Developments, in *Studies in Archaeology and History of Cirencester,* (ed. A.D. McWhirr), 15–17

Wacher, J.S., 1981 — *Cirencester Roman Amphitheatre*, Dept. of the Environment

Wacher, J.S. & McWhirr, A.D., 1982 — *Early Roman Occupation at Cirencester,* Cirencester Excavations I

Wade-Martins, P., 1980 — Excavations at North Elmham Park, 1967–1972, *East Anglian Archaeology*, Report no. 9, 247–374

Walters, H.B., 1926 — *Catalogue of the Engraved Gems and Cameos, Greek, Etruscan and Roman in the British Museum,* London

Warhurst, A., 1955 — The Jutish Cemetery at Lyminge, *Archaeol. Cantiana*, LXIX, 1–40

Waugh, H., and Goodburn, R., 1972 — The finds: non-ferrous objects, in *Verulamium Excavations,* (ed. S.S. Frere), 115–162

Webster, G., 1959 — Cirencester: Dyer Court Excavations, 1957, *Trans, Bristol Gloucestershire Archaeol. Soc.,* LXXVIII, 44–85

Webster, G., 1982 — Gazetteer of Military Objects from Cirencester, in *Early Roman Occupation at Cirencester,* (eds. J.S. Wacher & A.D. McWhirr), 109–117

Webster, P.V., 1976 — Severn Valley Ware: A Preliminary Study, *Trans. Bristol Gloucestershire Archaeol. Soc.,* 94, 18–46

Welcker, H., 1888 — Cribra orbitalia, ein ethnologish-diagnostisches Merkmal am Schädel mehrer Menschenrassen, *Arch. Anthrop.*, 17 (1): 1–18

Wells, C., 1962 — The Human Remains, in Reece, 1962, 62–70

Wells, C., 1964 — *Bones, Bodies and Disease,* London

Wells, C., 1968 — Osgood-Schlatter's disease in the ninth century?, *Brit. Med. J.,* 2, 623–4

Wells, C., 1973 — A Palaeopathological Rarity in a Skeleton of Roman Date, *Medical History,* 17 (4) 399–400

Wells, C., 1974a — Torus mandibularis in an early Scottish cemetery, *Paleopath. Ass. Newsletter,* 8, 7–9

Wells, C., 1974b — The results of 'bone-setting' in Anglo-Saxon times, *Med. Biol. Illust.,* 24, 215–20

Wells, C., 1974c — Osteochondritis dissecans in ancient British skeletal material, Med. Hist., 18 (4): 365–9

Wells, C., 1975 — Ancient obstetric hazards and female mortality, *Bull. N.Y. Acad. Med.,* 51, (11), 1235–49

Wells, C., 1976 — Ancient lesions of the hip joint, *Med. Biol. Illust.,* 26, 171–7

Wells, C., 1977 — Une curieuse blessure dans un squelette du deuxieme siècle A.D. (cimetière Romano-Britannique de Cirencester, comté de Gloucestershire, G.B.), *Trav. Doc. Centre Paléoanthrop. Paléopath.*, 4 (1): 9–19

Wells, C., 1980 — The Human Bones, in Wade-Martins, 247–324

Wells, C., 1981 — Discussion of the skeletal material, in *Excavations in Iona, 1964–1974*, (ed. R. Reece), 85–118

Wells, C., & Green, C., 1973 — Sunrise dating of Death and Burial, *Norfolk & Norwich Archaeol. Soc.*, XXXV, 435–442

Wenham, L.P., 1968 — *The Romano-British Cemetery at Trentholme Drive, York*, London

Whatley, E., 1894–5 — On the discovery of skeletons at The Barton, Cirencester; and other Roman finds of 1896, *Trans. Bristol Gloucestershire Archaeol. Soc.*, xix, 394–8

Wheeler, R.E.M. & Wheeler, T.V., 1928 — The Roman Amphitheatre at Caerleon, Monmouthshire, *Archaeologia*, 78, 111–218

Wheeler, R.E.M. & Wheeler, T.V., 1936 — *Verulamium: A Belgic and two Roman cities*, Soc. Antiquaries of London, XI, Oxford

Williams, D.F., 1977 — The Romano-British Black-Burnished Industry: an essay on characterisation by heavy mineral analysis, in *Pottery and Early Commerce*, (ed. D.P.S. Peacock), 163–220

Willmore, H.H., 1939 — Stone Coffins, Gloucestershire, *Trans. Bristol Gloucestershire Archaeol. Soc.*, 61, 158–171

Wilson, D.R., 1972 — Roman Britain in 1971: sites explored, *Britannia*, III, 339

Witts, G.B., 1883 — *Archaeological Handbook of the County of Gloucestershire*, Cheltenham

Wright, R.P., & Hassall, M.W.C., 1972 — Roman Britain in 1971: Inscriptions, *Britannia*, III, 352–3

Young C.J., 1977 — Oxfordshire Roman Pottery: The Roman Pottery Industry of the Oxford Region, *Brit. Archaeol. Rep.*, 43

INDEX

This index covers both the printed text and the material contained in five microfiche. References to pages in the printed text are in roman. Microfiche references are explained p. 22, and are in italic.